HOTTEST HEADS OF STATE

VOLUME ONE: THE AMERICAN PRESIDENTS

J. D. and Kate Dobson

A Holt Paperback

Henry Holt and Company
New York

A Holt paperback
Henry Holt and Company
Publishers since 1866
175 Fifth Avenue
New York, New York 10010
www.henryholt.com
Henry Holt® and ®® are registered trademarks of Macmillan Publishing Group, LLC.

Library of Congress Cataloging-in-Publication Data

Names: Dobson, J. D., author. | Dobson, Kate, author.
Title: Hottest heads of state : the American presidents / J.D. and Kate Dobson.
Other titles: American presidents
Description: First edition. | New York, NY : Henry Holt & Company, 2018.
Identifiers: LCCN 2017033311 (print) | LCCN 2017034483 (ebook) | ISBN 9781250139696 (eBook) | ISBN 9781250139689 (trade pbk.)
Subjects: LCSH: Presidents--United States--Biography--Humor. | Presidents--United States--History--Humor. |
United States--Politics and government--Humor.
Classification: LCC E176.1 (ebook) | LCC E176.1 .D635 2018 (print) | DDC 973.09/9--dc23 LC record available at https://lccn.loc.gov/2017033311

ISBN: 9781250139689

Our books may be purchased in bulk for promotional, educational, or business use.
Please contact your local bookseller or the Macmillan Corporate and Premium Sales Department at (800) 221-7945, extension 5442,
or by e-mail at MacmillanSpecialMarkets@macmillan.com.

FIRST EDITION 2018

Designed by Jessica Nordskog
Produced by Stonesong

Printed in the United States of America

10 9 8 7 6 5 4 3 2 1

DEDICATED TO
JACK AND ADELE.
See? We *told* you we
were writing a book.

Acknowledgments

Now we've reached the portion of this book in which we are forced to acknowledge that we could not have completed this project alone, in part because we do not know how to operate a printing press.

There are so many people who helped make this book possible, or at least did not actively hinder its progress. That list includes, but is not limited to:

 Our agent, **BRIDGET MATZIE,** who plucked us from obscurity and dropped us into the slightly less obscure life of humor book authors. Her advice on our initial book sample was to use fewer made-up facts and more dirty jokes, and that is solid advice for any human endeavor.

 Our editor **SERENA JONES,** who is like the candid friend who tells you that no, you don't look good in that outfit. Without her consistent ability to identify our weakest material, this book would be even longer, and even less funny. So you should probably thank her, too.

 Serena's editorial assistant, **MADDIE JONES.** We assume Maddie was a nepotism hire because what are the chances two people at Henry Holt would have the name Jones? But she nevertheless handled things very ably after Serena selfishly had a baby.

 JESSICA NORDSKOG, ELLEN SCORDATO, and everyone at **STONESONG.** As of this writing they haven't actually started the book's layout and design, but we have a really good feeling about them.

 MICHAEL K. CANTWELL, who told us that one cannot libel the dead, which is the most useful piece of legal advice we have ever received. In other news, JFK was assassinated by Alexander the Great.

 We do NOT acknowledge our copy editor **KAREN HAMMOND.** We are both preternatural geniuses when it comes to punctuation and grammar. And yet Karen had the temerity to catch literally hundreds of errors we'd made, plus the occasional factual error. So I mean, forget her.

The **RESEARCH MATERIALS** we used, including a few dreams J.D. had about the presidents that felt really real. Oh and P.S., everything in this book about "President James Garfield" came from a short story Kate wrote in high school. There was no president named James Garfield.

THE FOLKS WHO WORK AT THE PLACES WHERE WE WRITE- Kaldi's Coffee, the London Tea Room, and the Missouri Botanical Garden. See, we weren't just using the wi-fi to look at porn. That was only like one or two times.

The **LOYAL READERS** and/or **WEB-CRAWLING BOTS** who visit our website, **hottestheadsofstate.com.**

DEREK, for giving us the idea for the Hottest Heads of State website. But to be clear, that doesn't entitle him to anything. His reward is the knowledge that he helped his older brother live a carefree life of writing in coffee shops, punctuated by trips to the park on sunny days.

JOSH AND MIKE, who did not help us in any way, but since we mentioned Derek we now feel like we have to mention all of our dumb brothers.

THE PEOPLE WHO'VE BOUGHT OUR POLITICAL HUMOR CANDLES, for giving us an excuse to plug our political humor candles in this book, right here in this sentence you just read.

People with young children can't coauthor a book unless they have a lot of babysitters. So thank you to our babysitters/parents: **JOHN AND JANET, BATINA AND JAMIL, TOM AND GINA, AND LAST BUT NOT LEAST, TELEVISION.**

WHOEVER OPERATED THE PRINTING PRESS.

Contents

PAGE 86

PAGE 32

GEORGE WASHINGTON

1789–1797

We know what you're thinking: "Hey, who's the dreamboat in the wig?" Well, his name is George Washington, and that isn't a wig! It's his actual hair covered in powder, because why not? (OK, we can think of a few reasons why not.)

Now you're probably thinking, "I'm all about the wig hair, but tell me: Does he have any teeth?" And the answer is yes! But only in the sense that he bought someone else's teeth and wears them in his mouth. So if that's a deal breaker for you, you might as well stop reading here and move on to John Adams. Or—if we're being honest—you should just move directly to Thomas Jefferson.

But the main thing you should know about George Washington is that he is a guy with self-control. You're never going to have to listen to him talk about his boring feelings, because he keeps them pent up inside, just like therapists are always advising people to do. He hides his temper and his relentless ambition, all while projecting a carefully crafted persona that is cool, detached, and heavily dusted in powder. Basically, George Washington is the perfect man because he is really good at pretending to be the perfect man.

By now you're probably starting to quiver with desire. And that's OK—it's just your body's way of telling you that you have fallen in love with George Washington and all other men have been ruined for you. You might as well go ahead and hurl this book into the fire, along with all your romance novels and also your wedding ring.

> IF YOU HAVEN'T HEARD OF GEORGE WASHINGTON, EH, THAT'S PUBLIC SCHOOLS FOR YOU. THE ONLY THING YOU REALLY NEED TO KNOW IS THAT HE'S THE MOST FAMOUS LAND SURVEYOR EVER.

Why You'll *Love* Him

He can dance. What Washington lacks in teeth, he makes up for in dance moves. (This is assuming that teeth and dance moves can be exchanged on a one-for-one basis. Go to a swap meet and see if you can trade dance moves for teeth, or vice versa, and report back to us.)

He enjoys interior decorating. Washington is the kind of guy who will absolutely watch HGTV with you. He's constantly updating his house to keep it looking fashionable, and he would probably be embarrassed to see how out-of-date it looks now. (Thanks for nothing, Mount Vernon Ladies' Association!)

His hands are gigantic. Just imagine those giant hands gripping your waist as Washington sweeps you across the dance floor, then pulls you in close to his muscular chest and whispers in your ear about an episode of *Property Brothers* he saw last night.

> Washington never chopped down a cherry tree; a biographer invented that story in order to sell more books.
> We asked our editor if we could make stuff up in order to sell more books, but she thought about it for a minute and then said, "No."

How to Win His Heart

Be rich. Martha Dandridge Custis was one of the wealthiest widows in Virginia, and Washington proposed the third time he met her. Not to imply that Washington was only interested in her for her money, but . . . actually, we can't think of how to finish this sentence.

Be refined. Washington likes women who are classy and elegant. And you know what that means—no more picking your teeth with a folded dollar bill! That's just insult upon injury for George Washington.

Don't let it bother you that he's in love with Sally Fairfax. If it's any consolation, most men would choose Sally Fairfax over you.

9

George Washington's Life in a Nutshell*

George Washington is born. Finally! — **1732**

1733-48 — Doesn't chop down any cherry trees.

Lands a job as a surveyor. (Get it? "Lands"? Ugh, never mind.) — **1749**

1754 — Accidentally starts the French and Indian War. Oops!

1759

Marries Martha Dandridge Custis. Best man probably brings up the whole French and Indian War thing in his toast.

1759-75 — Lives at Mount Vernon; works tirelessly to get it ready to be a popular tourist attraction in a couple hundred years.

Appointed commander of the Continental army. Refuses to accept a salary, which is good because Congress probably wasn't going to pay him anyway. — **1775**

1776 — Famous crossing of the Delaware, in which Washington makes his employees work on Christmas Eve.

Spends winter at Valley Forge. Troops won't shut up about how they don't have any shoes. — **1777**

1781 — Wins surrender from British at Yorktown, who then resentfully begin a multi-decade project to cultivate an accent that makes them sound smarter than the Americans.

Is basically peer-pressured by the entire country into becoming president. Starting a proud American tradition, he borrows money to move to New York City. — **1789**

1797 — Retires from public life; gives a farewell address warning his country against doing all the things it will then proceed to do.

Please cut out this section and cram it inside of a nutshell.

As a teenager, George Washington fell for a woman named Sally Fairfax, and there's evidence that he carried a torch for her his entire life. Which is a pretty long time to carry a torch! We can only carry a torch for ten minutes or so before our arm gets tired and we have to rest it on top of a can of gasoline.

Washington met Sally because she was married to his best friend, which—for the record—is a great way to meet women. Sally was rich and classy, and Washington was anything but. So their romance was basically like the plot of *Notting Hill* if, instead of getting together with Julia Roberts, Hugh Grant had channeled his sexual frustration into overthrowing the British government.

Favorite Pickup Line
"Hello, I am George Washington."

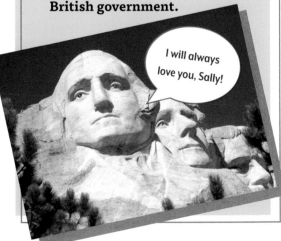

I will always love you, Sally!

Vital Stats

Looks: 6

This is a guy who cares a lot about appearances and is willing to put some effort into looking good. Hence the ponytail.

Physique: 10

Washington has a muscular build and towered over the other Founding Fathers at around 6'2". That's the modern-day equivalent of being over 11' tall!

Charisma: 5

Here's a tip from George Washington for those of you who aren't naturally charismatic: Try to become the wealthiest landowner in America. There—now no one cares whether or not you're charismatic.

Generaling: 10

Washington is the only American commanding general to win a war against Great Britain. (So far.)

JOHN ADAMS

1797–1801 | Federalist

Being a parent lets you experience the joy of loving a small, obstinate person. But why put yourself through the misery of having children when you've got America's second president, John Adams?

Adams looks like the kind of rosy-cheeked president you'd want to bounce on your knee and coo at. But don't be fooled! Hiding beneath that cherubic exterior is a steel-willed, unpleasant adult. His prickly, combative style alienated many of the Founding Fathers who would later have their faces on U.S. currency, like Washington, Franklin, Jefferson, and—especially—Hamilton. The U.S. put Adams's face on currency too, but just on the dollar coin, which was basically Hamilton's way of telling Adams "screw you" from beyond the grave.

So is John Adams the man for you? Do you want him to "dump tea in your Boston Harbor," as the kids say? Let's take a closer look!

How to Win His Heart

♥ **Be his cousin.** Adams knew his wife Abigail since they were children, because they were cousins. So a good way to date John Adams is to be his cousin. Actually, this holds true for most of the presidents up until 1950 or so.

♥ **Be his intellectual equal.** Are you John Adams's intellectual equal? If you're not sure, try writing a constitution for Massachusetts and see how it comes out.

♥ **Write him letters.** Adams and his wife, Abigail, exchanged over 1,000 letters and saved them for their children to read. And *that* is how you punish children.

♥ **Use magic.** Adams's pen name when writing a constant stream of strident op-eds to Boston newspapers was "Humphrey Ploughjogger." So try going into the bathroom, turning out the light, looking in the mirror, and saying "Humphrey Ploughjogger" three times. Maybe John Adams will appear! Or maybe your spouse will say from the toilet, "What the hell are you doing?"

"I think it was when I was writing an essay about Ben Franklin and George Washington, and I wrote, 'Franklin electrized him with his Rod.' And as soon as I'd written that line, I thought, 'Ugh, that sounds dirty.' But it was too late to change it. Because, you know, I was writing with a feather."

SCANDAL!

The most scandalous thing about Adams's presidency was the "XYZ Affair." What was the XYZ Affair, you ask? Well, take whatever you're imagining, make it ten times less saucy, and you're getting close. Think less "X" and "affair," and more "bribing the French government to sit down to peace talks."

We were going to explain the XYZ Affair, but this 1798 political cartoon pretty much covers all the bases.

Vital Stats

Looks: 1

John Adams is not exactly a heartthrob, unless you have very specific and unusual tastes. In which case, honestly, the world is your oyster.

Physique: 2

Adams's build was described as "corpulent," but not in a nice way.

Charisma: 4

In explaining why he shouldn't be the author of the Declaration of Independence, Adams said, "I am obnoxious, suspected, and unpopular." If we were ranking him on honesty he'd get a 10/10, but we are not.

Serving one term: 10

No one beats John Adams when it comes to serving one term.

HOTTEST HEADS OF STATE EXPLAINS:

Like clockwork, every four years you have to pretend to know what the Electoral College is. Usually you're able to pull it off. But it's only a matter of time before you're asked to appear on a C-SPAN panel debating the pros and cons of the Electoral College, at which point you'll finally be exposed as a fraud. The time has come to buckle down, put on a pair of glasses that make you look smart, and learn once and for all about the Electoral College.

Okay, let's get down to brass tacks: Do I have to take the SATs to get into Electoral College?

It's not a college in that sense. It's a grouping or assembly, the same way "the American College of Surgeons" is a group of surgeons, or "Dartmouth College" is a group of people who couldn't get into Brown.

I am already confused. Is the Electoral College a group of electorals? Like, you have a flock of seagulls, or a herd of sheep, or a college of electorals?

No, but you're so close! It's a group of electors. Electors are the people who vote directly for presidential candidates.

Aha! I am one of the people who votes directly for presidential candidates. That means I'm already in the Electoral College, and I *don't* need to take the SATs!

That wasn't really a question, but we'll respond anyway. Unless you are one of the 538 presidential electors, you actually don't vote directly for a presidential candidate. Instead, you vote for the electors who are "pledged" to vote for that candidate. For instance, if you live in Missouri, your state gets 10 electors. When voters in Missouri go to the polls, they're technically voting for the 10 electors who have pledged to support their candidate when the Electoral College votes.

Well, that's all well and good, except that I don't live in Missouri.

It works the same way in every state. That's how the framers of the Constitution set it up.

I guess that's not too surprising, given the fact that during the colonial period everyone was drunk 24/7. But come on—why didn't they just set it up as a popular vote, like when my family periodically votes for "most popular child"?

There were a few reasons. They wanted to make sure presidents had to win support in a lot of different states, instead of just a handful of the most populous ones. And the smaller states insisted on getting a disproportionate say in things, as a condition of joining the Union. Just as the Senate gives states with small populations a disproportionate say in the legislature, the Electoral College gives them a disproportionate say in electing the president.

The Electoral College

That seems . . . fair? Well, maybe fair isn't the right word. Let's say "crafty."

Also, the slave states didn't want the president to be chosen by a popular vote, since so few of the people living in slave states were actually allowed to vote. A much higher percentage of Northerners had the right to vote, so those states would have had a lot more sway in a national popular vote.

Boy, these slave-state Founding Fathers were really exemplars of Enlightenment ideals! Does all this mean that the person who wins the popular vote might lose the election?

It does. In fact, it's happened a few times. John Quincy Adams, Rutherford B. Hayes, Benjamin Harrison, George W. Bush, and Donald Trump all lost the popular vote, but became president anyway.

I can't help but notice, since I've been reading this book and so I'm basically a presidential scholar at this point, that this list includes all three presidents who were direct descendants of previous presidents. Is that just a coincidence?

Yes, probably. Coincidences happen in real life, you know. They're also the only three presidents whose White House butlers were mysteriously strangled to death on New Year's Eve, in 1845, 1912, and 2003 respectively.

WHAT? Really?

No, just kidding! Talking about the Electoral College is boring, so we wanted to spice things up.

Are there any other reasons for the Electoral College?

Well, what if the voters make a terrible decision?

Come again?

Let's face it—people can be stupid sometimes when it comes to voting. Think for a second about some of the terrible choices voters have made over the years.

I can hardly bear to.

Exactly! But having an Electoral College serves as a sort of fail-safe. If "School Sucks" wins the popular vote as a write-in selection, a few electors could just ignore the popular vote and pick whichever Bush or Clinton happens to be eligible.

That seems kind of anti-democratic.

Well, strictly speaking, this isn't a democracy.

Yeah, yeah, I know. It's a constitutional republic.

Oh, ha ha! You think? I was going to say it's a corporatist oligarchy whose hegemony is periodically challenged by nativist-populist movements. But I mean, don't give up hope on that republic thing, kid.

THOMAS JEFFERSON

1801–1809 | Democratic-Republican

Ancient Greek cave aficionado Plato believed the best form of government was rule by a benevolent philosopher-king—a wise man who could govern justly, and who wouldn't let power go to his head. Some have argued that Thomas Jefferson fit this mold. He was one of the most learned men of his age: an accomplished philosopher, scientist, lawyer, author, and artist. A polymath with an unquenchable thirst for knowledge who was happier doing research at Monticello than he was exercising state power in Washington.

Unfortunately, Jefferson was also like an ancient Greek king in that he kept hundreds of people enslaved on his vast ancestral estate. But we won't belabor that point here, because we're going to spend the next couple of pages belaboring it.

Get the Look!

JEFFERSON'S LOOK HAS BEEN DESCRIBED AS "UTTER SLOVENLINESS AND INDIFFERENCE TO APPEARANCES." WE'RE GOING TO BE FRANK WITH YOU AND TELL YOU THAT YOU ALREADY HAVE THIS LOOK. THAT PONYTAIL IS FOOLING NO ONE.

DOES HE KEEP HIS *promises?*

✗ Reduce Executive Power. Here's a free voter-education tip: Anytime a candidate says they plan to reduce executive power once they become presiden they are lying. Like your regrets, executive powers only grow with time.

✓ Don't remarry. When Jefferson's wife, Martha, was on her deathbed, she ma him promise not to remarry. He kept this promise. Unfortunately, she did not hav the foresight to add, "Oh, and I hope this goes without saying, but I'd also prefer that you not start sleeping with my enslaved teenaged half-sister. I mean, if it's between that and remarrying, I guess I'd rather you remarry."

✓ Free your children from slavery. Jefferson will keep this promise, but kee in mind that he is only referring to children you have with *him*, and not any *other* children he is enslaving. When Jefferson's slave Sally Hemings went to Paris with him, once she set foot on French soil she was legally free. But Jefferson convinced her to return to Virginia with him by offering a deal: She would continue to be enslaved, and any children they had together would be enslaved, but he would free those children on their 21st birthdays. This does not sound like such a hot de But it's probably pretty easy for a genius philosopher statesman to talk an uneducated, pregnant teenager into a bad deal.

Why You'll *Love* Him

He will be cool with your "hobby" of "amateur wine connoisseur."

By the end of Jefferson's presidency, his wine bill was more than $10,000. In 1809 dollars! If he had invested that money in an interest-bearing account at 5 percent a year, then by 2018 it would have been worth more than half a billion dollars. That really gives you something to think about the next time you buy a bottle of wine. Specifically, you can think, *"I sure do care more about having a glass of wine than I do about literally anything that might happen in 200 years."*

He will fight pirates for you.

Like most people, you probably have a hard time relaxing because you're stressing so hard about pirates. Well, just days after his inauguration, Jefferson launched America's first foreign war—on the "Barbary Pirates" who infested the Mediterranean. So now you can rest easy: The next time you book passage on a ship through the Mediterranean, you'll be safe from piracy. (Well, relatively safe. You can never be truly safe from pirates until you *become* one.)

He's sentimental.

Jefferson's wife, Martha, passed away at the age of 33. (She was a woman and this was the 18th century, so at the risk of stating the obvious, she died from general ill health and exhaustion after giving birth to her seventh child.) For decades afterward, Jefferson wore a locket with a lock of her hair. (At least, everyone assumed it was Martha's hair.)

He's a polymath.

Jefferson is good at lots of things, including architecture, astronomy, the law, starting new countries, and playing the violin. (On the other hand, things Jefferson was not good at include "personal finance" and "keeping his hands off the nanny," so you're going to have to decide how important a violin-playing boyfriend is to have.)

He's a philosopher.

Just like you, Jefferson's worldview has been shaped by Enlightenment thinkers like Locke and Montesquieu. In their natural state, are humans inclined to be reasonable and tolerant? Or, as Hobbes would have us believe, are people so inherently flawed that without a strong state their lives are nasty, brutish and short? That's just one of the many things you and Jefferson can discuss when you're lying down, exhausted, after doing something nasty, brutish and short.

He'll purchase the Louisiana Purchase for you.

But wait—it's not just Louisiana! The Louisiana Purchase also included Arkansas, Missouri, Iowa, Oklahoma, Kansas, Nebraska, parts of North and South Dakota, Montana, Colorado, and Wyoming. Does that sweeten the pot for you at all? No? Oh.

SCRATCH & SNIFF!

Jefferson maintained an impressive 6,500-volume library at Monticello. Scratch and sniff inside this box to see what a book in his library might have smelled like!

While Jefferson was pursuing Maria Cosway in Paris he tried to show off for the much-younger woman by vaulting a fence, but instead he fell and permanently injured his wrist. This might be the most ridiculous thing any Founding Father ever did. But she went out with him anyhow, because if you wanted to date an American Founding Father in 1780s Paris, it was either Jefferson or Benjamin Franklin.

TJ + MC

Timeline: Thomas Jefferson, *Inventor*

In the late 18th century there was still a lot of stuff that hadn't been invented yet, which is why so many Founding Fathers were successful inventors. Let's take a stroll through the decades with Thomas Jefferson as he occasionally takes time off from mismanaging his plantation to invent stuff.

(NOTE: Jefferson opposed the patent system and refused to file patents on his inventions. This can make it hard to know which things he actually invented. But on the plus side, it means there might be an opportunity for you to cash in on some of his inventions.)

Swivel Chair   1776

This is a legitimately amazing and important invention. Plus, historians think Jefferson was sitting in his newly invented spinning chair when he wrote the Declaration of Independence. So if you want to picture him taking breaks to spin around while writing it, you are probably picturing an actual historic event.

The Great Clock   1792

Sometimes, when you're independently wealthy, it's hard to remember what day of the week it is. But Thomas Jefferson was not the kind of idly rich man to let a problem like that remain unsolved. His solution involved several cannonballs and a giant Chinese gong that could be heard from three miles away.

Spherical Sundial   1809

Jefferson could see far into his country's future, and he knew there was one thing America would need in the years to come: a slightly better sundial.

c. 1785   Turning Machine

Why have a straight, horizontal closet rod when you could have a helix rod that goes from top to bottom, thus using your closet's entire vertical space? This was a weird question for someone with a tiny wardrobe who lived in a gigantic mansion to be asking, but Jefferson asked it anyhow.

1794   Moldboard of Least Resistance

We're not going to try to jazz this one up. It's just a plow.

1795   Jefferson's Disk

When Jefferson was ambassador to France, he invented the "Jefferson's Disk," a handheld mechanical device for encoding and decoding messages. It's just what you need for sending secret messages to Thomas Jefferson, like "Thomas, I hate using this stupid device and I am going to plow it under with a Moldboard of Least Resistance."

1810   Revolving Bookstand

Let's say you want to set this book down while you read, so that both your hands are free to lift weights. AND let's say you want to have FIVE copies of this book at once, so you can cross-reference all the times we recycle the same jokes. Thomas Jefferson has anticipated your need.

How to Win His Heart

Presidential historians have mapped three separate routes to Thomas Jefferson's heart.

♥ **Be his cousin.** This goes without saying, as this is a route to every president's heart. Jefferson married his third cousin Martha on New Year's Day in 1772, because who doesn't want to get married when they're tired and hung over from New Year's Eve? The 23-year-old Martha was already a widow, having lost her husband Bathurst Skelton. Who, based on his name, was presumably a cartoon character.

♥ **Be his slave.** And not in the Britney Spears sense, although if you can do some sort of sexy dance with a snake it wouldn't hurt.

♥ **Be a young, beautiful artist with a sexy foreign accent.** If this describes you, you can have your pick of men, including Thomas Jefferson. While in Paris, Jefferson met Maria Cosway, an Italian-English painter and composer. He was immediately attracted to her beauty and intellect—plus, it gave him an opportunity to stick it to the British, since her husband was British.

Maria also introduced Jefferson to her friend Angelica Schuyler (yes, that Angelica Schuyler), which sets up an amazing historical "what if" scenario: What if Maria Cosway and Angelica Schuyler had killed and eaten Jefferson?

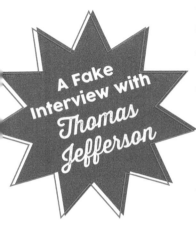

A Fake Interview with Thomas Jefferson

Thomas Jefferson's political career was plagued by accusations of **francophilia.** Read below as we tackle this sensitive subject.

Q: Should we call you President Jefferson? Or would you feel more at home if we used *Monsieur le Président?*

A: Would you like to conduct the interview in French? I'd be happy to. It's one of the seven languages I speak, along with English, German, Italian, Anglo-Saxon, Greek, and Latin.

Q: WE BET YOU'D LIKE TO CONDUCT THE INTERVIEW IN FRENCH! But that's a big *non*, mister. This is America and we'll speak English. French is for impersonating Miss Piggy, and Latin is for saying *"carpe diem"* when I have a second piece of pie.

A: So . . . did you have any questions?

Q: You were in Paris from 1784 to 1789. Just what exactly were you doing there for so long?

A: I was the American ambassador to France.

Q: Sounds like real a hardship post, having to live in Paris instead of rural Virginia.

A: Now you sound like *you* like France more than America. Do *you* like France more than America?

Q: We're asking the questions here! Do you admit that you tried to get the United States to align with France instead of Great Britain, our nation's closest, most special friend?

A: Yes, absolutely. Keep in mind that it had been only a few years since we fought a war against Great Britain, and it would be only a few years more before we fought another one.

Q: We don't even know what you're talking about. But anyway, do you admit that you were in Paris for the storming of the Bastille, and that you let the Marquis de Lafayette and other revolutionaries hold planning meetings at your house? How can you associate yourself with such a bloodthirsty, chaotic rebellion?

A: Well, I thought the French Revolution was pretty great, and I think an occasional bloody uprising is necessary in any free country. It's like I said after Shays' Rebellion in 1787: "The tree of liberty must be refreshed from time to time with the blood of patriots and tyrants. It is its natural manure."

Q: Why would you refresh a tree with manure?

A: . . . What would *you* refresh it with?

Q: We don't know. But not manure. We'd probably just leave it alone. Trees seem pretty self-sufficient.

A: I have to be honest: I'm not really a good farmer. I could be way off base on this whole "refresh your trees with manure" thing.

Vital Stats

Looks: 8

Jefferson looks pretty handsome in all his portraits. As he should, if he's the one paying the artist. If J.D. ever commissions a portrait of himself, people who see it are going to ask "Why do you own an oil painting of Brad Pitt?"

Physique: 8

One of Jefferson's workers at Monticello described him as "Six feet two and a half inches high, well proportioned, and straight as a gun barrel. He was like a fine horse—he had no surplus flesh." Which is a weird way to describe your boss, but maybe it was end-of-the-year bonus time.

Charisma: 3

Jefferson has a problem with mumbling. (Specifically, the problem is that he mumbles. He has no problem with it if *you* mumble.)

Sense of irony: 1

When Jefferson's presidency ended, he said he felt like "a prisoner, released from his chains." Ha! If you say so, Mr. President!

JAMES MADISON

1809–1817 | Democratic-Republican

Perhaps you're in the market for a tiny president* whom you can carry around in your purse, popping his head out occasionally to grumble about government tyranny. Allow us to introduce James Madison!

Sometimes great things come in small packages. Other times, shy and sickly things come in small packages. The point is, you don't know what is going to be inside of a small package until you elect it president. James Madison is a genius politician, but he's also nervous, prone to hypochondria, and got us into the War of 1812. (If you're not sure which war that was, it's the one that started in 1812.)

We know he doesn't sound amazing on paper. (At least, not on this piece of paper.) But Madison still managed to marry a woman who is gorgeous, vivacious, and—as if that weren't enough—great at saving paintings.

* Actual size: 5'4"

Why You'll *Love* Him

He's a nerd. You are reading a book about the U.S. presidents for fun right now, so don't try to tell us you're not into nerds.

He's the Father of the Constitution. You say you're not interested in guys with kids, but what if that kid was over 200 years old and made of paper?

You can give him piggyback rides. As your legs and back grow stronger, you'll eventually be able to upgrade to more of an Adams and then, finally, to a Taft.

He's best friends with Thomas Jefferson. Maybe he'll introduce you to Thomas Jefferson!

Madison's nickname is "Little Jemmie" for no other reason than because it is a great nickname.

Madison had two vice presidents, both of whom died in office. He didn't appoint a third, because he couldn't bear to kill again.

JAMES MADISON WROTE THE CONSTITUTION AND THE BILL OF RIGHTS! SO IT'S HIS FAULT THEY ARE BOTH SO BORING.

Here's a Tip

When Madison was courting Dolley Payne Todd, he asked her young cousin to write love letters to Dolley on his behalf. Madison would then read and approve all of the letters before they were sent to Dolley. This may sound strange, but it worked for James Madison, and it can work for you! It will be like a fun, sexy game between you, the object of your desire, and the object of your desire's cousin.

LOVE STORY

At the age of 43, Madison developed a crush on a hot young Quaker widow named Dolley Payne Todd. Like any normal guy, Madison decided to stalk his crush for a while before asking her out. He quietly interviewed her friends, he secretly investigated her family, and when everything checked out, bam!—he made his move.

His move was to ask a mutual friend to tell Dolley that he liked her. (The mutual friend was Aaron Burr. What a great guy!) We imagine their conversation as having gone something like this:

Aaron Burr: Hi, Dolley Madison! Whoops, I mean Dolley Payne Todd. I forgot that not everyone can see the future, like I can.

Dolley Payne Todd: Hello, Aaron Burr.

Aaron Burr: So, I have this friend . . .

Dolley Payne Todd: Pass.

Aaron Burr: Wait—hear me out! He's 17 years older than you, weighs about 100 pounds, and mistakenly believes he has epilepsy.

Dolley Payne Todd: I admit I'm intrigued. I've always wanted to date a guy with epilepsy, but I might be willing to settle for a guy who just thinks he has epilepsy. At 26 years old, I can hardly afford to be choosy.

Aaron Burr: No, you can't. Oh, and this is unrelated, but if I'm ever accused of treason and have to flee to Europe, would you mind helping me get a passport so I can sneak back into the country?

Dolley Payne Todd: Uh . . . sure.

How to Win His Heart

💜 **He's into younger women.** Are you a teenager? If so, James Madison might be interested. Also, good for you for reading a book!

💜 **Opposites attract.** Which means that if you want to attract James Madison, you'll need to be the most outgoing, charming, and stylish person ever. And tall. You're going to have be pretty tall.

Heartbreak!

Madison's first love was a 15-year-old named Kitty Floyd. He was 32 at the time, so . . . moving on. Kitty broke it off with him after she fell in love with someone her own age who probably didn't have crippling hypochondria. She gave Madison the news by sending him a letter that was sealed with dough, because this was somehow supposed to indicate that her feelings for Madison had "soured." And that is what you get for dating a 15-year-old.

Get the Look!

James Madison wears **ALL BLACK,** from head to toe, **EVERY DAY.** So go to your closet, put on your smallest all-black outfit, and go try to flirt with teenagers. It will be like Madison himself is walking the earth again, with his tiny pitter-patter!

Vital Stats

Looks: 3

Washington Irving once described Madison as a "withered little applejohn." Which I guess is better than calling him a big applejohn. You don't want *too* much applejohn.

Physique: 1

On the plus side, you can borrow his clothes!

Charisma: 2

Madison has all the charisma of a small, sickly man dressed entirely in black.

Having epilepsy: 5

Madison's epilepsy symptoms were psychosomatic. But if you *think* you're having a seizure, and you *look* like you're having a seizure, isn't that sort of the same thing as actually *having* a seizure? (No, it isn't. But we do think it deserves a 5 out of 10.)

How it really happened!

The following dramatization of how Dolley Madison rescued a portrait of George Washington from the White House in 1814 is based on a true story. (Specifically, the story of how Dolley Madison rescued a portrait of George Washington from the White House in 1814.)

DISCLAIMER: Any resemblance to persons living is an alarming coincidence, because this happened over 200 years ago. Any resemblance to persons dead is the result of our exhaustive research and scholarship.

DOLLEY MADISON: ART THIEF

A Play in One Act

Scene 1

SETTING: It is August 1814. The War of 1812 has been going on for a while (you can do the math), and the invading British Army is about to enter Washington, DC. Most people in the city have fled, and the White House has been evacuated except for DOLLEY MADISON and a few servants.

AT RISE: DOLLEY MADISON is in the White House dining room, along with the slaves PAUL JENNINGS and SUKEY. There is the sound of cannons firing in the background, ideally because actual cannons are being fired backstage. PAUL JENNINGS and SUKEY are frantically packing. DOLLEY MADISON is also packing, but less frantically. There is a large portrait of George Washington hanging on the wall. Don't skip this part—it will be important to the plot later!

DOLLEY MADISON
Let's see. I have a few boxes of important papers, a bunch of silver, my favorite red drapes, and a random clock. I think that's everything. Let's go be refugees!

(DOLLEY MADISON picks up a box and starts walking toward the door. As she passes the portrait of George Washington, she stops to stare at it for a moment. Then she drops the box with a loud thud.)

DOLLEY MADISON
Uh oh.

PAUL JENNINGS
(wearily) What's 'uh oh'?

DOLLEY MADISON
We forgot to pack this painting of George Washington!

PAUL JENNINGS

You mean . . . this painting here? The one that is eight feet tall and screwed to the wall?

DOLLEY MADISON

Yes!

PAUL JENNINGS

I don't know if I'd say we "forgot" to pack it. I think it's more like "we accurately assessed that there is no time to pack it."

DOLLEY MADISON

But I decided just now that it is a symbol of everything America stands for! We can't let it fall into the hands of the British.

SUKEY

Mrs. Madison, it is a very nice painting, but I'm worried that if we stay here any longer we will be killed. Even the mayor has come by, twice, to beg you to leave.

DOLLEY MADISON

Ah yes, I remember that. It was earlier today!

SUKEY

And what about those terrifying letters you've been getting from British admiral George Cockburn?

DOLLEY MADISON

Oh, that reminds me—I just received another letter from him today!
(Pulls a letter out of pocket and starts reading.)

"DEAR DOLLEY MADISON,
REMEMBER HOW IN MY LAST LETTER I SAID I WAS GOING TO BURN DOWN THE WHITE HOUSE WITH YOU IN IT? WELL FORGET ABOUT THAT, BECAUSE I'VE THOUGHT ABOUT IT SOME MORE AND DECIDED THAT INSTEAD I'M GOING TO CAP-TURE YOU AND PARADE YOU THROUGH THE STREETS OF LONDON WHILE PEOPLE THROW TOMATOES AT YOU. AND NOT IN A NICE WAY LIKE 'HERE IS A DELICIOUS TOMATO FOR YOU TO EAT,' BUT IN A MEAN WAY, LIKE 'HERE IS A TOMATO, AND I HATE YOU.'
LOVE, ADMIRAL GEORGE COCKBURN"

SUKEY

See? That's what I'm talking about it! Just forget about the painting—we need to get as far away from here as possible.

DOLLEY MADISON

But don't you see? If the British capture this painting of George Washington, it will be exactly as if they captured George Washington himself.

PAUL JENNINGS

(after a pause) Actually . . . that's not how paintings work.

DOLLEY MADISON

I hate to pull rank on you, but as the only person here who is not a slave I am going to have to insist that we carry this painting with us. By which of course I mean that you will carry it.

(CHARLES CARROLL enters, looking harried.)

DOLLEY MADISON

Ah, it's my good friend Charles Carroll! Not the Charles Carroll who signed the Declaration of Independence, of course, but his cousin who is also named Charles Carroll.

CHARLES CARROLL

Um, yes...I know who I am. Anyway, I just came over to escort you out of town, as promised. I saw that your wagon was packed full of drapes, so you must be all ready to go now?

DOLLEY MADISON

Oh Mr. Carroll, I'm so glad you're here. You can help us get this painting down from the wall.

CHARLES CARROLL

This...wait, we're doing what now?

(END OF SCENE)

Scene 2

SETTING: The White House dining room, half an hour later.

AT RISE: DOLLEY MADISON is supervising while PAUL JENNINGS tries to unscrew the painting from the wall. He is helped by FRENCH JOHN, the doorman, and THOMAS MCGRAW, the gardener.

FRENCH JOHN

Mrs. Madison, it's going to take us forever to unscrew this painting from the wall. And you know that it's just a copy of the original Gilbert Stuart painting, right? I feel like no one is talking about that.

THOMAS MCGRAW

And I'm just the gardener, so I don't really see why I need to be here at all...

(CHARLES CARROLL enters, looking panicked.)

CHARLES CARROLL

Mrs. Madison, my carriage is waiting outside. We really must leave right now.

DOLLEY MADISON

We're almost done, Mr. Carroll, no thanks to you! Now, if we can't unscrew the painting from the wall, we'll have to cut it out of its frame. But let's go very, very slowly so we don't accidentally damage the painting. I mean, really slowly.

(FRENCH JOHN uses a hatchet to break the outer frame, whatever that is, and PAUL JENNINGS starts cutting out the canvas with a knife.)

DOLLEY MADISON

Slower.

PAUL JENNINGS

(groaning) There.

DOLLEY MADISON

It is done!

CHARLES CARROLL

OK, let's get out of here.

DOLLEY MADISON

Wait! First I want to write all of this down in a letter to my sister.

(END OF SCENE)

Scene 3

SETTING: Outside, in front of the White House.

AT RISE: FRENCH JOHN and PAUL JENNINGS walk outside carrying the painting, followed by DOLLEY MADISON, THOMAS MCGRAW, SUKEY, and ANYONE ELSE I'M FORGETTING. CHARLES CARROLL is in his carriage.

DOLLEY MADISON

Uh oh.

PAUL JENNINGS

I'm going to pretend I did not just hear you say "uh oh."

DOLLEY MADISON

I just realized that if I am captured, the painting will be captured along with me!

CHARLES CARROLL

Yes. In fact, that might happen right here, on the White House porch, while we are standing around talking about it.

DOLLEY MADISON

(calling to passersby) Excuse me, gentlemen!

(TWO RANDOM GUYS walk over.)

DOLLEY MADISON

I was wondering if you would mind holding onto this painting for me, so that the British do not get ahold of it? Wait . . . you're not British yourselves, are you?

ONE OF THE RANDOM GUYS

No ma'am. At least, not yet.

DOLLEY MADISON

Perfect. Now, you should know that I recently decided this painting is a symbol of our entire country, so it's pretty important. Under no circumstances should it fall into the hands of the British. Save it if possible, but if not, destroy it.

CHARLES CARROLL

Destroy it? If destroying it was an option, why didn't we just destroy it ourselves an hour ago?

(RANDOM GUYS take the painting and walk off.)

DOLLEY MADISON

Yay, I'm a hero!

CHARLES CARROLL

(sarcastic) Oh yes. I'm sure Americans will be talking about this heroic act of bravery and valor for generations.

(Everyone climbs into the carriage, and the carriage departs.)

DOLLEY MADISON

(from off-stage) Uh oh. I forgot my parrot!

(END OF SCENE)

THE END

JAMES MONROE

1817–1825 | Democratic-Republican

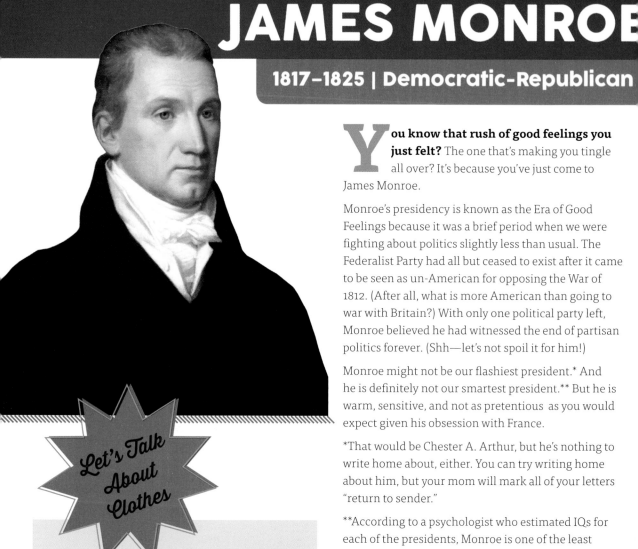

Let's Talk About Clothes

Sometimes people get stuck in fashion ruts, like your dental hygienist who wears a scrunchie. That's how James Monroe is. In the year 1820, he's still dressing like it's 1805! And yet he persists in wearing buckled shoes and knee breeches, even though they make him look like a time traveler from the very recent past.

You know that rush of good feelings you just felt? The one that's making you tingle all over? It's because you've just come to James Monroe.

Monroe's presidency is known as the Era of Good Feelings because it was a brief period when we were fighting about politics slightly less than usual. The Federalist Party had all but ceased to exist after it came to be seen as un-American for opposing the War of 1812. (After all, what is more American than going to war with Britain?) With only one political party left, Monroe believed he had witnessed the end of partisan politics forever. (Shh—let's not spoil it for him!)

Monroe might not be our flashiest president.* And he is definitely not our smartest president.** But he is warm, sensitive, and not as pretentious as you would expect given his obsession with France.

*That would be Chester A. Arthur, but he's nothing to write home about, either. You can try writing home about him, but your mom will mark all of your letters "return to sender."

**According to a psychologist who estimated IQs for each of the presidents, Monroe is one of the least smart presidents. He is also not a very smart dresser, but we didn't need a psychologist to tell us that.

IT'S EASY TO CONFUSE JAMES MONROE WITH JAMES MADISON.

If you have trouble telling them apart, just remember that James Madison is the short one, and James Monroe is the one about whom you know nothing.

Why You'll *Love* Him

He'll protect you from foreign entanglements. So if you want to date the King of Spain, you'll need to tell James Monroe to back off. If that doesn't work, hiss at him, like a cat.

He knows how to acquire weapons. While studying at the College of William and Mary, Monroe was part of a group of students who raided the royal governor's mansion and stole over 200 muskets and 300 swords. Which raises a lot of questions, mostly about why the governor was keeping so many muskets and swords at his house.

He's a Francophile. Monroe is like your college roommate who spent one semester in France and now won't stop talking about how pointy the Eiffel Tower is.

He's a soldier. Remember when George Washington crossed the Delaware River on Christmas Day to launch a sneak attack on the Hessian army? James Monroe was there, too! Not in the same boat though. It's not a good idea to put a bunch of future presidents all in one boat.

He'll go into personal debt for his country. Which is more important—having money, or having a noble husband who incurs huge amounts of debt in the course of serving his country?

ANSWER: Having money.

Sort-of Fun Facts

Monroe came very close to fighting a duel with Alexander Hamilton. Eventually they were talked out of it by—wait for it—Aaron Burr.

In what came to be called the Monroe Doctrine, James Monroe announced that the US would not tolerate any more European interference in the Americas. And that's why to this day Norway can't establish a colony in your driveway, however much it might want to.

At the Battle of Trenton, Monroe almost died after he was hit in the shoulder by a musket ball and it severed an artery. A doctor saved his life by clamping the artery shut. There—now you know how to treat severed arteries! We bet you can't wait to put that one to use.

Here's a Tip

Do you have any friends you'd like to rescue from prison? Sure, we all do. But before you waste a perfectly good cake by baking a hacksaw into it, here is something else you can try:

1. PUT ON YOUR NICEST CLOTHES—LIKE A TUXEDO, OR YOUR WEDDING DRESS.
2. RENT A FANCY CAR. MAYBE ONE OF THOSE LIMOS WITH A HOT TUB IN THE BACK.
3. VISIT YOUR FRIEND IN PRISON.

The warden will be so intimidated that he might decide to let your friend go. This is basically how James Monroe's wife rescued the Marquis de Lafayette's wife from a Parisian prison during the French Revolution. Monroe also funneled money to the marquise so that she could travel to Austria and reunite with her husband. Who was in prison. But the Austrian emperor gave her special permission to join her husband in prison, which she did. And they lived there together, in solitary confinement, for two years. Oh, and their daughters were there, too. (If you're thinking this would be a great premise for a sitcom, then you need to back off and stop stealing our ideas for sitcoms.)

FAMOUS FRIENDS

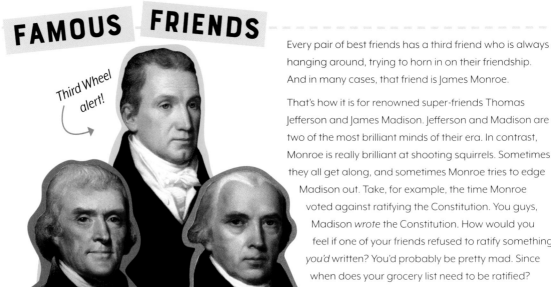

Third Wheel alert!

Every pair of best friends has a third friend who is always hanging around, trying to horn in on their friendship. And in many cases, that friend is James Monroe.

That's how it is for renowned super-friends Thomas Jefferson and James Madison. Jefferson and Madison are two of the most brilliant minds of their era. In contrast, Monroe is really brilliant at shooting squirrels. Sometimes they all get along, and sometimes Monroe tries to edge Madison out. Take, for example, the time Monroe voted against ratifying the Constitution. You guys, Madison *wrote* the Constitution. How would you feel if one of your friends refused to ratify something *you'd* written? You'd probably be pretty mad. Since when does your grocery list need to be ratified?

What Is the Missouri Compromise?

Pop QUIZ

a. When you and your spouse are arguing over where to move, but you agree to take Missouri off the list.

b. A deal struck by Congress that admitted Missouri to the Union as a slave state but prohibited slavery in all other territories north of the 36°30' parallel. It also conjured Maine into existence.

c. Just like "going Dutch" means to split the bill on a date, a "Missouri Compromise" is when one person pays for dates north of the 36°30' parallel, and the other person pays for dates south of the 36°30' parallel.

d. When you have a disagreement with someone from Missouri, and he offers to settle it by flipping a coin, so you give him a coin, and he runs off with it. You've just been "Missouri Compromised"!

Answer:
The answer is (b). It was one of several failed attempts to settle the national dispute over slavery by agreeing to have the United States be just a *little bit* of a slave nation, just as one can be just a little bit pregnant.

Favorite Pickup Line

"Just lie back and relax. The Era of Good Feelings is about to start."

Vital Stats

Looks: 4

He does have a very cute dimple on his chin. As he leans in toward you, just try to focus your eyes on that.

Physique: 7

Monroe is tall, broad, and comes with a free musket ball lodged in his shoulder, like the prize in a box of cereal.

Charisma: 4

You know you're not very charismatic when you lose an election to James Madison.

Jailbreaks: 8

While serving as Minister to France, Monroe not only helped free the Marquis de Lafayette's wife from prison, he also convinced French revolutionaries to release Thomas Paine. So if you get put in prison in France, try dropping Monroe's name and see if that does the trick. (If you don't know how to speak French, what you want to say is *"Le fantôme vengeur du président américain James Monroe va me libérera et vous tuer tous."*)

JOHN QUINCY ADAMS

AW, LOOK—HE LIKES YOU!

If you haven't figured it out yet, John Quincy Adams is John Adams's son. What a crazy coincidence that they would both become president!

The expression "Absence makes the heart grow fonder" will never feel more true than when you're dating John Quincy Adams. After you haven't seen him for a few months, you'll forget all about how moody and controlling he is and just remember the good stuff, like how he has really pointy eyebrows. As the weeks go by, you might even find yourself taking out a miniature portrait of him so you can gaze at it for a while, and . . . eh, actually, let's just put that back in the drawer. Maybe instead you should reread his most recent letter—you know, the one where he calls you shallow and immature? No? Never mind, then!

The good news is that John Quincy Adams is absent a lot, so you'll have plenty of opportunities to grow fond of him. As a prominent diplomat, he travels all over the world, and sometimes you won't be invited. Other times you are invited, but your children aren't, and then you don't get to see them for six years. So maybe don't get too attached to your children. (Which is good advice anyway when you're living in the 19th century.)

Part of what makes John Quincy Adams so difficult to live with is that he despises everything pleasurable, like spending money and being lazy, and he only enjoys things that are unpleasant, like cold baths and working for the government. He's also pretty bossy. One time his wife, Louisa, decided to put on a little blush before going to a party. When Adams saw it, he wiped it right off her face. Another time she wouldn't let him wipe it off, so he left for the party without her. So much for having a fun night out in Prussia!

But this is the price you have to pay to be in a relationship with the most brilliant man ever elected president and the greatest diplomat in our nation's history. So it sort of balances out, right?

Oh, and also his mom hates you.

Why You'll *Love* Him

He'll assign you reading lists. Remember how in school, your teachers made you spend summer vacation reading a bunch of boring books? You've had a sweet taste of what it's like to date John Quincy Adams!

He'll make you send him written progress reports on the aforementioned reading lists. It's just like your sexy-but-stern professor fantasy, but without the "sexy" part. (He makes up for it, though, by being extra stern!)

There's an alligator living in his bathtub. The Marquis de Lafayette gave John Quincy Adams an alligator. You like alligators, right? Great! Maybe just use the bathroom before you come over.

Let's Talk About Clothes

John Quincy Adams was the first president to wear pants. That's right—pants! You don't even want to know what all of those other presidents were doing before pants came along.

Heartbreak!

JOHN QUINCY ADAMS was almost engaged to a woman named Mary Frazier, but his mom convinced him to call it off. He was crushed and remained bitter about it for years. But the real heartbreak is that our sixth president was so easily pushed around by his mom.

IT IS I, ABIGAIL ADAMS, ADDRESSING YOU FROM THE PAST THROUGH THE MEDIUM OF THIS BOOK. HELLO! THAT IS ALL I HAD TO SAY.

In the election of 1824, none of the candidates for president won a majority of electoral votes, so the decision was kicked to the House of Representatives. That is the system our Founding Fathers put in place so they could mess with us.

Andrew Jackson thought he had it in the bag, possibly because he didn't know how to count, and he was furious when he lost to John Quincy Adams. He accused Adams of striking a "corrupt bargain" with influential congressman Henry Clay, in which Clay traded his support to Adams in exchange for the position of secretary of state. But if there's one thing Andrew Jackson is good at (other than styling his hair), it's plotting revenge. He and his supporters spent the next four years trashing Adams's reputation and blocking him in Congress so effectively that his presidency was pretty much a failure.

So now you know the story of the election of 1824! And you shall carry a terrible curse until you tell someone else the story of the election of 1824. (Sorry, we probably should have mentioned that earlier!)

Did you know John Quincy Adams spoke six languages?
See if you can identify all of them!

☐ **English**

☐ **French**

☐ **Dutch**

☐ **Latin**

☐ **German**

☐ **Greek**

☐ **Mandarin**

☐ **Swahili**

☐ **C++**

☐ **Na'vi**

☐ **Expressive glares**

☐ **Whatever it is that whales speak**

Vital Stats

Looks: 4

We know Adams *looks* evil, but he really isn't evil. He's just kind of a crappy boyfriend.

Physique: 8

Adams likes to suffer, so he loves exercising. He would start each day with a refreshing swim in the Potomac River, nude. It was a simpler time then, when if you saw a naked body in the Potomac, you would just think, "Hey, there's the president!"

Charisma: 3

Adams described himself as "a man of reserved, cold, austere, and forbidding manners." And this was in his *diary*, which is where most of us go to lie about ourselves.

Diplomacy: 10

Some people think John Quincy Adams is the greatest diplomat in American history. Others will never forgive him for negotiating an end to the War of 1812 without demanding that Britain give us Canada as a pet.

Favorite Pickup Line

"I need to get my library card, because I'm checking you out!"

(Said while speaking to a book)

35

CANADA, OUR ANCIENT ENEMY

Like a sprawling barbarian horde, Canadians have for centuries peered jealously across the border at their civilized neighbor to the south, waiting for an opportunity to catch us off guard. And it takes a steel-willed president to keep these icy foes at bay. How have the U.S. presidents fared in this, their most solemn and sacred responsibility? Overall, pretty poorly.

Sometimes, you want a strong man who will protect you and keep you safe, from Canada.

GEORGE WASHINGTON

In 1775, the Continental army invaded Canada in the hopes of convincing Québec to join the colonies in their rebellion against Britain. While persuading a bunch of French Canadians to become Americans sounds like a can't-miss plan, amazingly, it didn't pan out. Washington was commander of the Continental army rather than president at the time, but we're still going to ding him for this one.

JAMES MADISON

Madison knew that the only languages Canadians understand are English, French . . . and force. When the British Empire kept making Americans join the British navy, Madison responded by trying to make Canada join America. U.S. forces invaded Canada at several points along the border, and even managed to capture parts of Ontario. (Which would feel like a more significant accomplishment if we knew what an Ontario is.)

MARTIN VAN BUREN

In 1837, a group of patriotic Canadians and Americans who shared the simple dream of overthrowing the Canadian government were attacked in U.S. waters on their ship *Caroline*, which was then set on fire and sent over Niagara Falls. Even though sending a flaming warship over Niagara Falls is awesome, Martin Van Buren knew he needed to respond, and that his response needed to be stronger than simply saying, "Guys that was awesome." We think a massive invasion of Canada would have been appropriate, but instead he got an apology, which is better than nothing.

"No no, we insist, you climb up first. We're going to watch so we can warn you if the ladder starts to look unstable."

of your visit, try telling them "War Plan Red." This might trigger "Defense Scheme No. 1," Canada's war plan for a counter-invasion of the U.S. That plan involves crossing the border and capturing Albany, and we're OK with that.

If you're a maritime firefighter, here's a tip: You can put out a burning ship by sailing it over Niagara Falls.

JAMES K. POLK

Dreamboat James K. Polk won the presidency, at least in part, by promising to annex the Pacific Northwest all the way up to Alaska. But once in the White House, he settled for the current border, because he was afraid of going to war with Canada and Mexico simultaneously. That, right there, should have disqualified him from the presidency. Part of the presidential oath of office should be, "I hope I get to go to war with Canada and Mexico simultaneously."

ANDREW JOHNSON

In 1866, a group of more than 1,000 Irish-American Civil War veterans invaded Canada from Buffalo as part of a convoluted scheme to force the British Empire to grant Ireland independence. They won their first couple of battles against the Canadian militia, but then President Johnson—who was always looking for new ways to fail—ordered the U.S. Army to stop them. When you hear people say it's a tragedy that Lincoln didn't get to finish his second term, this is probably what they're talking about.

CALVIN COOLIDGE

While Calvin Coolidge was commander-in-chief, the U.S. military created "War Plan Red," a strategy for war with Britain that consisted primarily of a massive invasion and occupation of Canada. Under War Plan Red, U.S. forces would invade "Crimson" (Canada's code name) from North Dakota, the Midwest, the Great Lakes, and Vermont. So the next time you lose a bet and have to go to Canada, when the customs officer asks for the purpose

HERBERT HOOVER

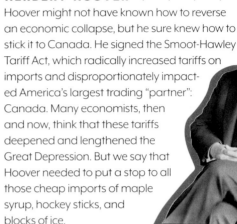

Hoover might not have known how to reverse an economic collapse, but he sure knew how to stick it to Canada. He signed the Smoot-Hawley Tariff Act, which radically increased tariffs on imports and disproportionately impacted America's largest trading "partner": Canada. Many economists, then and now, think that these tariffs deepened and lengthened the Great Depression. But we say that Hoover needed to put a stop to all those cheap imports of maple syrup, hockey sticks, and blocks of ice.

HARRY S. TRUMAN

In 1948, Newfoundland held a referendum on whether to remain a British territory, gain independence, or join Canada. Harry S. Truman, probably because he was too busy waving that "Dewey Defeats Truman" newspaper around, failed to press for a fourth option to be included on the ballot, "Join the winning team: America!" And that's why everyone in Newfoundland is so sad all the time, even to this day.

RICHARD NIXON

Finally, a president who knows how to stand up to those bullies in Ottawa. In a speech to the Canadian Parliament in 1972, Nixon essentially broke up with Canada, saying, "It is time for us to recognize that we have very separate identities," "we have significant differences," and "I've met someone else." (He didn't say that last part, except maybe to himself, under his breath.) Richard Nixon didn't become president to make friends, folks. He did it to make *enemies*.

37

ANDREW JACKSON

1829–1837 | Democrat

Are you ready for the most intense, romantic, and terrifying relationship you've ever had? Because we'll be honest—you don't look ready.

The main thing you need to know about dating Andrew Jackson is that you can never, ever break up with him. South Carolina tried breaking up with him once, and that's why to this day South Carolina is a smoking wasteland incapable of supporting human life. Jackson's troops also tried breaking up with him, and he stopped them by holding them at gunpoint. (There was some dispute over whether they were deserting, or their enlistments were just up. As it turns out, when Andrew Jackson is your commanding officer, your enlistment is never up. You are bound into service for life, just like when you join the Girl Scouts.)

Clearly this is a man who does not deal with abandonment well. Some historians argue that's because his entire family abandoned him (by dying) when he was pretty young—but shouldn't that make him really *good* at dealing with abandonment?

Anyway—if you can get past what is obviously a huge red flag, then you and Andrew Jackson will probably be very happy together. He has the elegant manners of a wealthy gentleman, the sex appeal of a dangerous bad boy, and the hair of a character from *Fraggle Rock.* Plus he's a national celebrity and a champion of the common man! (But only the common men who are white and who have not offended him somehow. Which narrows down the list considerably.)

> IT'S HARD TO RESIST A MAN IN UNIFORM. YOU JUST WANT TO REACH OUT AND UNBUTTON ONE OF THOSE LITTLE BRASS BUTTONS. THEN ANOTHER, THEN ANOTHER, THEN ANOTHER, THEN ANOTHER, THEN . . . WELL, YOU'RE PROBABLY GOING TO BE HERE FOR A WHILE. (JUST WAIT UNTIL YOU SEE HIS PANTS!)

Why You'll *Love* Him

He invades Florida whenever he feels like it. Andrew Jackson isn't the kind of guy who waits for official orders before invading Florida. He invades Florida whenever he decides that Florida needs invading. Which is surprisingly often! Or maybe not that surprising, if you've ever been to Florida.

He doesn't care if you're married. If you've made the mistake of marrying someone other than Andrew Jackson, you might think that there is no hope for romance between you and Andrew Jackson. But that could not possibly be further from the truth. Jackson married Rachel Donelson Robards even though she was sort of already married, and it was no big deal. Well, it was kind of a big deal to her first husband. But not to Andrew Jackson.

He'll defend your honor. Jackson will gladly kill anyone who gives you the side-eye. He'll also kill anyone who gives the side-eye to the person who gave you the side-eye. Uh oh, now he's just getting confused!

He is in possession of a large amount of cheese. If you like cheese, then you're in luck, because cheese is widely available at grocery stores everywhere. But if you like cheese and you're dating Andrew Jackson, then you're *really* in luck, because Jackson has a 1,400-pound wheel of cheese that he received as a gift from a (presumably well intentioned) dairy farmer. A lesser man might hoard all of that cheese for himself, but Jackson will happily share it with you. He's actually trying to get rid of it anyway, because the stench is overpowering. Bottoms up!*

This is what people often say before drinking a mug of cheese.

Pop QUIZ

Test your knowledge of Andrew Jackson by seeing if you can identify whom he killed versus whom he only threatened to kill.

	Killed	Threatened to Kill
The Governor of Tennessee		
Beloved statesman Henry Clay		
His own vice president		
Famous marksman Charles Dickinson		
Everyone in South Carolina		
About 4,000 Cherokees		
The National Bank		
Soldier who refused to clean up after breakfast		

See next page for answers!

ANSWER KEY

The Governor of Tennessee: Threatened to kill.

Jackson was supposed to duel Tennessee governor John Sevier, but Sevier's horse ran away with all of his weapons, so instead Jackson just chased him around the woods for a while.

Henry Clay: Threatened to kill.

Upon leaving the White House, Jackson said he had only two regrets. One was that he never shot Henry Clay.

His own vice president: Threatened to kill.

The other was that he didn't hang John C. Calhoun.

Charles Dickinson: Killed.

Jackson was in a LOT of duels, but only one duel ended with him killing a man, and that man was Charles Dickinson. When you look at it that way, Jackson actually showed a lot of restraint! And yet, when people talk about him, the word "restraint" never comes up.

Everyone in South Carolina: Threatened to kill.

As president, Jackson got into a showdown with South Carolina when they announced they were going to ignore any federal laws they didn't like. (Specifically, the law that required them to pay tariffs.) Jackson was ready to march an army into the rebellious state, but then South Carolina backed down, and he was probably secretly disappointed.

About 4,000 Cherokees: Killed.

Also as president, Jackson signed the Indian Removal Act, which forced Native American tribes to hand over their ancestral homelands in exchange for a forced death march. A lot of people died along the way (hence the term "death march"), but it was especially hard on the Cherokee tribe, about a fourth of whom perished. And then the ones who survived had to live in Oklahoma.

The National Bank: Killed.

Jackson told Martin Van Buren, "The bank, Mr. Van Buren, is trying to kill me, *but I will kill it.*" And he *did* kill the bank, in defiance of both Congress and most of his cabinet, by withdrawing all of the government's money. It was only later that he learned the bank was never actually trying to kill him, because it was a bank.

Soldier who refused to clean up after breakfast: Killed.

A teenage soldier under Jackson's command got into trouble when he refused to pick up the bones that some other soldiers had thrown on the ground during breakfast. (We don't know what they had been eating for breakfast, and we don't want to know.) The young soldier resisted arrest, so he was charged with mutiny and executed. This came back to haunt Andrew Jackson when his political opponents used it against him during his presidential campaign. Hopefully it also came back to haunt Andrew Jackson in the form of some sort of ghost.

How to Win His Heart

💜 **Be in danger.** Andrew Jackson wants to be the knight in shining armor who rescues you from danger. In fact, he insists on it. So if you're not currently in danger, you'll need to manufacture some kind of danger. Maybe the danger could involve quicksand, like if you accidentally ate a bunch of quicksand.

💜 **Be attractive.** Andrew Jackson prefers to be surrounded by good-looking people, and he will be more inclined to rescue you if you're naturally beautiful. Incidentally, this is also true of EMTs.

💜 **Be loyal.** After Andrew Jackson saves your life, he'll expect you to be loyal to him forever. (This is true of EMTs, too!)

Sort-of Fun Facts

Jackson started a gunfight in the streets of downtown Nashville. OK, technically the other guy was the first to pull out a gun. All because Andrew Jackson was chasing him with a whip. Come on—if you don't want to be chased with a whip, then you have no business going to Nashville.

Jackson defeated the British at the Battle of New Orleans and instantly became a national hero. Apparently no one cared that (1) the War of 1812 was already over, (2) he declared martial law in New Orleans and refused to lift it even after the British had left, (3) he imprisoned a state senator who said that martial law should be lifted, and (4) he imprisoned a judge who said he couldn't imprison a state senator. We'll stop the list there, but you get the idea: Jackson is an amazing hero of democracy who should definitely be on the twenty-dollar bill.

Vital Stats

Looks: 7

If you saw Andrew Jackson on the street, you probably wouldn't describe him as "handsome." "Striking" seems more appropriate, especially since he might literally be striking someone at the time.

Physique: 6

Jackson's body is long, lean, and contains more than the average number of bullets. (The average number is zero.)

Charisma: 10

Obviously Andrew Jackson is dripping with charisma. Otherwise there would be very little to recommend him as a human being.

Getting assassinated: 0

A mentally ill man tried to shoot Andrew Jackson in the back, but his gun misfired. So he pulled out another gun, and *that* gun misfired. And then Andrew Jackson started violently beating the guy with his walking cane. Later it was determined that it was a 1 in 125,000 chance that both guns would misfire that day. (It was probably a 1 in 3 chance that Andrew Jackson would beat someone with a cane that day.)

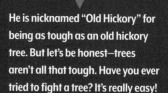

He is nicknamed "Old Hickory" for being as tough as an old hickory tree. But let's be honest—trees aren't all that tough. Have you ever tried to fight a tree? It's really easy!

Jackson was born in a log cabin, starting a trend among presidents that has proven almost as popular as the trend of being born extremely rich.

MARTIN VAN BUREN

Let's face it: You're not getting any younger. So are you finally ready to settle? Perhaps with a man who's just OK? What if we told you that the term "OK" was literally invented to describe one specific man? Getting interested? No? Well, then you're in the perfect frame of mind to learn about Martin Van Buren.

Van Buren is a schemy politician and Andrew Jackson protégé who basically invented the "political machine" system that greased the wheels of American politics for decades. He's the kind of guy who isn't going to judge you for anything, no matter how sketchy, and who would probably be willing to get you a job as a postmaster, if you're into that kind of thing.

If the prospect of a nice, plum job at the post office *isn't* enough to catch your eye, Van Buren is also (sort of) the origin of the word "OK." He hailed from Kinderhook, New York, and sometimes went by "Old Kinderhook," because back then, people liked their presidents good and old, like a nicely aged giant wheel of cheese. Van Buren's campaign decided to use "Vote for OK" instead of "Vote for Martin Van Buren" as their slogan, because they were lazy. Their Whig opponents countered with "Haha, 'OK' stands for 'Oll Korrect' because Van Buren doesn't know how to spell 'All Correct' because he is stupid."

That's a pretty sick burn, and it helped popularize the term "OK" as something that means, basically, "all correct." But as it turns out, people don't care whether or not the president can spell, so Van Buren won the election anyway. (That's why he's in this book!) But a crushing economic depression kept him from winning his party's nomination for reelection, and he had to run as the candidate of the anti-slavery "Free Soil" party. He lost, perhaps because people took the name "free soil" too literally, and no one was in the market for a bunch of dirt, at any price. The one immutable law of American politics is that no one wants a bunch of free dirt.

> **MARTIN VAN BUREN WAS ANDREW JACKSON'S DEVOTED PROTÉGÉ. AND NOT JUST WHEN IT CAME TO HAIR!**

Why You'll *Love* Him

To protect her privacy, Van Buren did not mention his wife Hannah a single time in his autobiography. This is a tradition many men carry on to this day in their Tinder profiles.

. . . .

He has an accent! Unfortunately, that accent is "Dutch."

. . . .

He's available! He is one of the only presidents who entered the White House single. In lieu of an actual wife, his 20-something stepdaughter Angelica served as his First Lady, which isn't creepy at all.

Here's a Tip

Martin Van Buren grew up in a tavern. Now, this isn't a parenting book, but if you want your children to grow up to be as successful as Martin Van Buren, why not try raising them in a tavern? Better yet—raise just one of them in a tavern, and keep the others at home as a control group.

WE ASKED . . . WHAT WAS YOUR MOST EMBARRASSING MOMENT?

> "
> There was this one time that the governor of Missouri ordered all Mormons in the state 'exterminated.' Mormon leader Joseph Smith asked me for help, and I told him, 'Your cause is just, but I can do nothing for you; if I take up for you I shall lose the state of Missouri.' Ugh, I cringe every time I remember the look on his face! But in my defense, I did end up winning Missouri.
> "

**Young Martin Van Buren is giving you his "come hither" look!
(Do not go hither.)**

Van Buren famously defused a tense situation on the Senate floor by walking over to the guy who was yelling at him (Henry Clay, who was the *worst*) and asking to borrow a pinch of snuff. You can try this too! But be careful, because there's a small chance they will actually have snuff. And then you're going to have to do some snuff.

Get the Look!

YOU DON'T HAVE TO DO ANYTHING TO GET THIS LOOK! THIS IS THE KIND OF LOOK THAT COMES TO YOU, WHETHER YOU LIKE IT OR NOT.

Vital Stats

Looks: 3

Martin Van Buren looks like a really convincing shopping mall Santa who has taken off his wig and beard during a bathroom break. And this scenario doesn't feel impossible. Who knows what kind of lives these mall Santas lead!

Physique: 3

Early in his career Van Buren worked as a town clerk, so he has that stereotypical "town clerk" build.

Charisma: 5

Van Buren is a great dealmaker, but he isn't the kind of guy who could charm the pants off of you. So that's a relief.

Nickname: 8

"Hey, come meet my friend Martin. Or, as we like to call him, 'Little Magician.' Get a few cups of rum punch in him, and you'll find out why!"

If you ever took the time to read the Federalist Papers, you'd know the Founders intended for presidential elections to be won by the hottest candidate. And yet, far too often, the American voters have cast their votes based on considerations like "Is he in my political party?" or "Would I enjoy having a beer with him, even though I don't like beer?" Here are some almost-presidents who slipped away.

John Frémont
(RAN FOR PRESIDENT IN 1856)

John Frémont was a famous explorer. Here he is exploring the inside of his coat.

Henry Clay
(RAN FOR PRESIDENT IN 1824, 1832, 1840, 1844, 1848)

Clay, known as "The Great Compromiser," ran for president no fewer than five times. He was beaten by men such as Andrew "I beat people literally, not just in elections" Jackson, Zachary "I've never voted" Taylor, and William "I think I'm coming down with something" Harrison.

George McClellan
(RAN FOR PRESIDENT IN 1864)

One way you know we're not ancient Rome is that when a commanding general like George McClellan wants to run the country, he challenges the incumbent in an election, instead of just marching his troops into the capital. The other ways you know we're not ancient Rome are 1) more cars, and 2) fewer orgies.

GOT AWAY

Alton B. Parker
(RAN FOR PRESIDENT IN 1904)

You only have to look at Alton B. Parker's big, soulful doe eyes to know that, in the 1904 presidential election, Teddy Roosevelt is going to take him down like a big, soulful doe.

William Jennings Bryan
(RAN FOR PRESIDENT IN 1896, 1900, 1908)

William Jennings Bryan lost three presidential elections, was fired as Woodrow Wilson's secretary of state, and was counsel for the "evolution is a bunch of hokey" side in the Scopes Monkey Trial. And yet he's best known for his "cross of gold" speech opposing the gold standard, which he gave at the 1896 Democratic National Convention. You, too, can make people forget about your shortcomings by giving a speech about the gold standard. In fact, we guarantee that if you climb onstage at the Democratic National Convention and start ranting about the gold standard, that's what you'll be known for.

Charles Evans Hughes
(RAN FOR PRESIDENT IN 1916)

If you're feeling sad that Charles Evans Hughes lost the 1916 election to Woodrow Wilson, console yourself with the fact that he was obviously better-suited to other careers. For example: 1) polar expedition leader, 2) viking, 3) walrus.

Alf Landon
(RAN FOR PRESIDENT IN 1936)

Alf Landon was able to shoot arrows that made people fall in love, but 1936 just wasn't a GOP year.

George McGovern
(RAN FOR PRESIDENT IN 1972)

In the 1972 election, even George McGovern's good looks couldn't overcome Richard Nixon's . . . what? What did Nixon have that McGovern didn't? Dark malevolence? Jowls? Apparently the silent majority demanded jowls.

John McCain
(RAN FOR PRESIDENT IN 2008)

Instead of nominating John McCain in 2008, the Republican Party should have nominated this photo of John McCain.

Al Gore
(RAN FOR PRESIDENT IN 2000)

Our only consolation is that a President Gore would probably have enslaved us all deep beneath the earth, mining for solar panels.

Mitt Romney
(RAN FOR PRESIDENT IN 2012)

Stop for a second and think about the fact that "Mitt" sounds like an actual name. Mitt Romney. Mitt Romney. It sounds normal, right? That's the indelible mark Mitt Romney has left on America.

WILLIAM HENRY HARRISON

1841–a little later in 1841 | Whig

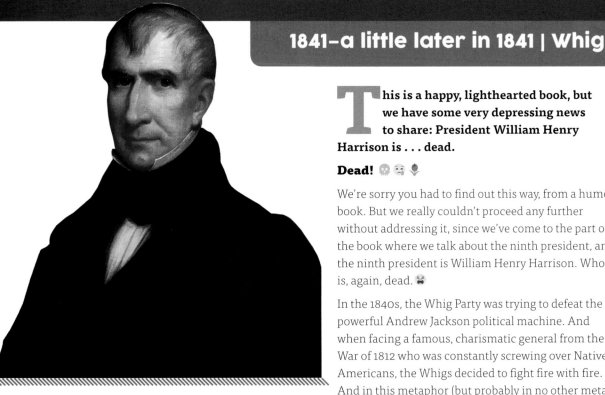

This is a happy, lighthearted book, but we have some very depressing news to share: President William Henry Harrison is . . . dead.

Dead! 💀 😵 🌷

We're sorry you had to find out this way, from a humor book. But we really couldn't proceed any further without addressing it, since we've come to the part of the book where we talk about the ninth president, and the ninth president is William Henry Harrison. Who is, again, dead. 💀

In the 1840s, the Whig Party was trying to defeat the powerful Andrew Jackson political machine. And when facing a famous, charismatic general from the War of 1812 who was constantly screwing over Native Americans, the Whigs decided to fight fire with fire. And in this metaphor (but probably in no other metaphor, ever) the "fire" was William Henry Harrison.

Unfortunately for his legacy, Harrison was taken far too soon. Not in the sense of age—he was 68, which is a longer life than someone born in 1773 has any right to hope for. Rather, he was taken too soon into his presidency. Harrison died on his 31st day in office, and his greatest accomplishment as president was giving the physicians in Washington something interesting to work on for a few days.

So, sadly, William Henry Harrison is not available for you to date. But you know what they say: If you miss one President Harrison, just wait awhile, because another one is bound to come along.

TRUE FACT THAT IS ALSO A
DOUBLE ENTENDRE

To show your support for Harrison (if he weren't dead 😵) you might be asked to "ROLL HIS BALLS." These were gigantic, 10-foot leather-and-tin balls covered in Harrison campaign slogans that supporters would roll from campaign stop to campaign stop, as a gimmick. In fact, this is the origin of the phrase "keep the ball rolling." So the next time someone says he wants to keep the ball rolling, picture him grunting and sweating as he rolls Harrison's balls. There—that meeting about end-of-year revenue projections just got more interesting!

Why You'll *Love* Him (Even Though He Is Dead 🏠)

He is a gold medalist. Congress awarded Harrison a gold medal for his performance during the War of 1812. Of course, this was in the days before they started testing generals for performance-enhancing drugs, so Harrison's record must always have an asterisk next to it.

He will help you rebel against your dad. Harrison wanted to marry 19-year-old Anna Symmes, but her father denied them permission. So the young couple eloped and honeymooned at "Fort Washington," which was not a resort town, or a rustic lodge, but a literal frontier army fort. When Anna's father demanded to know how Harrison could possibly support a family, the future president replied "Sir, my sword is my means of support." The historical record does not indicate whether Anna's father rolled his eyes.

His nickname is Tippecanoe. He got it by winning the Battle of Tippecanoe. This is a great nicknaming system, which is why we've nicknamed Dwight D. Eisenhower after his 1944-45 victory over the Germans in the famous Battle of the Bulge.

He did not live in a log cabin. Harrison's father was a wealthy governor of Virginia and a signer of the Declaration of Independence. But Martin Van Buren's campaign tried to tar Harrison as an uneducated hick who wanted to sit around a log cabin drinking hard cider. This backfired when Harrison's campaign took the insult and ran with it, giving away hard cider in log cabin-shaped bottles at campaign stops. And that's 1840s America for you! You might die of sepsis from getting a hangnail, but at least presidential campaigns were giving away liquor in novelty bottles.

Timeline: William Henry Harrison's *presidential daybook*

MARCH 4, 1841	MARCH 5-25, 1841	MARCH 26, 1841	MARCH 26– APRIL 3, 1841	APRIL 4, 1841
Be inaugurated. Don't wear a coat, despite the freezing rain. This will definitely make you look vigorous despite your age, and not like someone who is too old to know how to dress himself.	Spend all day, every day, meeting with people who want jobs in your administration. Boy, being president is everything that you dreamt it would be, in that one horrible nightmare where the presidency was an endless series of job interviews.	Tell your doctor you're feeling a little weak and anxious. (NOTE TO READER: If it's the 1840s and you're feeling sick, *don't* tell your doctor.)	Gradually deteriorate as doctors throw things at the wall to see what sticks. (Nothing "sticks," except in the sense that they "stick" a bunch of things into your body.)	Die. Now you belong to the ages, William Henry Harrison.

Top 7 "Medical" Treatments for *William Henry Harrison*

Get ready to have everything you think you know about William Henry Harrison shattered. Are you ready? He probably did not die of a case of pneumonia caught while giving his inaugural address. His likely cause of death was enteric fever, which he developed because the White House water supply was contaminated with raw sewage.

Doctors at the time weren't sure what was wrong with him, so they tried everything in their toolkit. Here are just some of the treatments they inflicted on President Harrison.

OPIUM Sure, this one *sounds* great. But put down your opium pipe for two seconds, hippie, and listen: Opiates make you constipated, which is the last thing you want if you have an enteric fever like typhoid. Plus, constipation gives 19th century doctors an excuse to do what they were already itching to do: Give you enemas.

STANDARD ENEMAS Before later revisions, the Hippocratic Oath began, "First, do no harm. Second, give round-the-clock enemas, no matter what's wrong with the patient."

LEECHES Having your body covered in leeches is a good way to take your mind off all the enemas.

VIRGINIA SNAKEWEED ENEMAS Unfortunately, nothing is going to take your mind off these.

DRINKING MERCURY The original Hippocratic Oath *also* instructed, "Try having the patient drink some mercury, and see what happens. Remember, no one lives forever!"

HOT BRANDY TODDY Oh thank God. Let this man expire with some dignity.

Pop QUIZ

William Henry Harrison achieved national fame for defeating the British at the Battle of the Thames. Where was this battle?

a. Surely it was on the Thames River, which runs through London, in England. If Harrison became one of the most famous men in America by winning a battle against the British called the Battle of the Thames, it must have been in England.

b. Just please don't tell me it was in Canada or something.

c. Again, I'd like to repeat my request that it not turn out that the battle was in Canada. We'd rightfully mock the British if they made a huge deal out of a victory against us called

the Battle of the Potomac and it was actually in Guam.

d. b and c

Answer: Sadly, the answer is (d). Please, we implore you: To salvage what's left of our national dignity, refer to this conflict as the "Battle of Moraviantown" the next time it comes up at a girls' night out.

Sort-of Fun Facts

Harrison was the last president born a British subject. Unless you count Barack Obama, of course. Obama was born in England, as "Merlin." But he is living backwards through time, so it's hard to say whether he or Harrison counts as the "last."

He's no George Washington. His parents were friends with George and Martha Washington, but young Tippecanoe ignored one of the central elements of Washington's success: Distilling whiskey. Harrison built a distillery at his hilariously named Indiana estate "Grouseland," but quickly closed it after deciding he didn't like seeing the effect of whiskey on people. In contrast, Washington's reaction on seeing his whiskey's effect on people was to contentedly count his money.

He went toe-to-toe with Jefferson on slavery. But not in a good way. As governor of the Indiana Territory, Harrison pushed for slavery to be spread to Illinois and Indiana. President Jefferson undermined him by clandestinely funding the construction of antislavery churches throughout the territory. (But before you pat Jefferson on the back *too* much, keep in mind that one of Jefferson's main objections to expanding slavery was that it would mean more African Americans.)

Vital Stats

Looks: 3

At the time, people thought Harrison was handsome. Of course, there was also a lot of free hard cider floating around.

Physique: 7

You're not going to be attracted to William Henry Harrison for his body. You're going to be attracted to him because you always fall for men you can't have, and you can't have William Henry Harrison, because he is dead.

Charisma: 4

Harrison got his start in the army by convincing a few dozen Philadelphian street toughs, ne'er-do-wells, and rogues to join his military unit and follow him to Ohio. And you have to be pretty persuasive to convince Philadelphians to move to Ohio for *any* reason.

Cursed:

Gather 'round the fire, children, and hear the tale of the "Curse of Tippecanoe." Some people believe that Harrison's victory at the Battle of Tippecanoe put a curse on the U.S. presidency. Specifically, the curse "Every president elected in a year that is a multiple of 20 will die in office." That sounds to us like a lot of math for a curse, but it held true for 120 years. Ronald Reagan, elected in 1980, was the first such president to live out his term since James Monroe. The lesson? You cannot curse someone magically shielded by Nancy Reagan's arcane wards and protections.

JOHN TYLER

1841–1845 | Whig (sort of)

The room was silent, except for the drip, drip, drip of fetid water hitting the floor as the creature approached the dais. Lurching down the aisle, it trailed pond scum and matted reeds like the train of a wedding dress.

"Tell me again why the vice president is a swamp monster?" one congressman whispered to another.

"It was the only way we could carry Virginia," someone behind him hissed.

It had been two days since the funeral of William Henry Harrison, and in the midst of the shock and confusion, no one had anticipated how swiftly and decisively the hitherto forgotten vice president John Tyler would emerge from its lair deep in the marshes of Virginia to claim the presidency as its own.

"I am just a humble creature from the swamp," Tyler's address to Congress began. "But now the ancient swamp gods have called on me to serve as your president. And to be clear, I will not be the 'acting president.' I distinctly heard the swamp gods say 'president.' If you attempt to send me letters that address me as 'acting president,' I will send the letters back to you unopened and, as with everything I touch, completely covered in slime."

There was a long pause, and the audience shifted uncomfortably in their chairs.

"I have taken an important vow today," the creature finally continued. "I vowed to defend the human Constitution. And I will keep that vow, especially the parts about states' rights, and the part that says swamp people are allowed to kidnap land people and enslave them in our underwater peat mines."

There was a smattering of applause from the congressmen who had not been listening closely, and the creature descended from the podium with a loud sloshing sound.

Sort-of Fun Facts

★ John Tyler believed in "sulphur hydrotherapy." This should surprise no one.

★ Tyler consumed large doses of mercury because he believed it to be good for his health. (Mercury is poisonous to humans, but may or may not be poisonous to creatures born of the swamp.)

★ When the Civil War broke out, Tyler was the only former president to side with the Confederacy, which has somewhat tarnished his otherwise unblemished reputation.

When the creature first spotted the beautiful and vivacious young woman, it felt a stirring in the empty cavity where its heart should be, but which instead held a second stomach. It was a sensation the creature hadn't felt since before its wife passed away, four long months ago. In that moment, the creature knew that it would not rest until it had wrapped this woman in its slimy limbs and dragged her back to the swamp to make her its queen.

At first, the lovely Julia Gardiner refused the president's advances, because come on. She was only 21, and although the creature claimed to be ageless, most people put it at around 52. For two years, she declined its proposals of marriage and promises of more duckweed than she could dream of. But the creature persisted, and it convinced Julia and her family to join it at a boat party that promised to be fun and free of tragic accidents. Unfortunately, there was a tragic accident: One of the boat's cannons exploded, killing several people, including Julia's father. When Julia found out, she fainted—right into the president's outstretched "arms."

Julia was devastated, and Tyler took advantage of her grief to convince her to accept one of its tentacles in marriage. And the couple lived happily ever after! If you have a sinking feeling in your stomach right now, don't worry—that's the feeling of having just read a really romantic story!

Why You'll *Love* It

It does as it pleases. Swamp creatures do not view themselves as subject to the laws of man, so they are definitely not going to take orders from the dumb Whig Party. Tyler was nominally a Whig but ignored party directives. So the Whigs in Congress expelled Tyler from the party and refused to pay to fix up the White House. (Years of neglect had turned the building into a decaying quagmire, where presumably Tyler felt perfectly at home.)

It refuses to mingle with commoners.
The commoners are mostly fine with this.

It pushed to annex Texas. If you enjoy having Texas as a part of the United States, thank John Tyler! If you don't, you can visit John Tyler's house in Virginia and throw eggs at it.

It will chase you. Tyler had a crush on a young woman named Julia Gardiner and would literally chase her around the White House. Onlookers commented that this behavior did not seem very presidential, but this was when people still believed that there should be standards for how presidents behave.

Vital Stats

Looks: 3

Maybe it's just us, but we think John Tyler looks a bit like a swamp monster.

Physique: 2

John Tyler is as thin as someone who survives on nothing but cattails, washed down with large amounts of mercury.

Charisma: 1

No.

Number of Children: 15

Tyler has fathered more children than any other president. There—that seems like a good, frightening note to end on!

HOTTEST HEADS OF STATE EXPLAINS:

I went to a wig party one time in college. I wore a Beatles wig. But not the kind of Beatles wig you're thinking of. This was more 1975 John Lennon. My girlfriend went as Yoko Ono, and we lay on the floor to recreate the famous Rolling Stone cover. Then my uncle kicked me out of the party and said it wasn't a wig party, it was a BBQ for my cousin's high school graduation. I still have the wig, though. I use it to get out of jury duty.

Umm . . . OK. The Whig Party wasn't *that* kind of wig party. It was a political party in the first half of the 1800s. It had nothing to do with wigs.

NOTHING to do with wigs? Are you trying to tell me that no one in it wore a wig?

Well, probably some people in the Whig Party wore wigs. But it's spelled w-h-i-g. The "h" is silent.

Can I just say that "the h is silent" would be a great password for a secret, underground speakeasy hosting a wig party?

You are not wrong. But did you have any questions about the Whig Party?

Where did they get the name "Whig"?

By the early 19th century, the word *whig* had come to stand for "anti-tyranny." Say . . . do you like etymology? We'd love to tell you all about how "whig" derives from "whiggamore," a Scots term for horse-driver. It is a thrilling tale that begins with Oliver Cromwell and war-wracked 1640s Britain.

No thank you. In fact, I insist you not tell me about it. But I would like to hear about how the Whigs were anti-tyranny.

To be more precise, they were anti–Andrew Jackson. In the 1830s, Jackson had accumulated a lot of power, and the Whig Party represented a broad coalition of people opposed to him: southern planters, northern industry, the anti-Masonic movement. And, more generally, people who didn't think the president should be a despot, and who opposed Jackson's ruthless treatment of Native Americans.

That sounds like a platform I could get behind, especially the anti-Masonic part. Were there ever any Whig presidents?

Yes, four of them.

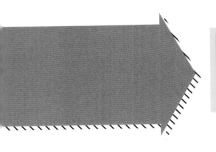

The Whig Party

Four so far, right? Does this book have some kind of anti-Whig bias? I am so sick of the mainstream humor book media. Your job is to report the facts, not opine on whether or not there will be additional Whig Party presidents.

OK. Four so far. William Harrison, John Tyler, Zachary Taylor, and Millard Fillmore.

Who?

Exactly. The Whigs didn't really leave their mark on the office, except that they were prominent among the presidents who failed to prevent the Civil War.

Still, it's impressive that they elected four presidents.

Actually, they only elected two presidents. But both of them died shortly after taking office, so their vice presidents took over. Abracadabra, two Whig presidents were turned into four! It's like cutting a worm in half.

That seems like a weird coincidence. Both of the Whigs who were elected president died in office? Is this what inevitably happens to presidents who dare to challenge the Freemasons and their iron grip on history?

At the risk of dignifying that question with an answer, no. Although if you want to fall down a rabbit hole into the dark, twisted heart of American conspiracy theorizing, Google "did the Freemasons assassinate Zachary Taylor?"

Maybe later. Right now, I'm pretty jazzed up to vote Whig this coming Election Day. How can I figure out who the Whig candidates are for my local school board, mosquito abatement district, and so forth?

We've got some bad news. The Whig Party disbanded in 1856, after fracturing over the issue of "Are members of minority groups actual human beings?" One part became the Republican Party. The other became the anti-Catholic, anti-immigrant "American Party," better known as the "Know-Nothings."

Man, that is bad news. When I vote, can I just write in "THE WHIG PARTY, BLAM!"

You could do worse.

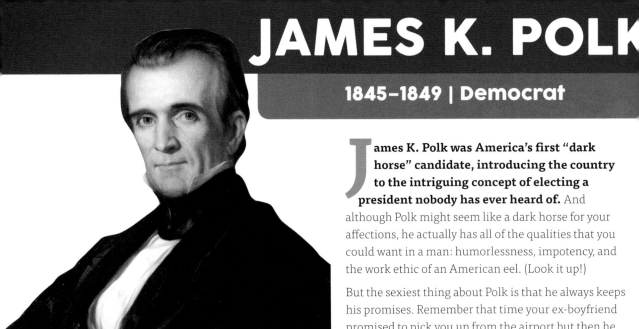

JAMES K. POLK

1845–1849 | Democrat

James K. Polk was America's first "dark horse" candidate, introducing the country to the intriguing concept of electing a president nobody has ever heard of. And although Polk might seem like a dark horse for your affections, he actually has all of the qualities that you could want in a man: humorlessness, impotency, and the work ethic of an American eel. (Look it up!)

But the sexiest thing about Polk is that he always keeps his promises. Remember that time your ex-boyfriend promised to pick you up from the airport but then he didn't, and you've been living at the airport ever since? That would never happen with James K. Polk. For one thing, he would never promise to pick you up at the airport. But when he *does* make a crazy promise, he keeps it. One time, he even kept four promises!

So after fulfilling all of his campaign promises in only four years, Polk retired without seeking a second term. He knew the key to showmanship is to leave the people wanting more. (Then a few months later he died, because he was overly committed to the principles of showmanship.)

> IF YOU'RE LOOKING FOR A BOYFRIEND WHO WORKS ALL OF THE TIME AND THEN DIES, THEN PUT AWAY YOUR BINOCULARS, BECAUSE HE'S RIGHT HERE! AND ALSO BECAUSE THAT IS A WEIRD WAY TO LOOK FOR BOYFRIENDS.

Here's a Tip

James K. Polk is always working, so he needs a partner who is prepared to spend a lot of time alone, pursuing solitary hobbies. Here are some ways you can stay busy while your presidential boyfriend is busy invading Mexico or whatever.

Go to church. That's one day down, six to go!

Pretend to needlepoint. This is more rewarding than actual needlepointing.

Become his secretary. Polk's wife, Sarah, basically functioned as his secretary. It was a lot like the movie *Secretary,* except with less spanking and more working quietly without any spanking.

DOES HE KEEP HIS *promises?*

☑ **Reestablish an Independent Treasury**

No one knows what this means, so when Polk promised to do it and then later said he'd done it, everyone just shrugged and went back to riding horses or farming cotton or whatever.

☑ **Lower Tariffs**

Finally, hard-working Americans could afford to import opium!

☑ **Acquire California and New Mexico**

As long as the Mexicans were already angry at the U.S. for annexing Texas, Polk figured he might as well start a war with them and take some of their land.

☑ **Settle the Oregon Boundary Dispute**

This is where the slogan Fifty-four forty or fight! came from. Now you know the story behind your mom's tattoo!

Get the Look!

Just tell your hairdresser, "Give me the James K. Polk!"

WE ASKED . . . WHAT IS YOUR DREAM VACATION?

" The president does not have time for vacations. Or time to dream about vacations. Or time to answer questions about dream vacations. Actually, OK . . . I guess I did have time for that last one. "

Vital Stats

Looks: 9

Come up with your own sexy pun involving the word "polk," and insert it here: _____. There, now you've coauthored a book!

Physique: 5

As it turns out, working constantly is not great for your health. Some historians even say Polk worked himself to death, though that's not technically true unless what he was working on was drinking contaminated water.

Charisma: 2

Polk is all business, all the time. If you're like that too, then great! You and James K. Polk will be very happy together. (By "happy," we mean, "joylessly grinding through one project after another, year after year, until finally achieving the sweet release of death.")

Mullet: 10

It feels like these other presidents aren't even trying.

ZACHARY TAYLOR

1849–1850 | Whig

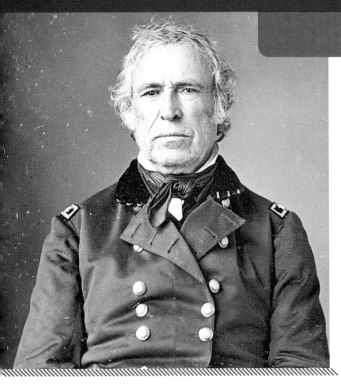

Zachary Taylor is the president who most resembles a hobo. But because he died less than a year and a half into his term, we will never know what kind of hobo he might have eventually become.

Taylor is a simple man of simple pleasures, like wearing tattered clothing and drinking contaminated milk. Unfortunately, the latter led to his death from cholera. And the former led to him being repeatedly mistaken for a farmer. (No offense, farmers!)

Until he ran for president, Taylor had never voted. And we're only assuming that he voted in his own election. No one really knows what goes on inside those voting booths, and maybe Taylor was just having a quick snack of canned beans.

Although he might not sound like much of a catch, there are a lot of perks that come with dating a 19th-century war hero. Like getting to live in a tent! And, well, that's it actually. Tents are pretty fun, though.

Here's a Tip

If you want to test potential mates for historical knowledge, try introducing yourself by saying, "My friends call me 'Old Rough and Ready.'" If they look shocked, it's because they're impressed you know so much about Zachary Taylor!

ZACHARY TAYLOR DIED 16 MONTHS INTO HIS TERM. EVER SINCE THEN, THE NUMBER 16 HAS BEEN UNLUCKY FOR U.S. PRESIDENTS. SOME PEOPLE SAY THAT'S WHY THE WHITE HOUSE DOESN'T HAVE A 16TH FLOOR!

"It was probably the time I was kidnapped on my way to Washington for my inauguration. I was supposed to catch the steamer *Tennessee* and take it upriver. But some other boat pulled up first, in the hopes of tricking me into getting on, and I got on. I guess I'm pretty easy to kidnap!"

Let's Talk About Clothes

Taylor is known for his trademark "bedraggled" look, which he achieves by wearing clothing that is **oversized** and in a state of **extreme distress.** It took a while for this look to catch on, but 150 years later, **"grunge"** was born! Then three years later grunge was over, to everyone's **collective relief.**

But this raises an important question— Does each new president get a new mattress, towels, etc.? Maybe we don't want to be president after all!

Vital Stats

Looks: 2

Despite his low score, we can see how someone would be into Zachary Taylor. It would be like loving an old, well-worn shoe that is also walleyed.

Physique: 1

Taylor has a barrel-shaped body with weirdly long arms and weirdly short legs. So his figure leaves something to be desired. (Specifically, normal proportions.)

Charisma: 4

Taylor is about as charismatic as a grizzled, barrel-shaped hobo. Which is to say, sort of.

Spitting: 10

Of all the presidents, it is believed that Zachary Taylor had the most accurate aim when it came to spitting tobacco onto the White House floor. Of course, some argue that when it comes to spitting on the White House floor, what matters isn't accuracy, but *volume.*

How to Meet a
PRESIDENT

The world is full of U.S. presidents. But for some reason, it can be hard to actually meet one. Here are some foolproof, time-tested strategies for "randomly" meeting the president of your dreams. Just don't tell him you obsessively plotted the whole thing for months while sitting naked inside your incense-choked shrine to him! That's the kind of thing you want to save for a first date.

Richard Nixon

Identify the SKETCHIEST NEARBY LOCATION. Depending on where you live, this might be a dive bar down by the docks, a dark alley, or a cornfield at midnight under a pale crescent moon. Go there, take out your wallet, and start visibly counting your money. When someone hits you on the back of the head with a sap, that's Richard Nixon!

Jimmy Carter

You've been looking for an excuse to attend the SOUTHERN PEANUT GROWERS CONFERENCE. Well, this is your chance! The odds are approximately 50/50 that Jimmy Carter will attend this annual trade group meeting, and if he's there, you'll find him at the nightly dance party.

Harry S. Truman

Truman worked as a postman, and if there's one thing we've learned from film noir movies, it's that the mail recipient/postman relationship is fraught with sexual tension. Figure out WHEN YOUR MAIL GETS DELIVERED, and surprise Harry S. Truman in a sheer negligée. If you open the door and discover that your postman *isn't* Harry. S Truman, just pack up your things, move to a house on a different mail route, and try again. Repeat as necessary.

Teddy Roosevelt

Purchase the **BEST ANIMAL COSTUME** you can afford—for example, a grizzly bear costume. Go for a long walk in the Adirondack Mountains. Eventually Teddy Roosevelt will drop out of a tree with a knife in his teeth. Quickly remove your bear mask and say, "Teddy Roosevelt, my name is [insert your name]. I'm not actually a bear. But do you think you could 'bear' to go on a date with me?"

(Important note: Only use this line if you're dressed as a bear. For other animal costumes, use "I'd be 'lion' if I said I didn't find you attractive," "If we go out for drinks I promise I won't 'boar' you," "It will 'tick' me off if you don't ask me to dinner," etc.)

Any other president

Attend one of his $1,000-a-plate reelection campaign fundraiser dinners. When it comes time for you to shake his hand, use your middle finger to tickle his palm, and give him a long, languid wink. (Please note: At John F. Kennedy fundraisers, you don't need to pull stunts like this to seduce him. Everything is already included in the price of your meal.)

Andrew Jackson

Start a "BATTLE OF NEW ORLEANS" study group. Andrew Jackson will show up for the first meeting, because if there's one person who loves talking about the Battle of New Orleans—and there is, in fact, one person—it's Andrew Jackson.

Gerald Ford

Meeting Gerald Ford is easy—you just need to **BE PRESIDENT,** and appoint him to be your vice president. Then he'll *have* to meet you. If you hit things off and start dating, you'll have the hot, cat-and-mouse dynamic that comes with dating someone who has a lot to gain if you die.

MILLARD FILLMORE

1850–1853 | Whig

After spending some time with Zachary Taylor, you're probably excited to meet a guy who knows how to read.* Introducing Millard Fillmore.

Even though Millard Fillmore was Zachary Taylor's vice president, the two men didn't meet until after they'd won the election. And they discovered pretty quickly that they didn't have much in common. For example, Millard Fillmore was a polished and dignified intellectual, and Zachary Taylor looked like he found his clothes in an abandoned train car.

Now, the hot-button issue at the time was slavery. Congress was debating whether or not to pass the Compromise of 1850, which was supposed to defuse tension between free and slave states by giving both sides a little bit of what they wanted. For example, free states would get to admit California into the Union, and slave states would get to arrest anyone accused of being a runaway slave and conscript them into slavery. So . . . win-win, right?

President Taylor did not weigh in on the debate, because he was too busy drinking a glass of milk he'd found in the trash. After Taylor died of cholera, Fillmore became president and pushed Congress to pass the Compromise of 1850. And, as with all compromises, it blew up in his face and destroyed his entire political party. (Which was just the Whigs, so no big deal!)

Still, it's hard to blame Fillmore, because a lot of people are under the mistaken impression that compromises are a good way to solve problems. But take our word for it: Compromises are terrible. It is so, so much better to just vanquish your enemies.

*Just kidding! Zachary Taylor *did* know how to read. He did not know how to write.

> *Did you know* that Millard Fillmore was the first president to have a bathtub in the White House? No? Well good, because it isn't true. It's just a story that was invented by journalist H.L. Mencken, because he wanted something fun to write about during WWI. And there's nothing like an anecdote about bathtubs to raise the troops' spirits!

Why You'll *Love* Him

He doesn't smoke, drink, or gamble. Which means more cigars, liquor, and gambling money for you!

He lacks emotion. This is also good. More emotions for you!

He loves learning. When he was apprenticing as a clothmaker, Fillmore kept a dictionary handy and memorized the definitions of words in between doing whatever it is clothmakers do. (Probably something involving cloth!)

How to Win His Heart

❤ **Be his teacher.** Millard Fillmore married his high school teacher, so this is a tried-and-true way to win his heart. Even if you're not a teacher by trade, there's probably still a lot you could teach to Millard Fillmore. Like how to use a microwave.

❤ **Enjoy long walks.** A lot of people *say* they enjoy long walks when they're creating a profile on a presidents-only dating website. But Millard Fillmore really means it! One time he walked 150 miles to Buffalo, New York, for what we can safely assume was the most disappointing vacation ever.

❤ **Don't join the Freemasons.** Millard Fillmore got his start in politics by working for the Anti-Masonic Party. So if you want a future with him, you will have to resist that secret society's ancient and seductive call.

Vital Stats

Looks: 5

No biography of Millard Fillmore would be complete without mentioning that he looks exactly like Alec Baldwin. We're talking to you, biographer Paul Finkelman!

Physique: 7

One account described Fillmore as having the "chest of a woodsman." We're not sure whether this means a heavily muscled chest or a chest full of axes. Either way, it's something we'd like to see.

Charisma: 2

Millard Fillmore has the charisma of a sexy robot, like Data from *Star Trek,* or Wall-E.

Enthusiasm for milk: 10

If you offer to buy Millard Fillmore a drink, he'll probably order a glass of milk. Just tell him, "Sure, coming right up!" and then climb out the fire escape.

FRANKLIN PIERCE

Hello, who is this handsome hunk of president? We'll give you a hint: His name is at the top of the page in large letters.

Franklin Pierce is nicknamed "Handsome Frank" because . . . actually, you can probably figure it out. But what a lot of people don't realize is that Pierce is more than just a handsome face. He also has great hair! It's black and curly and combed at an angle so rakish that you could literally comb your own hair with a rake and it would not be this rakish. Combine that with his deep voice and natural charm, and you've got one of the most attractive men to ever be a terrible president.

Pierce's worst move was signing the Kansas-Nebraska Act, which allowed the residents of new territories to vote on whether or not to allow slavery. We know, we know—it sounds like an amazing idea! But in practice, it resulted in pro- and anti-slavery groups moving to Kansas and shooting each other. After Pierce's first term, he was not nominated for a second. In fact, his own party's slogan was "Anybody but Pierce." And that is how they ended up with James Buchanan.

So Pierce wasn't very good at being president. But in his defense, that's only an important quality to have if you happen to be president. And besides that one flaw, he is pretty much perfect: handsome, charming, outdoorsy, and a notorious alcoholic. (So yeah, you'll have to keep an eye on that last one.)

> WOULD YOUR SIGNIFICANT OTHER FIND IT STRANGE IF YOU INSISTED ON CALLING HIM "PRESIDENT PIERCE" IN BED? WE GUESS YOU'RE GOING TO FIND OUT!

How to Win His Heart

♥ **Be shy, sickly, and kind of a downer.** This is how historians describe Pierce's wife, Jane, so you're going to have to be even *more* shy, sickly and down if you want to steal him away from her.

♥ **Be a teetotaler.** Jane didn't like it when her husband drank and required that his wine glass be placed upside-down at White House dinners, which made it harder to pour him a glass of wine, but still not impossible.

Why You'll *Love* Him

He was fun. Drinking! Wrestling! Fishing! Well, maybe not fishing.

He has a knack for remembering people's names. Finally, a boyfriend who won't make you wear a nametag.

He tried to annex Cuba. Pierce doesn't get enough credit for trying to sneakily annex Cuba. Just think: If he had been successful, you might be living in Cuba right now, sitting on the beach and smoking a cigar with your dad, Fidel Castro.

WHEN HE WAS YOUNG

If you think it's a coincidence that Franklin Pierce and Franklin Pierce's horse have the same hairstyle, then you don't know Franklin Pierce.

Pierce is considered one of the worst presidents in American history, basically because he didn't prevent the Civil War. But you know who else didn't prevent the Civil War? EVERYONE. George Washington, Abraham Lincoln, your dad, etc.

FAMOUS FRIENDS

Franklin Pierce was close friends with renowned writer Nathaniel Hawthorne! And Nathaniel Hawthorne had a famous friend, too—President Franklin Pierce!

Vital Stats

Looks: 10

We think we have adequately covered this.

Physique: 7

Pierce gets a 10 for his broad shoulders and slim waist, but a 0 for taking care of his liver. (That averages out to a 7.)

Charisma: 8

Pierce has a deep voice and so much natural charm that he could talk down an angry mob. And one time he did talk down an angry mob. But that's a story for another book. You have to write it though! We're sick of writing books.

Wrestling: 8

If you wrestle with Franklin Pierce you will probably lose, but you will still come away feeling like you've won.

FAVORITE
PRESIDENTIAL RECIPES

Glass of Milk

Zachary Taylor

Let some milk sit out for a few days during a muggy, Washington, D.C., summer. Then take a sip and see what happens! Remember: Any glass of milk that doesn't kill you will only make you stronger.

Mug of Beer

John Adams

Take mug of beer and toss it out the window. Pour yourself a nice civilized mug of cider.

'Possom and Taters

William Taft

Acquire a Georgia opossum weighing at least 25 pounds. Clean by soaking in a vat of hot lye water (taking care not to drink the vat of lye water and be poisoned). Rinse thoroughly, then roast at 350°F until tender, periodically basting the opossum in its own delicious opossum juices. Cook the potatoes somehow (you can figure this out!) and arrange on platter. Serve for Thanksgiving to horrified family members, explaining that opossum is William Taft's favorite food. You might also have to explain who William Taft is.

Gin, Neat

Richard Nixon

Pour 8 ounces of gin into a coffee mug, no mixer. Drink. Wander the halls of the White House cursing at the portraits of your predecessors while Henry Kissinger nods and takes notes.

Lincoln Logs

Abraham Lincoln

Add 4 cups water, a pinch of cumin, and a bay leaf to a pressure cooker. Bring to a boil, then add the contents of a box of Lincoln Logs. Cook until wood is soft. This meal is a great way to stay lean, like Abraham Lincoln.

Raw Bear Liver

Theodore Roosevelt

Enter the woods and kill a wolf. Gut the wolf and drape its viscera around your shoulders. Wait for the scent to attract a bear. Kill bear. Remove bear's liver. Salt and pepper to taste.

Birthday Cake
John F. Kennedy

Tell your staff you'd like a birthday cake. When they bring it in, check to see if Marilyn Monroe is hiding inside. If she isn't inside, request a different cake.

Cold, Wet K-rations
Dwight D. Eisenhower

Dig a trench in your yard. Sit in trench until it rains. Open one can of K-rations, wait for rain to moisten, then eat with the tip of a knife, all while cursing the futility of war.

What Someone Else Is Eating
Lyndon B. Johnson

If you see something that looks good on the plate of the person sitting next to you, just start eating off their plate. There: Now you're the president of dinner.

Scrambled Eggs, No Polk
James K. Polk

Combine 8 eggs, 1/2 cup of milk, and a dash of salt. Beat vigorously. Melt 2 tablespoons butter in a frying pan, add egg mixture, and scramble. Do NOT invite James Polk to enjoy them with you because then they are just regular scrambled eggs.

Jelly Bean Surprise
Ronald Reagan

Pour jelly beans into a bowl.

Boiled Peanuts
Jimmy Carter

As winter's grip loosens and the land warms, sow peanuts across the modest breadth of your land, working from sunup 'til sundown, falling into bed each night exhausted but content. In the fall, harvest the peanuts, boil, and salt them. Don't eat them, though, because you're not some sort of hedonist. Just live with the knowledge that you have lust in your heart, for boiled peanuts.

Pretzels
George W. Bush

Open a bag of pretzels. Put one in your mouth, chew for 30 seconds, then chew for another 30 seconds, then swallow. Let out a sigh of relief. Repeat.

Hamburger, Well-Done
Bill Clinton

Have the Secret Service take you to McDonald's to get a hamburger. Tell the cashier you'd like it "well-done." He'll know what you mean!

JAMES BUCHANAN

1857–1861 | Democrat

You can feel his eyes on you from across the room. When you finally brave a glance in his direction, you confirm it—he is definitely staring at you. With his head cocked to one side, he swirls his glass of cognac. Your eyes meet, and he winks.

Well, technically, it's not a wink—he's just got this weird thing where he's nearsighted in one eye and farsighted in the other, so he has to close one eye to see across the room. Still, you feel your face flush, as if your body can't help but react to him. You turn away, but out of the corner of your eye, you see him moving toward you—with short, quick steps on his abnormally small feet. He navigates through the crowd until he's so close that you feel the heat radiating off of his large frame. You take a deep breath and turn to face him, craning your neck to meet his gaze.

"Hello," he says. His voice is higher than you were expecting, and nasally (in a sexy way). "My name is James Buchanan." He holds out two fingers, presumably offering you some kind of miniature handshake.

"I know who you are," you gasp, suddenly feeling out of breath. His head is tilted to one side again, and he's gazing at you as if you are the most interesting person in the world. (You're not. It's just his weird eye thing!)

That's when he leans in close, so close that you can smell the brandy on his breath. "Hey," he whispers, his lips brushing against your ear. "I'm sorry about that whole thing with the Civil War."

That's always the part where you wake up, sweaty and tangled in your sheets. Why does this keep happening to you? Why must President James Buchanan come to you every night in your dreams? It's almost as if your subconscious is trying to tell you something. You turn on your lamp and stare at the portrait of Buchanan that's hanging next to your bed. Is it possible that, without even realizing it, you've developed feelings for the 15th president?

Let's Talk About Clothes

Instead of wearing a tie, Buchanan wears a **CRAVAT,** which is what it's called when you stuff a piece of fabric down the front of your shirt. Not only does this look good, it's also a great way to steal fabric!

Why You'll *Love* Him

He's single. Maybe we should have mentioned this earlier, but most of these guys are married. Sorry!

He likes to party. He was even expelled from Dickinson College for drunken carousing. Later he defended himself by explaining that he only did it so that he would be popular.

He might be celibate. How important is sex to you in a relationship? If you're not sure, then dating James Buchanan is a good way to find out.

He can hold his drink. Are you sick of men dropping their drinks on you? That won't happen with James Buchanan! Not only does he know how to hold a drink, he is also capable of drinking large quantities of alcohol without it having any apparent effect on him. Except, you know, gout.

He's into guys. If you are male and have been feeling sad because none of these presidents are attracted to you sexually, then we (might) have good news!

ARE YOU A "BUCHANEER"? THAT'S WHAT YOU CALL SOMEONE WHO IS REALLY INTO JAMES BUCHANAN. LIKE WILLIAM RUFUS KING, FOR EXAMPLE.

Sort-of Fun Facts

★ Before getting into politics, James Buchanan made a small fortune as a successful lawyer. If you think you can't get rich by becoming a lawyer, you are mistaken!

★ Buchanan spent four decades in politics, serving in both houses of Congress and as Polk's secretary of state. Andrew Jackson appointed him minister to Russia, saying, "It was as far as I could send him out of my sight . . . I would have sent him to the North Pole if we had kept a minister there." Ahh—never change, Andrew Jackson!

★ Was James Buchanan the boyfriend of Vice President William Rufus King? Historians say: Maybe! They did live together for ten years, and Andrew Jackson referred to them as "Miss Nancy" and "Aunt Fancy," if that counts as evidence of anything besides Andrew Jackson's being a jerk.

★ If you ask James Buchanan who caused the Civil War, he'll say it was those lousy abolitionists. You shouldn't feel like you need to ask him though.

Timeline: Let's Get Ready to Have a *Civil War*

A lot of people give James Buchanan a hard time because the Civil War basically started on his watch. And now it's our turn to give him a hard time!

MARCH 4, 1857
James Buchanan is inaugurated. So far, so good!

MARCH 6, 1857
In the *Dred Scott* decision, the Supreme Court rules that the federal government cannot ban slavery from new states or territories. Buchanan is relieved to finally have this settled. He figures that now everyone will finally stop arguing about slavery. And who knows, maybe they will! We'll just have to wait and find out.

DECEMBER 9, 1857
Buchanan tries to get Congress to accept a pro-slavery constitution for Kansas called the Lecompton Constitution. The anti-slavery half of his party is like, "That's it, we're done with this guy."

FEBRUARY 6, 1858
While debating the Lecompton Constitution, a violent brawl breaks out in the House of Representatives. It's almost as if this is foreshadowing something . . . but what?

NOVEMBER 6, 1860
Abraham Lincoln wins the presidential election. But don't be sad, we still have four more months to enjoy the presidential antics of James Buchanan.

DECEMBER 20, 1860
South Carolina secedes from the Union. Buchanan says that it is illegal for states to secede, but that it is *also* illegal to *stop* states from seceding. If only there were some way to change the laws!

JANUARY 9, 1861
Mississippi secedes from the Union. Also, troops in South Carolina fire on a federal ship. So . . . is James Buchanan sure he doesn't want to do anything about this? Maybe we should check with him again.

JANUARY 10, 1861
Florida secedes from the Union. Oh well, at least we still have Alabama.

JANUARY 11, 1861
Alabama secedes from the Union. Noooooooooooo!

JANUARY 19, 1861
Georgia secedes. Do we have to keep saying "from the Union" each time? That's implied, right?

JANUARY 26, 1861
Louisiana secedes. Now everyone has to celebrate Mardi Gras in Missouri.

FEBRUARY 1, 1861
Texas secedes. The real question is, when did we agree to let Texas back in?

MARCH 4, 1861
Abraham Lincoln is inaugurated. You know how sometimes when you leave a job, you secretly hope that the next guy will mess everything up so that all of your old coworkers finally realize how wonderful you were? Yeah. That did not happen to James Buchanan.

The closest Buchanan came to marrying was when he was engaged to a woman (!) named Ann Coleman. Ann broke off their engagement after accusing Buchanan of not showing her enough affection. A few days later, she died of a broken heart. Yes, apparently that's a real thing! Ask any doctor in 1819.

Buchanan always used this story to explain why he never married. But other people have their own theories as to why he never married, including: He's homosexual, he's asexual, he just hasn't met the right person yet (you), he's secretly the pope. (That last one is ours!)

Here's a Tip

A fun way to tease James Buchanan is to ask him how many states there were in the Union when his term as president began compared to when it ended.

Vital Stats

Looks: 6

And who is this tall drink of hair gel? Oh that's right—it's James Buchanan!

Physique: 4

One biographer described Buchanan as resembling "an erect, two-footed tyrannosaur." When compared to the other presidents, we're going to say that puts him at about a 4.

Charisma: 4

Buchanan has a sharp legal mind, and if there's one thing the American people love, it is listening to complicated legal arguments.

Ability to grow facial hair: 0

There is no evidence that Buchanan ever needed to shave, whereas most presidents leave behind a trail of beard clippings.

ABRAHAM LINCOLN

1861–1865 | Republican

If you're reading in bed, you're going to want to turn on the lights for this one.

Picture, if you will, a giant, gaunt man with sunken cheeks and shadowed eyes, draped in a dark suit and silk top hat. When he speaks, it is in an eerily high-pitched, backwoods drawl. He is obsessed with death. And he is very, very skilled with an axe.

Pretty spooky, right? But we're actually just talking about Abraham Lincoln! And there's no reason to be scared of Abraham Lincoln, unless you're a local bully, a confederacy, or a tree.

As you may be aware, Lincoln led the United States in its defeat of pro-slavery separatists in the 1861–1865 Civil War, and most historians consider him to be our greatest president. This is patently unfair, since no other presidents have had a chance to win a civil war, and maybe they would have done *even better* than Lincoln. But that's historians for you. Unfair.

Here's a Tip

Don't go to the theater with Abraham Lincoln. He is too tall and will block everyone's view of the stage. He shouldn't ever go to the theater, and you shouldn't be encouraging him.

WHEN HE WAS YOUNG

You know what they say about the size of a man's hands! (They say the bigger his hands, the more likely it is he will save the Union.)

Why You'll *Love* Him

He's good with an axe. Growing up on the frontier, Lincoln became a skilled rail-splitter and woodcutter. (And not the kind of "rail splitting" and "woodcutting" you're thinking about. Get your mind out of the gutter!) And here's a job-hunting tip: If you need to give your résumé some pop, try adding "good with an axe."

He's a wrestler. When Lincoln moved to New Salem, Illinois, the leader of a local gang called the Clary's Grove Boys challenged him to a fight. With the whole town watching, Lincoln picked the gang leader up by the neck and shook him, then offered to take on the rest of his gang one by one. Instead, the gang leader offered his hand in friendship. Lincoln took over the Clary's Grove Boys, and one of his first acts as their leader was getting them to stop putting townspeople inside barrels and rolling them down hills.

He's a Whig. The next time someone tells you that the GOP is the "Party of Lincoln," point out that Lincoln spent most of his career as a Whig. Then, urge them to follow Lincoln's example and join the Whig Party, because people, we can make this happen.

He has a sense of humor. Lincoln arguably has the best sense of humor of any president. Here is a joke of his that you can use: Once, President Lincoln was visited by a man who started giving him a bunch of unsolicited policy advice. After two hours of this, Lincoln grabbed the man's leg and said, "Mr. Harvey, what tremendous great calves you have got!" This is a hilarious and fail-safe way to end your meetings at work. Maybe forever!

He's a storyteller. When you grow up in a one-room, firelit log cabin, you learn how to tell long stories to pass the time, and Lincoln was a mesmerizing and entertaining storyteller. If he settles down in a rocking chair and starts to spin a yarn, just say, "Abe, I have great news. TV has been invented."

SCANDAL!

As you may recall from trying to flirt with your Latin teacher, *habeas corpus* is Latin for "you may have the body." But *habeas corpus* isn't just an awkward Latin come-on. It also stands for a bedrock principle in Western legal thought: the government can't just lock someone away and deny them trial or due process.

But what if you *really want* to have the army arrest someone you think is a Confederate sympathizer and detain them without trial indefinitely? This is exactly what Lincoln wanted to do, so he decreed a suspension of the writ of *habeas corpus* in some parts of the country. U.S. Chief Justice Roger Taney issued an order that Lincoln had no right to suspend *habeas corpus*. But Lincoln ignored him and did it anyway, joining the club of "presidents who have ignored Supreme Court decisions." This is a club that just includes Lincoln and Andrew Jackson.

Generally speaking, you should never join any club that includes Andrew Jackson. But in Lincoln's defense, Chief Justice Taney also wrote the *Dred Scott* decision. If you're going to ignore any Supreme Court Justice, it should be Taney. In fact, if you're both black and a U.S. citizen, you're ignoring his *Dred Scott* decision right now! We genuinely wish Taney were here to see it.

Abraham Lincoln, Attorney at Law

Lincoln is a self-taught lawyer, which is the best kind if what you're hoping for is a case that is *interesting*. Here are some of Lincoln's greatest hits:

Lincoln successfully defended his cousin "Peachy" on murder charges, presumably by pointing out to the jury that the guy was named "Peachy."

A witness claimed to have seen Lincoln's client commit murder by the light of the moon. Lincoln, in a dramatic moment, pulled out a *Farmers' Almanac* and showed that there was no moon that night. So if you're ever on trial for murder and your lawyer pulls out a copy of the *Farmers' Almanac*, breathe a sigh of relief.

Lincoln was hired by a high-powered East Coast legal team for a corporate case in Chicago. They wanted someone cheap and local, and when you think "cheap and local," you think "Abraham Lincoln." But then the trial was moved to Cincinnati, so they replaced him with a different lawyer.

But they didn't tell Lincoln they'd replaced him, and he showed up in Cincinnati eager to try the big case. Upon seeing him, his replacement, a Pittsburgh lawyer named Edwin Stanton, said, "Where did this long-armed baboon come from?" And Lincoln was made to sit in the audience instead of with the other lawyers, because they were embarrassed by how weird and dorky he looked.

Then, seven years later, Lincoln made Stanton his secretary of war, and together they won the Civil War. So, the moral of this story is that if you humiliate your coworkers, it will probably turn out great in the end . . . and it might even save the republic!

DIY PROJECT:

Abraham Lincoln and Mary Todd didn't create a wedding scrapbook. But that shouldn't stop you from creating one for them! We promise it won't be creepy at all. To help you get started, here are some ideas for what a scrapbook of their magical day might include.

LINCOLN'S WEDDING DAY LETTER TO MARY

On the day of their wedding, Lincoln decided that on second thought, maybe he *didn't* want to marry Mary Todd. So he wrote her a breakup letter telling her he didn't love her and asked his close friend Joshua Speed to deliver it. Speed, to his credit, urged Lincoln to tell Mary directly. (Although maybe Speed also thought it would be weird for *him* to deliver the letter, given that he and Lincoln had been sharing a bed for three years.*)

CALENDAR WITH NOVEMBER 4, 1842 CIRCLED

This is the day that Abraham and Mary announced that their engagement was back on, and also that they were going to get married that same day. To capture some of the romantic magic, make sure to include what Lincoln said when a friend asked him where he was going: "To hell."

*But just as friends! Good, good friends who sleep in the same cozy double bed every night and send each other letters signed "Yours forever," just like you do with *your* friends.

BEST MAN REMARKS

Lincoln's best man later captured some of the future president's giddy mood that day, noting that Lincoln "looked and acted as if he were going to the slaughter." That sure sounds like wedding day jitters to us!

ROBERT LINCOLN'S BIRTH CERTIFICATE

The Lincolns' son, Robert, was born nine months to the day after their wedding. Do you know what *isn't* nine months long, contrary to popular belief? The human gestation period.

Happily ever after!

Are you Abraham Lincoln's Soul Mate?

You know you've made a connection with someone when you can finish each other's sentences. Let's see if you can do it with Abraham Lincoln.

Four score and seven years _____.
    a.   ago.
    b.   is a long time to go without brushing your teeth.

A house divided against itself cannot _____.
    a.   stand
    b.   really be called a house, per se.
             What you're thinking of is a duplex.

With malice toward none, with charity for _____.
    a.   all
    b.   none, but at least I don't have any malice.

Now we are engaged in a great civil _____.
    a.   war
    b.   war reenactment, so I don't want to see any
             cell phones out there.

The angels of our better _____.
    a.   nature.
    b.   nativity set. Those are the angels I want to use
             for the diorama. Please go get them, they're
             under my pillow.

Government of the people, by the people, and for the _____.
    a.   people
    b.   love of God, we've tried that since 1776;
             when are we going to finally admit that it
             doesn't work and just install a king?

Sort-of Fun Facts

★ Lincoln had a rural Kentucky accent, pronouncing get as "git," there as "thar," and so forth. So the next time someone demands you recite the Gettysburg Address from memory, just mumble incoherently in a fake twang.

★ Lincoln thought the Declaration of Independence was a better expression of freedom, justice, and equality before the law than the Constitution, what with its "We'll count slaves as three-fifths of a person," and similar fine print. And he has a point! It just goes to show that if you need a moving articulation of individual liberty, don't pick a slaveholder like James Madison to write it. Pick a slaveholder like Thomas Jefferson.

★ Lincoln's mother died of food poisoning, and his family moved to Illinois because they were fleeing an outbreak of contaminated milk. And yet his favorite food was imported oysters. If it's the 1800s, you probably shouldn't eat oysters that have been imported from any farther away than you can *throw* an oyster.

Vital Stats

Looks: 3

There are a lot of reasons to love Lincoln, but most people—including Lincoln himself—would agree that looks are not one of them. Although for a dissenting view, Lincoln's personal secretary said Lincoln's face, *"moved through a thousand delicate gradations of line and contour, light and shade, sparkle of the eye and curve of the lip."* Sounds like his secretary was getting a lot done at work and definitely *not* just spending all day gazing at Lincoln.

Physique: 8

Too often, we think of Lincoln as tall and scrawny. Lincoln *is* tall and very skinny, but also bizarrely strong. There are multiple, credible stories of him lifting loads up to 1,000 pounds, which some humans can do, but usually not ones who look like Lincoln. He would win bets by picking up barrels of whisky that weighed several hundred pounds and drinking from them. And in his very first political speech, he spotted a violent troublemaker in the crowd and literally picked him up and threw him. That crowd only had room for one violent troublemaker, and it was Lincoln!

Charisma: 7

Lincoln exercises a magnetic pull on people, but he is awkward in social interactions, afraid of women, and a poor orator. When he delivered the Gettysburg Address, it flopped. And only afterward, when people read it in print, did they start thinking it was halfway decent. Fortunately for Lincoln, his moral courage, vision, and strength comes through in his writing, and people in the 19th century were a lot more likely to read his statements than hear or see them. In fact, it's fun to imagine what kinds of presidents we would have today if radio and television had never been invented.

No, wait. Not "fun." What's the opposite of fun?

Ability to grow facial hair: 7

Amazingly, Lincoln's beard made its first public appearance at his inauguration. Did this surprise beard help cause the Civil War? Before you answer "no," try to imagine what would have happened if Barack Obama had shown up on his inauguration day with a full, luxuriant beard. (What would have happened is a civil war.)

PRESIDENTIAL

★ BEST BEARDS ★

TREND REPORT

Thomas Jefferson once wrote that all men are created equal . . . except when it comes to growing beards!

OK, technically Thomas Jefferson only wrote the first part, and the rest was written by Walt Whitman. We've done an exhaustive search of presidents' chins and narrowed it down to the top five best beards to serve as commander-in-chief (of beards). Join us as we take a look back through history to see which presidents have the best beards, and by extension are the best presidents.

5 ABRAHAM LINCOLN

4 ULYSSES S. GRANT

Lincoln lands in the #5 spot because part of his beard is missing, and what remains is styled to look like a tiny curtain. He adopted this look on the advice of an 11-year-old girl who thought he would look more handsome with facial hair. And she was right! If nothing else, it distracts from whatever is going on with his ear.

OK, NOW we're talking. (Talking about beards!) Ulysses S. Grant's beard is everything that a beard should be: facial hair covering a man's lower cheeks and chin.

CONGRATULATIONS, JAMES A. GARFIELD!

Garfield doesn't top many lists of presidential superlatives, except for "most quickly assassinated," but you have to admit, the guy really knows how to grow a beard. (The secret is to sit there and do nothing!)

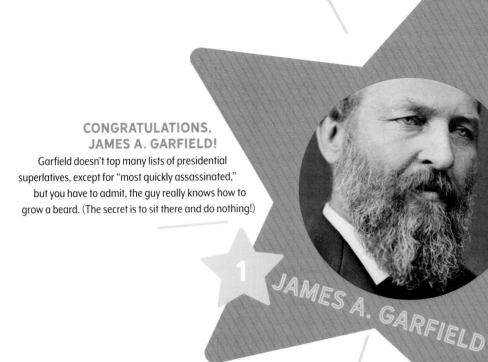

1 JAMES A. GARFIELD

3 BENJAMIN HARRISON

2 RUTHERFORD B. HAYES

Are you into Santa? *Really* into Santa?
Since you've probably already been banned from your local mall, why not try sitting in Benjamin Harrison's lap? His frosty white beard will tickle your cheek as you lean in close to ask him for a present. (Hopefully you asked for a new import tariff, because that's what you're getting.)

Rutherford B. Hayes's beard is so long and dense that you just want to run your fingers through it and—uh oh, your fingers got stuck! Hayes is not going to be happy with you when he wakes up.

ANDREW JOHNSON

1865–1869 | Democrat

You're now on page 82, and you're probably getting nostalgic for page 38, when you got to meet Andrew Jackson. Well, we've got good news. Just 28 years after Jackson's term ended, another hot-tempered, populist, hillbilly demagogue from Tennessee became president. Let us introduce you to the president named Andrew who *isn't* on the twenty-dollar bill: Andrew Johnson. (Or "Andy" to his friends, like you and Abraham Lincoln.)

Like some of our greatest presidents, Andy Johnson grew up poor and uneducated. Unlike some of our greatest presidents, Johnson was not one of our greatest presidents. His only real political skills were 1) whipping up crowds with fiery speeches, and 2) not betraying the Union. And you're probably just as good as him at at least one of those things.

When the South seceded, Johnson was the only sitting senator from a Confederate state who remained loyal to the United States. That's how he got the job as Lincoln's running mate. But Johnson only opposed secession because he had grown up poor and resented the Southern plantation aristocracy—not because he opposed slavery. He was fine with slavery. But hey, no one's perfect! And that's especially true of Andy Johnson.

Heartbreak!

Andrew Johnson's first love was a girl named Mary Wood. But when he proposed to her, she turned him down . . . even though he had sewn her a quilt! We hate to tell this to all the teenage boys out there who are sewing quilts for their crushes, but if you want to win someone's heart, you'll need to sew TWO quilts.

Here is an editorial cartoon criticizing Hollywood actor Tommy Lee Jones for vetoing the Freedmen's Bureau Act, which was intended to help freed slaves during Reconstruction.

Why You'll *Love* Him

You want excitement. After siding with the Union, Johnson had to flee Tennessee under gunfire from angry Confederate sympathizers. When was the last time you were chased out of your state by an angry mob? If you can't remember off the top of your head, then it's been too long, and it's time to entwine your fate with that of Andy Johnson.

You enjoy hearing about Andrew Johnson. In an hour-long speech about George Washington, Johnson referred to himself more than 200 times. And he still had time to squeeze in the accusation that a couple members of Congress were trying to have him assassinated.

You love mice. It can be a hard to find a guy who loves mice! Well, maybe you just haven't been looking in the right place: the White House. When President Johnson wasn't busy sewing his own clothes or undermining Reconstruction, he was tending to a family of mice in his bedroom by leaving out water and flour for them. He called these mice his "little fellows." So if Johnson ever asks you to come to his bedroom to see his little fellow, one way or another, you are in for a memorable experience.

Sort-of Fun Facts

Johnson vetoed the Civil Rights Bill of 1866, arguing that it discriminated against whites in favor of African-Americans. Yes: politicians were claiming reverse discrimination ONE YEAR AFTER EMANCIPATION.

Johnson was a tailor by trade, and even after he became president he continued making his own clothes. It sounds ridiculous, but in retrospect, we'd probably all be better off if he'd spent even *more* of his presidency sewing.

SCANDAL!

When you hear that President Johnson was impeached, you probably think, "Ooh, did he lie about having an affair with an intern? Tell me more!" Sadly, to the best of our knowledge, Johnson did not have affairs with any interns. He was impeached because he kept trying to sabotage Reconstruction. If only the Constitution's framers had had the foresight to limit impeachable offenses to "hot sex scandals," he would have been fine.

Timeline of Andrew Johnson Not Being a *Drunkard*

The peerlessly eloquent Abraham Lincoln once said of his vice president, "Andy ain't a drunkard." Nevertheless, alcohol played a key role in Andy Johnson's life.

MARCH 4, 1864: Johnson wakes up with a hangover on Lincoln's inauguration day, and asks outgoing Vice President Hannibal Hamlin for some whiskey. (By the way, this is a solid first-day-at-a-new-job ice breaker: Ask your predecessor if he has any whiskey.) Johnson goes on to give a rambling and obviously drunken inauguration speech. Afterward, he goes into hiding while Washington society mocks him. Just imagine how much worse all that teasing and bullying would have been in an age of social media. It gets better, Andy Johnson! (Well, not for you personally, Mr. Vice President. For you, it's just going to keep getting worse.)

APRIL 15, 1864: The conspirators who killed Abraham Lincoln planned to murder Andrew Johnson and Secretary of State William Seward the same day. Seward's would-be assassin almost succeeds. But the man assigned to shoot Johnson gets drunk at the hotel bar instead. (Don't worry, George Atzerodt: This book is a judgment-free zone when it comes to getting drunk at the hotel bar.)

SUMMER, 1866: During the 1866 election, Johnson decides to go on a speaking tour around the country. His advisors urge him to stick to a script, but instead he goes off-the-cuff and relies on one of the golden rules of public speaking: Compare yourself to Jesus. At stop after stop, President Johnson says that like Jesus, he wants to forgive. Specifically, he wants to forgive white Southerners, and stop punishing them with things like the 14th Amendment granting citizenship to freed slaves. You know, just like Jesus would do. In response, Republicans spread the rumor that Johnson was drunk. And you know what? If you're comparing yourself to Jesus and criticizing the 14th Amendment, hopefully you *are* drunk.

How to Win His Heart

Here is a foolproof, five-step process for winning Andy Johnson's heart, based on his courtship of Eliza Johnson.

♥ **Be a teenager.** If you're not already a teenager, become one. This happens a lot in movies so we're confident you can figure it out.

♥ **Keep an eye out for handsome teenagers moving to town.** Extra points if he's an illiterate runaway tailor's apprentice, like Johnson was. (Also, if you have illiterate runaway tailor's apprentices roaming the streets of your town, please alert OSHA.)

♥ **Pick the handsome teenage runaway tailor's apprentice who looks the most like Hollywood actor Tommy Lee Jones.** Carry an 8.5 X 11 inch glossy of Tommy Lee Jones around and hold it up next to their faces to compare, if needed.

♥ **Teach him to read and do basic math.** Just sit him down in front of *Sesame Street* for several hundred hours until he picks it up.

♥ ***Voilà!*** You've given him the gift of knowledge, and now he will give you the gift of marriage to a penniless teenager.

Here's a Tip

If you ever accidentally become president, do what Andy Johnson did: **DON'T HAVE A VICE PRESIDENT.** This will make the Senate less likely to remove you from office, because your successor would be the pro–women's suffrage Senate president pro tem. And if there's one thing the Senate likes less than your efforts to block Reconstruction, it's women getting the vote. (On second thought, this tip is pretty specific to Andrew Johnson.)

Let's Talk About Clothes

If someone claims to be a **professional tailor** and this is how his clothes fit, you need to consider the possibility that he is **lying.** And if he's lying about that, he might also be lying about why he wears 19th–century suits.

Vital Stats

Looks:

Andrew Johnson looks exactly like Tommy Lee Jones. We can't assign a rating to Tommy Lee Jones any more than we could assign a rating to the sun overhead, or the earth beneath our feet. Who are we to judge such things?

Physique: 6

Johnson wasn't known to be particularly athletic. But as an accomplished tailor, he had very talented hands, if you know what we mean. (We mean he can sew you some great outfits!)

Charisma: 8

Johnson had a plainspoken, direct style that appealed to his Tennessee constituency, and he was a rousing public speaker. The Richmond newspaper *Whig* called him the "the most unscrupulous demagogue in the Union," which sounds pretty charismatic to us! Plus we implicitly trust anything printed in *Whig*.

Impeached: 10

Getting impeached *sounds* easy, but Johnson is one of only two presidents to have actually pulled it off. (As of this writing.)

ULYSSES S. GRANT

Do you sometimes feel frustrated that your boyfriend is such a loser? He got kicked out of the army, and you're living in the woods, broke, because he has no marketable skills?

Well, keep in mind that this describes exactly the situation of Ulysses S. Grant after he and his wife, Julia, got married. Following a series of professional failures, he was reduced to selling firewood on street corners in St. Louis, which is about as lucrative and prestigious as it sounds. But just six years later he was the commanding general of all Union forces, and five years after that he was in the White House.

Eleven years is a pretty short time to go from "Hi, I live in the woods, oh sorry that was my stomach rumbling, I'm very hungry, all the time" to "Hi, I live in the White House because I am the president." And so before you dump your boyfriend, keep in mind that this kind of radical transformation could happen in your life, too! Then, go ahead and dump him, and find a guy more like Ulysses S. Grant. He could become president!

But that doesn't necessarily mean he'll be a *good* president.

To anyone who says that history doesn't remember vice presidents, we have two words for them:

Schuyler **Colfax.**

Why You'll *Love* Him

He knows how to ride a horse. During the Mexican-American war, Grant rode a galloping horse down a sniper-lined street and hung off one side, to use the horse as a shield. This made him famous for his horsemanship. Apparently, that's how you're supposed to ride a horse.

He is a leather man. Grant had a leather store called "Grant & Perkins" that sold harnesses, saddles, and other leather goods. So let your imagination run wild on what kind of a "leather store" this was.

He respects the dead. Let's face it: Someday, your pet canary is going to die. When this happens, some boyfriends would be quietly guessing whether it will fit down the toilet. But not Ulysses S. Grant! When Julia Dent's pet canary passed away, Grant built it a tiny yellow coffin and arranged for eight fellow army officers to attend its funeral.*

He tries to protect civil rights. Grant created the Justice Department and used it and the army to fight the KKK and other armed groups that terrorized and subjugated blacks. For a while he was pretty successful, and a number of black politicians were elected to Congress. But eventually the armed groups and their political allies won, and blacks in former Confederate states essentially lost the vote they had so recently gained. Don't let anyone tell you that terrorists never win.

*Unfortunately he was not able to provide this same level of ceremony at his inaugural ball, when the temperature plummeted and the hundreds of canaries in cages suspended from the rafters started freezing to death and raining down on the dance floor. Grant was pretty superstitious, and he probably didn't view a rain of dead, frozen canaries at his inaugural ball as a positive omen for his presidency.

He is a great writer. Grant's autobiography was so good that some people suspected Mark Twain had ghostwritten it. That is almost certainly not true. And besides, if Mark Twain writes your memoirs you shouldn't keep it a secret, because that's a lot more impressive than being a good memoirist.

His father might not come to your wedding if he disagrees with your parents about something. Slavery, for example, which is the reason he skipped Ulysses and Julia's wedding. Oh well, more cake for you!

WHEN HE WAS YOUNG

In the 1840s, officers were always trying to achieve an "hourglass" figure.

Grant's administration accomplished a lot in eight years, if you include scandals. In his defense, Grant himself was a man of integrity. But he was also a man of incompetence when it came to judging character, and a man of laziness when it came to overseeing employees. (It's not a great defense.)

If you saw this picture in GQ you would not think it was a photo from 1864. You would think, **"Huh, I guess Civil War uniforms are in this season."**

How to Win His Heart

♥ **Cross your eyes.** Grant's wife Julia was born with crossed eyes, and after they got married she considered having surgery to fix them. Grant's response to this plan was, "*I like them just as they are, and now, remember, you are not to interfere with them. They are mine.*" Which is sort of sweet? Although it's also a *little* creepy for your husband to claim ownership of your eyes.

♥ **Get your brother to room with him.** Julia met Grant through her brother, who was Grant's roommate at West Point. You can try this same angle, but it might take some doing. Especially if you don't currently have a brother.

♥ **Have clairvoyant dreams.** Throughout her life, Julia had dreams she thought predicted the future. *Your* best shot at having a prophetic dream is to have lots and lots of dreams, because statistically speaking, some of them will probably come true. So you're going to need to spend more time asleep. This will have the added benefit of making your shoes last longer.

Here are a few lifehacks from Ulysses S. Grant, perfect for hacking up your life.

CHANGING YOUR NAME

If you need to change your name, you can do it the hard way, through the legal system, or the easy way, by stealing a name and date of birth from a tombstone. Or you can do what Grant did: His given name was Hiram Ulysses Grant, but the congressman who wrote his nomination letter to West Point accidentally wrote "Ulysses S. Grant." And Grant just decided to roll with it because honestly who cares what your name is.

LEAVING THE ARMY

Eventually, the day will come when you'll want to leave the army. But how? Well, you could do what Grant did—start drinking a lot and moping around because you miss your family, and your commanding officer will encourage you to resign. But be careful: If a civil war breaks out, the army might decide it doesn't care about your drinking after all.

NEGOTIATING

When Grant wanted Britain to pay for damage done by warships they'd sold to the Confederacy, he drove a hard bargain. He told them they could either pay us $2 billion in gold, or give us Canada. (They counteroffered with "How about we keep Canada and don't give you any gold?" which Grant accepted.)

Vital Stats

Looks: 9

Just look at him. He's looking at you, after all. In fact . . . we'd say he's having a hard time looking away!

Physique: ?

Grant insisted on absolute privacy when naked. This means history has handed down no daguerreotypes of a bathing General Grant. Which, in turn, means that the photo of him you inherited from your great-great-grandmother is probably a fake.

Charisma: 1

Grant is quiet and reserved. If you want to get him talking, try swearing or telling a dirty joke, because he hates both and will scold you. And we can tell that you secretly want Grant to scold you.

Nickname: 10

Grant was dubbed "The Butcher" by the press after taking about 50,000 casualties in a month. To which he should have replied, "Guys, if you think 50,000 casualties a month is a lot, just wait seventy years. There are going to be more casualties than that on the first *day* of the Battle of the Somme." But he couldn't, because it would have revealed his secret.

RUTHERFORD B. HAYES

Maybe you're not looking for anything too flashy. Maybe you just want a boyfriend who is safe, family-friendly, and won't leave you stranded by the side of the road. So tell us—what will it take to get you into a Rutherford B. Hayes today?

Rutherford B. Hayes is not very exciting. But neither is toast, and people still love toast. Plus Hayes is a Civil War hero and three-term governor of Ohio, which is more than most toast can say. He's also politically moderate, he doesn't smoke or drink, and he has a passion for travel that was ignited by his first visit to Fremont, Ohio.

So what could anyone possibly find objectionable about Rutherford B. Hayes? Well, what if we told you that Hayes only won the presidency because a special Republican-led commission awarded him 20 electoral votes that both sides claimed to have won? And what if we told you that the Democrats only accepted his presidency after Republicans agreed to withdraw federal troops from the South, effectively ending Reconstruction and federal efforts to protect the rights of black Americans living in former Confederate states? You'd be OK with all of that? Oh. Well, it sounds like you're pretty easygoing! You would probably get along great with Rutherford B. Hayes.

> BEFORE YOU ELOPE WITH RUTHERFORD B. HAYES, WE FEEL COMPELLED TO WARN YOU THAT "RUTHERFORD" IS A FAMILY NAME.

How to Win His Heart

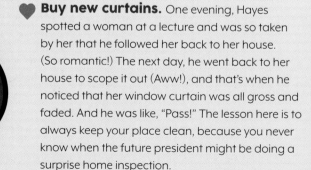

♥ **Don't drink.** Hayes banned alcohol from the White House. So you're going to have to either give up drinking or finally make that throw pillow with a bag of wine hidden inside that you've been talking about all these years.

♥ **Buy new curtains.** One evening, Hayes spotted a woman at a lecture and was so taken by her that he followed her back to her house. (So romantic!) The next day, he went back to her house to scope it out (Aww!), and that's when he noticed that her window curtain was all gross and faded. And he was like, "Pass!" The lesson here is to always keep your place clean, because you never know when the future president might be doing a surprise home inspection.

Why You'll *Love* Him

He likes routine. This makes him easier to stalk!

He won't mind living with your mother. After marrying Lucy Webb, the newlyweds moved in with Lucy's mother. Hayes wrote in his diary that he found this arrangement "most agreeable." Other things that Hayes found agreeable included law school and Burlington, Vermont. So maybe don't take his word for it.

He'll defend you in a murder trial. Hayes' legal career first took off after he served as the defense lawyer in two high-profile murder cases. Though we should probably mention that one of his clients was sentenced to life in prison, and the other one was put in an asylum. So . . . hopefully you finished reading this paragraph before murdering anyone.

Pop QUIZ

In the election of 1876, the Democratic party came up with all sorts of creative ways to commit voter fraud. One method was to print voting ballots that would trick illiterate Republicans into voting Democratic. Now is your chance to find out if YOU are smarter than an illiterate Republican, by seeing if you can identify which of these ballots is fraudulent!

This is the Democratic Presidential Ticket, not the
REPUBLICAN PRESIDENTIAL TICKET

FOR PRESIDENT
Samuel Tilden of New York

REPUBLICAN PRESIDENTIAL TICKET

FOR PRESIDENT
Rutherford B. Hayes from Ohio
(Don't hold that against him!)

Nothing says **"Republican"** like an elephant!

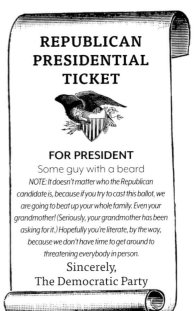

REPUBLICAN PRESIDENTIAL TICKET

FOR PRESIDENT
Some guy with a beard
NOTE: It doesn't matter who the Republican candidate is, because if you try to cast this ballot, we are going to beat up your whole family. Even your grandmother! (Seriously, your grandmother has been asking for it.) Hopefully you're literate, by the way, because we don't have time to get around to threatening everybody in person.
Sincerely,
The Democratic Party

ANSWER: All three ballots are fraudulent! If you don't believe us, try inserting one into a ballot box on the next election day and see what happens. (What will happen is that you will be arrested.)

Sort-of Fun Facts

Hayes moved to Cincinnati because one of his friends told him about Cincinnati and he was like, "Man, I gotta get in on that!"

He first got involved in politics because he could not help but be sucked in by all of the energy and excitement surrounding the Whig party.

Hayes began the tradition of the White House Easter Egg Roll, and now every year thousands of confused children are made to roll eggs across the White House lawn with a spoon.

MINI POSTER!

It's hard to get through a whole day without looking at a photo of young Rutherford B Hayes. That's why we've included this Rutherford B. Hayes mini-poster for you to cut out and put in your locker. If you don't have a locker, just tape it to your windshield.

(*Safety warning:* If you do tape it to your windshield, make sure you won't need to crane your neck to look at it. Eyes straight ahead on the road, and/or on Rutherford B. Hayes!)

Vital Stats

Looks: 6

Before you make up your mind about this one, you need to look at a photo of him from when he was young. It's like a song you can't get out of your head.

Physique: 6

Like everything else with Hayes, there's nothing to complain about here. But there's also nothing to be excited about, like a third arm.

Charisma: 4

Hayes is not an especially memorable speaker, which is why you can't remember any of his speeches.

Civil War service: 8

Hayes was the only president to be wounded fighting in the Civil War, and he was wounded a lot. At one point he was even reported to be dead! And who knows, maybe he *was* dead, and some other guy stole his identity and grew a gigantic beard to disguise his face. The more we think about it, this is definitely what happened.

1881–a few months later | Republican

The more you learn about James Garfield, the more you are going to fall in love with him. Which is too bad, because he has already been spoken for—by me, Kate!

With that in mind, you're probably better off not reading this section on Garfield, unless it's an emergency. Like if you're writing a paper on James Garfield that's due tomorrow, and this was the only book about presidents available from the library, because you have a terrible library.

James Garfield is a self-made man—by which I mean that he pulled himself out of poverty through hard work, and not that he assembled his own body out of atoms like Doctor Manhattan in *The Watchmen*. (Although that would have been impressive, too, in its own way.) Garfield's family was desperately poor—so poor that the future president didn't own a pair of shoes until he was four. In spite of his shoe-related hardships, Garfield rose quickly in the world. And the secret to his success is simply that he's a really good guy. It just goes to show that anyone can become president, if they're friendly, hardworking, handsome, brilliant, mesmerizingly charismatic, and male.

There is every indication that Garfield would have been an amazing president, if he hadn't been shot in the back by a mentally ill man who wanted to be ambassador to France. In an ironic twist, assassinating the president made that guy even *less* likely to be appointed ambassador to France.

MAYBE YOU DIDN'T REALIZE THAT AS YOU READ THROUGH THIS BOOK YOU WERE SUPPOSED TO BE CALLING "DIBS."

Why ~~You'll~~ I *Love* Him

He's modest. Garfield never "toots his own horn," which means both that he does not brag about himself and also that he does not play the horn.

He hates slavery. I don't know about you, but I could never be with a man who was OK with slavery.

He doesn't hold a grudge. Garfield can't bear to stay mad at anyone. This is a very important quality to me, because I am constantly wronging loved ones.

He's affectionate. Don't be surprised if, instead of shaking your hand, Garfield pulls you in for a hug. He's like that with everyone! It definitely doesn't mean he's interested in you.

He loves to play with his kids. Which means more time for me to sit back and watch TV!

He loves his mom. I'm not actually all that crazy about this one.

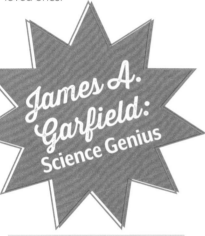

James A. Garfield: Science Genius

Despite having a bullet lodged in his back, Garfield might have survived if the doctors treating him WOULD HAVE WASHED THEIR FREAKING HANDS. But even in death, Garfield has contributed way more to science than you ever have. (I'm talking to you, Stephen Hawking!)

METAL DETECTORS

Alexander Graham Bell invented the metal detector while trying to locate the bullet in Garfield's back. So when you finally find that chest of pirate gold buried on the beach, make sure you thank James Garfield! And his assassin. And Alexander Graham Bell, I guess.

AIR-CONDITIONING

The air conditioner was invented to keep Garfield's recovery room cool, and there is literally nothing I love more than air-conditioning. (Sorry, kids!)

ACCEPTANCE OF GERM THEORY

After Garfield died, American surgeons finally accepted that washing their hands and sterilizing their instruments wasn't a total waste of time, depending on whether or not they wanted their patients to live.

JAMES GARFIELD VS. MATT DAMON'S CHARACTER IN GOOD WILL HUNTING

	James Garfield	Matt Damon's Character
Born into poverty	James Garfield's family was so poor they had to work on a farm instead of doing something more fun, like competing in dressage.	In the opening scenes of *Good Will Hunting*, we can tell that Matt Damon's character is really poor because he has no furniture in his house but a weirdly large amount of furniture in his front yard.
Was a school janitor	Another student might be teased for working part-time as the school janitor, but being covered in soot all the time only made James Garfield even sexier.	Matt Damon keeps the hallway floors at MIT so clean that you can and should eat off of them.
Self-taught lawyer	In his spare time, James Garfield taught himself law. His first case was before the Supreme Court, and he won! Which sounds impressive, but if you think about it, the odds are 50/50.	Matt Damon uses his vast knowledge of the law to defend himself from a variety of criminal charges, including "mayhem," which I think means he cut off someone's leg.
Good at math	James Garfield discovered an original proof of the Pythagorean Theorem while chatting with some fellow congressmen about math. If you've ever spent time on Capitol Hill, you know how congressmen are always gabbing about math!	Struggling with your math homework? Just hang it on the wall inside any building on MIT's campus and Matt Damon will come and do it for you while you're asleep. This is one of the perks of living in Cambridge.
Ladies man	At one point, James Garfield had three girlfriends. Well, technically it was two girlfriends and one fiancée.	Matt Damon is so charming that Minnie Driver gives him her phone number. If you've ever met Minnie Driver, then you know how hard it is to convince her to give you her phone number.

Timeline of James A. Garfield
Blasting Through Every Barrier
Life Puts in His Way

1831 James Garfield is born, weighing a whopping 10 pounds. So he is even great at parasitically siphoning nourishment from his mother.

 **1851** Enrolls in college. Pays his tuition by working as the janitor.

1852 Promoted from janitor to professor. So he's either an amazing student or this is a terrible school, or both.

 **1856** Promoted from professor to school president, even though he is only 26. (So it probably is a terrible school.)

1861–1862 Joins the Union army and, with no military experience, leads his regiment into battle against a more experienced, better equipped Confederate general. Stays up all night coming up with a zany scheme to trick the rebels into thinking he has more men than he really does. And his plan works, because he is James Garfield and his plans always work, except for his "Don't get assassinated" plan.

 1880 Gives an off-the-cuff speech at the Republican convention nominating someone else for president. His speech is so amazing that everyone decides to nominate Garfield instead. So on the one hand, he failed to get his candidate nominated. But on the other hand—pretty good speech!

Match wits with James Garfield by seeing if you, too, can come up with an original proof of the **Pythagorean theorem.** (Here's a hint: If your last line isn't "$a^2 + b^2 = c^2$", then you've taken a wrong turn somewhere.)

a

c

b

If c is the hypotenuse of a right triangle and a and b are the other two sides, prove that the square of the hypotenuse is equal to the sum of the squares of the other two sides.

WHEN HE WAS YOUNG

Sorry, this feels mean—dangling James Garfield in front of you, even though he can never be yours!

James Garfield's mother wanted nothing more than for her youngest son to get an education. But Garfield didn't listen to her, because the sea was calling him. (It was saying, "Hey, James Garfield! It's me, the sea. Come live on top of my head!")

Unfortunately, Garfield lived in rural Ohio, and the closest thing to a sea was the Ohio and Erie Canal. Fortunately, the canal was also calling to him. (It said, "Hey, James Garfield, I'm just as good as the sea! Only slightly narrower and full of mud.") So at age 16, Garfield left home and took a job aboard a canal boat.

Garfield's story might have ended here, because he didn't know how to swim, and he kept falling into the canal. In six weeks, he fell into the canal 14 times. After almost drowning, Garfield decided to give up his dream of a life at sea and return home. After all that he'd been through, school was starting to look pretty good. (Well, it looked OK.)

WARNING! NO LIFEGUARD ON DUTY!

JAMES GARFIELD IS THE LAST OF OUR PRESIDENTS TO HAVE BEEN BORN IN A LOG CABIN, BECAUSE AMERICANS WERE FINALLY STARTING TO FIGURE OUT THAT LIVING IN A LOG CABIN IS NOT AS FUN AS THE LOG INDUSTRY WOULD HAVE YOU BELIEVE.

Vital Stats

Looks: 8

I could gaze into those pale blue eyes all day. (OK, maybe not ALL day! 12 hours max.)

Physique: 9

James Garfield has the broad, muscular shoulders of a man who has repeatedly pulled himself out of a canal.

Charisma: 9

Garfield has been able to seduce me even though he is nearly 150 years older than me and communicates solely through the medium of history books. That's charisma!

Filial devotion: 10

Garfield had his mother move into the White House with him and personally carried her up and down the stairs, I guess because she was really lazy.

CHESTER A. ARTHUR

1881–1885 | Republican

Wait, don't just skip this page! We know it might not seem like it on its face, but the truth is, you could do a lot worse than Chester A. Arthur.

Sure, you're skeptical. America was skeptical at first, too. Upon hearing the news that Arthur was to become president, one prominent Republican cried out, "Chet Arthur? President of the United States? Good God!" And that guy was his *friend*.

No one minded when Arthur was the vice president, because America will let literally anyone be vice president. Arthur got the job in order to appease a group of Republicans known as the Stalwarts (because they were "stalwart" in their support of Ulysses S. Grant and government corruption in general. It's kind of refreshing how upfront they were about it!) The leader of the Stalwarts was a guy named Roscoe Conkling, and Arthur was his loyal sidekick. They were just like Batman and Robin, if instead of fighting crime, Batman and Robin handed out government jobs in exchange for donations to the Republican Party.

When James Garfield was assassinated, the entire country collectively banged their foreheads against the wall when they realized that Chester A. Arthur was in line to become president. But you know what? Arthur rose to the occasion. He blew off Roscoe Conkling and instituted a civil service based on merit rather than greasy bags of cash. He built up the navy, urged Congress to pass new civil rights legislation, and fought discrimination against Chinese immigrants. In the end, America was pleasantly surprised by Chester A. Arthur. Or, if not pleasantly surprised, it was at least mildly indifferent. And we think that if you give him a chance, you'll be pleasantly surprised, too. Or at least mildly indifferent.

> Chester A. Arthur *might* have been Canadian. Either that or he was from Vermont, which some say is just as bad.

Why You'll *Love* Him

He has style. Of course, you already knew this. You can tell just by looking at him—this is a man who has his finger on the pulse of appropriate whisker length.

He's a gourmand. That means he likes fancy food, not that he is some kind of half-man, half-gourd. Although that would be pretty great, too, if you like decorative gourds.

He doesn't like to work. This is probably what made the job of vice president so appealing to him in the first place.

He makes a good sidekick. And you've been wanting a sidekick! He can ride in a side-car attached to your regular car, and then you won't have to sit in the same car with him.

He's in touch with his emotions. This is a nice way of saying that he cries a lot.

Chester A. Arthur will never complain that you're spending too much time on your hair.

SCANDAL!

When there has been an attempt on the president's life, whom do you first suspect? That's right: the vice president.

After James Garfield was shot, rumors started flying that Chester A. Arthur was involved. It didn't help that Garfield's assassin shouted out "I am a Stalwart, and Arthur will be president!" while he was being dragged away by police. In fact, that definitely made things worse. But once investigators looked into Arthur's tearful, puppy-dog eyes, they could tell that he'd had nothing to do with the assassination. Well that, or they just decided that they didn't care to investigate any further. Either way!

CAUGHT ON ~~FILM!~~ CLOTH!

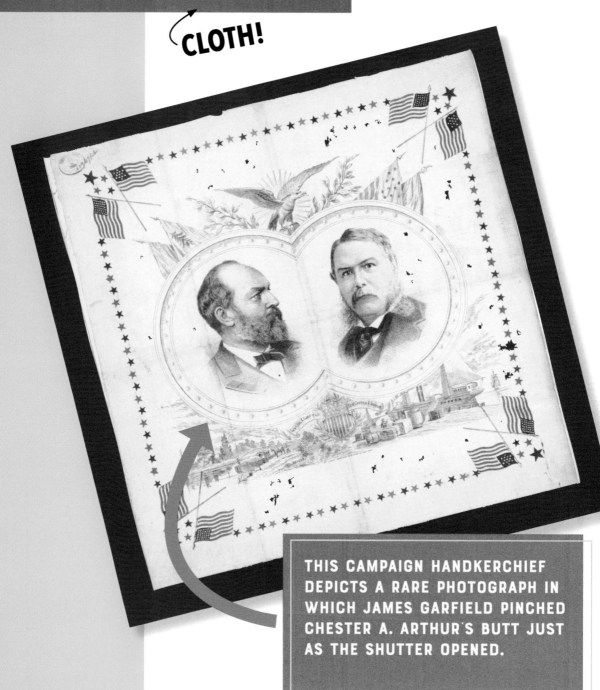

THIS CAMPAIGN HANDKERCHIEF DEPICTS A RARE PHOTOGRAPH IN WHICH JAMES GARFIELD PINCHED CHESTER A. ARTHUR'S BUTT JUST AS THE SHUTTER OPENED.

If you want to help Chester A. Arthur achieve great things, all he needs is a little encouragement. After James Garfield was shot, Arthur started receiving letters from a strange woman who urged him to prove his critics wrong by becoming a great president. It's hard to say how much these letters influenced Arthur, but he did save them, and he even surprised this woman by showing up at her house one day. She was so shy that she would only speak to him from behind a curtain. So our tip is that you should hang curtains in your house, so you have a place to hide in case Chester A. Arthur ever stops by.

Vital Stats

Looks: 1

With his sad brown eyes and equally sad brown whiskers, Chester A. Arthur looks like a seal. And not one of those cute seals, either. One of those scary seals that crawls into your house through a drain pipe.

Physique: 2

"Seal" isn't a body type many people are into. If you don't believe us, try creating a dating profile that describes your body as "seal-like," and see what happens. (Do not agree to meet with anyone who responds. He or she might be a seal!)

Charisma: 3

Arthur is easy to get along with, but he's not the kind of guy who steals the limelight. Somehow, this was true even when he was the president.

Pants: 10

How does a man who owns 80 pairs of pants become president of the United States? Well, part of the answer is that the guy who was *elected* president got assassinated.

match the Mistress to her Potus

♥ 1789–1960 ♥

It can be pretty hard for politicians to remain faithful to their wives. As former Speaker of the House Newt Gingrich once explained, "There's no question at times in my life, partially driven by how passionately I felt about this country, that I worked far too hard and things happened in my life that were not appropriate." Specifically, cheating on his wife.

It's hard to know what lesson to take from this, other than that you should include "I promise to keep my passionate feelings about America under control" in your wedding vows. But the upshot is that throughout history, many U.S. presidents have stepped out on their wives and "entered the Oval Office," so to speak. Test your knowledge of White House infidelities by seeing if you can match each mistress to her presidential lover!

Important notes:

1 We've included some affairs that are only strongly rumored. Why include rumors? Because it's important to spread rumors, or else they will gradually die out.

2 What about slaves? Human relationships are complicated, but we don't think the Venn Diagram of "enslaved women" and "consenting partners" has a TON of overlap. So we've chosen to omit the many cases in which presidents either probably or definitely slept with women they'd enslaved.

DRAW A LINE MATCHING THE PHOTO OF EACH PRESIDENT TO HIS ALLEGED MISTRESS(ES)

Dwight D. Eisenhower

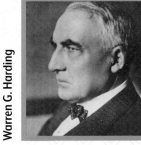

Warren G. Harding

James A. Garfield

Woodrow Wilson

Franklin D. Roosevelt

Carrie Fulton Phillips

Lucy Mercer

Lucia Calhoun

Rebecca Selleck

Kay Summersby

Nan Britton

Mary Peck

Marguerite "Missy" LeHand

 +

REBECCA SELLECK AND JAMES GARFIELD

Garfield dated Selleck in college even though he was already engaged to someone else back home. But what does "engaged" really mean, anyway? We looked it up, and it means "partly embedded in a wall"!

 +

LUCIA CALHOUN AND JAMES GARFIELD

Haven't we all succumbed at one time or another to the raw sexual magnetism of newspaper reporters, with their fedora hats and ink-stained fingers?

 +

NAN BRITTON AND WARREN G. HARDING

Although "Nan Britton" sounds like an alternate character name for Mrs. Doubtfire, she was actually a Marion, Ohio, teenager with a huge, all-consuming crush on her father's friend Warren Harding. Her dad learned about the crush because she had literally wallpapered her bedroom with pictures of Harding. (We've all been there!) When he told Harding about this, the senator agreed to talk to her. And he did! Later, she had his baby.

 +

CARRIE FULTON PHILLIPS AND WARREN G. HARDING

Do you think you're working hard enough to change the world? Well, while you were signing some online petition, Carrie Fulton Phillips was having an affair with Harding and blackmailing him to oppose war with Germany in 1917. When Harding ran for president, Phillips also blackmailed the Republican Party, getting a lifetime pension for herself and, awkwardly, her husband. She used this pension to live the kind of life we all dream of—walking her dogs around the neighborhood wearing nothing but a mink coat (and shoes).

 +

MARY PECK AND WOODROW WILSON

The fun thing about vacationing in Bermuda is that you never know when you're going to meet the governor of New Jersey and start having an affair with him. Bermuda's tourism bureau should bring this up more often!

 +

MARGUERITE "MISSY" LEHAND AND FRANKLIN D. ROOSEVELT

If your husband ever comes home and announces that he met an intriguing woman named "Marguerite LeHand," you should be concerned.

 +

LUCY MERCER AND FRANKLIN D. ROOSEVELT

When Eleanor Roosevelt discovered that FDR was having an affair with her social secretary, FDR promised to end it. So it's weird that Mercer was with him 26 years later when he suffered a stroke while having his portrait painted. (Was this a Titanic-style "Paint me like your French girls" portrait? Hopefully!)

 +

KAY SUMMERSBY AND DWIGHT D. EISENHOWER

Regardless of whether this affair really happened, we can all agree that the most awkward part of sleeping with your chauffeur is the moment you tell them you want the chauffeur hat on. (After that, it's smooth sailing!)

GROVER CLEVELAND

1885–1889 | Democrat

"Call me Uncle Jumbo!" That's what Grover Cleveland would say to you right now, if he weren't terrified of women.

Fortunately for you, Grover Cleveland *is* terrified of women, so you will never have to hear those words spoken aloud (unless you are reading this book aloud right now, perhaps to your partner, as part of a romantic evening of reading aloud to one another about Grover Cleveland). But once you get past Cleveland's shyness and awkwardness, you'll be rewarded with a man who is decent,[1] honest,[2] and shaped like a giant rectangle.[3]

> SOMETIMES WHEN YOU LOVE SOMEONE, YOU SEE THAT PERSON'S FACE EVERYWHERE—WHETHER YOU'RE WALKING PAST BUFFALO CITY HALL OR SWIMMING THROUGH A POOL OF THOUSAND-DOLLAR BILLS.

[1] Except for that one incident where he *might* have fathered an illegitimate child and then had the child's mother committed to a mental asylum. (To be clear, he definitely slept with a woman and then had her involuntarily committed to an asylum, but he may or may not be the father of her child.)

[2] Unless you count the time he told everyone he was going fishing, when really he was having half of his jaw and upper palate surgically removed. To make his alibi more credible, he had the great (?) idea to have this operation onboard a yacht. Does this really count as a lie, though? It's more of a lie of omission.

[3] His body is shaped like a giant rectangle!

Why You'll *Love* Him

He's honest. Cleveland built his career on a reputation for being unflinchingly honest. If you've never dated someone who is extremely honest, then you are in for a real barrel of laughs. (Sorry, that was a lie! You're in for a barrel of very candid feedback about your outfits.)

He works hard. This is a guy who went from being mayor of Buffalo to president of the United States in just three years, and the only way to pull that off is by working really hard. You should definitely mention this to the current mayor of Buffalo if you run into him, or if you have his phone number.[4]

He hates the press. No one hates the press more than you and Grover Cleveland. The press is always hounding Cleveland for sordid details about his personal life, and they rejected your idea for a comic strip about a family of clams, tentatively titled, "Clams!"

He's not afraid to say "no." Cleveland used the veto more times than any other president in a single term. Don't even *try* asking him to give you a pension for serving in the Civil War, because we can tell you right now what his answer will be. (It will be no.)

You can call him "Sheriff." Technically you can call anyone sheriff, but Grover Cleveland really did start his political career as the sheriff of Buffalo, so he won't find it as confusing as other people do.

SCANDAL!

Before you commit to a relationship with Grover Cleveland, perhaps you want to hear a little more about this woman he allegedly forced himself on, impregnated, and then locked in a mental asylum. Or maybe not. It's really up to you!

The woman's name is Maria Halpin, and Cleveland's version of the story is that he did sleep with Maria, but so had a lot of his friends. (So far so good, right?) Cleveland was single at the time, and his friends were all married, so Cleveland agreed to support the child in order to protect his friends' reputations, because that's what good friends do. (FYI to our friends.)

By this point, you're probably so impressed with how forthcoming Grover Cleveland has been that you're ready to elect him president right now. But wait, there's more! After the baby was born, Cleveland used his political connections to have Maria put in an asylum, supposedly because she was drinking too much, and then he put the baby up for adoption against her wishes. The whole thing almost makes you rethink having an affair with Grover Cleveland!

[4] 716-851-4841

LOVE STORY

The romance between Grover Cleveland and Frances Folsom was like something out of a fairy tale. But one of those creepy, old-timey fairy tales. Let's take a look back at their love story.

1864 - THEY MEET. Frances is introduced to her father's law partner and best friend, the 27-year-old Grover Cleveland. Cleveland gives Frances a baby carriage as a gift, because she is a baby.

1875 - TRAGEDY STRIKES. Frances's father dies in an accident caused by his reckless driving. (Specifically, his reckless driving of a carriage.) Cleveland starts supporting Frances and her mother. She calls him "Uncle Cleve," because he is practically her uncle.

1882-1884 - ROMANCE STRIKES. Frances goes away to college, and Cleveland begins writing her letters. He eventually falls in love with her, which is one of the dangers of having a pen pal.

1885 - THE ENGAGEMENT. Cleveland proposes to Frances, and she accepts. Word gets out that the president is engaged, but everyone assumes he is engaged to Frances's mother, because that would have been a reasonable thing to have happened.

1886 - THE WEDDING. Cleveland, now almost 50, marries 21-year-old Frances in a private ceremony at the White House. America breathes a sigh of relief that President Cleveland didn't choose to be both the groom and also the surrogate father who gave the bride away.

1886 - THE TERRIFYING DISCOVERY. Wanting to find out what happened to Cleveland's seven previous wives, all of whom mysteriously vanished, Frances breaks into the "forbidden room" in the White House basement, where—to her horror—she discovers the missing wives' mummified remains. (Just kidding! But it seems plausible, doesn't it?)

His friends call him "Big Steve," which is a fairly cryptic nickname unless you happen to know that his first name is Stephen. He goes by his middle name, Grover, for reasons that will become apparent as soon as you say the name "Stephen Cleveland" aloud.

He was in the process of moving to Cleveland (for obvious reasons) when he made the classic mistake of stopping in Buffalo, New York. Like a black hole from which not even light can escape, the city of Buffalo sucked him in, and he was not able to break out of its icy grip until he'd subdued it by becoming its mayor.

His enemies call him the "Buffalo Hangman," because when he was sheriff he occasionally had to hang people. (And, presumably, buffalo. If the buffalo had committed a serious crime.)

WHEW. NOW THAT'S OVER, AND YOU'LL DEFINITELY NEVER HAVE TO SEE THIS GUY AGAIN!

Vital Stats

Looks: 1

In physical descriptions of Cleveland, somehow the word "ham" always seems to come up.

Physique: 1

Cleveland has very broad shoulders, but it's hard to tell because his chest, stomach, and legs are also very broad.

Charisma: 1

Although he is not an inspiring speaker, he makes up for it by memorizing all of his speeches, which blew people's minds. You can find out for yourself how charismatic this is by memorizing one of Grover Cleveland's speeches and delivering it at parties, on the subway, etc.

Pants: 5

We have checked into this, and Grover Cleveland owned an average amount of pants.

BENJAMIN HARRISON

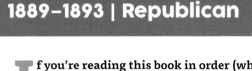

1889–1893 | Republican

If you're reading this book in order (which is how you're supposed to read books, FYI), then you've just seen a photo of Grover Cleveland, and you probably thought to yourself, "Boy, I'd like to be in a Grover Cleveland sandwich, if you know what I mean."

Well, we don't know what you mean, but Benjamin Harrison does, because he served between Grover Cleveland's first and second terms. This turned out to be the most memorable thing about the Harrison presidency.

Why did America decide to take a break from Grover Cleveland and have a four-year dalliance with Benjamin Harrison? A lot of reasons, but one might be America's sublimated desire for a hereditary monarchy, which manifests every few decades in the form of Adamses, Bushes, etc. (The "etc." is Roosevelts.) Benjamin Harrison was the grandson of President William Henry Harrison, who is remembered for taking something everyone does (dying) and making it historic and noteworthy.

It's a little surprising that America was willing to roll the dice on another Harrison presidency after the first one petered out after a few weeks, but Harrison turned out to be a decent guy who knew how to give a nice, succinct inaugural speech. Among other things, he was way ahead of his time on race: He funded education for the children of freed slaves, he made Frederick Douglass an ambassador, and he opposed the Chinese Exclusion Act (which was exactly what it sounds like).

On the other hand, he was kind of a weird uncle. But we'll get to that in a second.

Favorite Pickup Line

"What do you say we leave the lights on tonight? Because electricity just got installed in the White House, and I'm afraid of touching the light switch. Also, let's do this every night because I am probably going to be scared of electricity for a while."

Why You'll *Love* Him

BENJAMIN HARRISON'S FAVORITE FOOD IS CORN. SO THAT'S WHY YOUR TRAP ISN'T WORKING— YOU NEED TO BAIT IT WITH CORN.

Some guys are reluctant to introduce you to their families, but not Benjamin Harrison! For his honeymoon, he took his first wife, Caroline, to his hometown of North Bend, Ohio, a tiny hamlet whose sole attraction was his grandfather's gigantic, monumental tomb. I bet they didn't get much sleep on that honeymoon!

Harrison's presidency was riven by angry, divisive debates . . . over *what do we do with all this extra money.* These are the kinds of fights you want to have with your spouse.

He understands work-life balance. As president, Harrison tried to wrap things up at the office by noon so he could spend the rest of the day goofing off with his grandkids. For a gilded-age quasi-aristocrat, we'll call that a full day's work.

He fights big corporations. And we know you'll love that! Unless you're a big corporation that has become sentient and is reading this book.

SCANDAL!

Oh, there really wasn't anything scandalous in Benjamin Harrison's presidency. Pretty ho-hum.

Well, unless you count the time his wife died, and he married a woman younger than either of his children.

But Mary Dimmick was pretty mature for her age—in fact, she had a very impressive job! She worked at the White House, as his wife's secretary.

Now, to be fair, there might have been some nepotism involved when she was hired. Because she was also his wife's niece.

But other than marrying his own niece, there really wasn't any scandal to speak of in the Harrison administration!

Harrison was the first president to have his voice recorded. So, yes: You can change your ringtone to Harrison saying, "I was present at the first Pan-American Congress." It's a great way to meet people who share your interest in Benjamin Harrison.

During the 1888 presidential election, Harrison decided that instead of campaigning around the country, he'd just sit on his porch in Indianapolis and wait for throngs of people to come to him. The Indianapolis Bureau of Tourism keeps urging presidential candidates to try this proven strategy, but so far they've had no takers.

Harrison's daughter Mary founded an investment newsletter for women called *Cues on the News*. So . . . we hate to be the bearers of bad news, but you're going to need to come up with a different name for your investment newsletter for women.

Here's a Tip

If you and your significant other ever decide to take a five-week vacation through the western states, do it the way Benjamin and Caroline Harrison did: aboard your own five-car, lavishly outfitted train, with ˙THE PRESIDENTIAL SPECIAL˙ written on it in giant gold letters. This gold lettering will make a great conversation piece during the long, boring stretches of track through the desert, because you can use it to start yet another of the endless arguments about the gold standard that dominated the 19th century.

Well, yes. But when it comes to Harrison, that's like having someone promise, "I will eat a really huge breakfast." He might keep his promise, but you're not too excited about it. (Unless you're running a diner, in which case, jackpot!)

✓ **High protective tariffs on imports.** Under Harrison's presidency, the McKinley Tariff Act raised tariffs on goods ranging from carpet to tin plates. This made it a lot more expensive for Americans to build houses out of carpet and tin plates.

✓ **A modernized navy.** But you have to keep in mind this meant modern by 1889 standards, which probably just meant that there always had to be at least one sailor on board who wasn't drunk.

✓ **Pensions for Civil War veterans.** This is how Harrison solved the most vexing problem facing his presidency—what to do with all the money the government was making from tariffs on carpet and tin plates.

Vital Stats

Looks: 5

He's the last president to have a beard. And no, we don't mean "most recent." We mean last.

Physique: 2

Let's just say that he had a body only a low-level White House staffer hoping to marry the president could love.

Charisma: 5

This one is hard to score. Harrison was a famously magnetic public speaker, but in smaller groups, he was so cold and aloof that people called him "The Human Iceberg." On the other hand, that is such an awesome nickname that we feel compelled to reward him with at least a 5.

Goat chasing: 4

Harrison's grandkids kept a goat named "Old Whiskers" at the White House, and one day it escaped and Harrison chased it down Pennsylvania Avenue while wearing a top hat and carrying a cane. But we're still only going to give him a 4 out of 10 because we don't know if he caught the goat. If we were rating him on willingness to chase goats, he'd get a 10/10. But we're not.

WHEN HE WAS YOUNG

Caroline Harrison met her future husband because her father was a science professor, and Harrison was one of his students. Which is a great way to meet men who look like this!

HOTTEST HEADS OF STATE EXPLAINS:

Throughout the 19th century, some of the same policy debates kept coming up over and over again in presidential elections. "How much more land should we take from Mexico?" "What did we decide to do about slavery again?" And, "Should we use the gold standard?"

What is the gold standard, you might ask? Please allow us to use our deep knowledge of monetary history to explain. You might even call this the gold standard of gold standard explanations.

What is the gold standard?

Hopefully you don't have any money in your wallet, because you've already spent it buying additional copies of this book as gifts for your friends, or just as an investment. But if you *do* have any money, it's probably made of paper. The gold standard is when paper money is "backed" by gold.

Do you mean "backed" as in decorated? Like it has a gold foil backing? Because that sounds a lot better than our current non–gold foil system. Please sign me up for the gold standard.

No. "Backed" means that for every dollar of paper money, there's a dollar's worth of gold somewhere that the paper bill represents. That way, the value of the paper money isn't theoretical—the paper is a stand-in for actual physical stuff. This gives people more confidence in it. They don't have to worry that one day they'll wake up and it'll just be a worthless piece of paper, like that IOU from your kids for "one hug." Under the gold standard, money is usually "convertible," which means you can trade it in to the central bank for gold.

"Convertible" currency should mean currency that you can trade in to the central bank for a convertible car. Or currency that has a convertible printed on it. Or currency that you can only use for transactions while you're *in* a convertible. But that aside, convertible currency sounds amazing. I would almost always rather have a tiny gold pebble than a dollar bill. Are there any other benefits to the gold standard?

It helps control inflation, since the amount of money in the economy is limited by the amount of gold in the country's vaults. But there are also some downsides.

The Gold Standard

Well, of course. Like, what happens if a super villain steals all the country's gold? Doesn't the currency then lose all value?

It sounds like you're ready to start on your economics dissertation! Actually, the main downside is that your rate of economic growth is restricted by the size of your gold reserves. If you want to add 50,000 jobs to your economy, you have to acquire enough gold to back enough new dollar bills to pay those workers. And you're probably not mining gold that fast!

That sounds like a mining problem, not a currency problem. Other than lazy, unproductive miners, why did the gold standard become so controversial in the 19th century?

During the Civil War, the U.S. government wanted to spend more money than its precious metal holdings permitted (don't we all!), so it started printing "fiat" money that wasn't really backed by anything except for "come on guys, we're the U.S. government." This fiat money was controversial, for the same reason that you'd have some questions if the IRS paid your tax refund in polka-dotted bills that said "United Statez of America." Sure, it's coming from the government, but is it "real" money? Will stores accept it? So a lot of people wanted the U.S. to return to a "bimetallic" gold-and-silver standard after the war. For decades, this was a central issue in presidential elections.

Zzzzz . . . what, huh? Oh, sorry, I fell asleep there for a second. It sounds like those must have been some really riveting presidential debates.

Well, people had a lot fewer entertainment options back then.

I do have one question before we wrap up. Why gold? It doesn't seem like it has any more inherent value than paper, since it isn't actually good for anything useful. Why not iron or copper or something?

Because gold is shiny and yellow and very scarce.

Those are dumb criteria. I have a new plan. Copper has inherent value, because it's used for wiring. So let's back currency with copper. But to make sure copper is *scarce*, we'll need to destroy most it. Maybe by launching it on a giant rocket into the sun.

Actually, now that I think about it, that sounds complicated.

Well, monetary policy *is* pretty complicated. But on the plus side, a project to launch most of the Earth's copper into the sun would create a lot of jobs.

GROVER CLEVELAND
AGAIN
1893–1897 | Democrat

Have you ever broken up with a guy and then started dating Benjamin Harrison, but later thought, "Hey, maybe that first guy wasn't so bad after all"? Then you know exactly how America felt about Grover Cleveland.

By serving as both the 22nd and 24th president, Grover Cleveland has forever ruined all attempts to number the presidents. But we refuse to devote a second chapter of this book to Grover Cleveland's life story—that's exactly what he wants us to do. Instead we're going to use this space to make a list of romantic fantasies involving Grover Cleveland.

USE THIS LIST ON FIRST DATES TO WEED OUT PEOPLE WHO DON'T SHARE YOUR INTEREST IN PRESIDENTIAL HISTORY.

TOP 12

Fantasies involving GROVER CLEVELAND

1 Having sex with him two nonconsecutive times.

2 He puts on nothing but his SHERIFF'S STAR; you go on a crime spree in downtown Buffalo.

3 Something involving his MUSTACHE.

4 You read him a list of your romantic fantasies, and he vetoes all of them.

5 Challenging him to a game of STRIP POKER. But instead of stripping off your clothes, you take turns stripping paint off of an old piece of furniture. (Follow this up with a game of "applying wood stain poker.")

6 You are the submissive; he is the dominant. But he believes in reducing EXECUTIVE POWER, so he doesn't give you any commands or try to dominate you. Eventually, you fall asleep.

7 Having sex on the shoulder of the highway under a "YOU ARE NOW ENTERING CLEVELAND" sign.

8 ROLE PLAY: He plays himself, as president of the United States, and you play the woman he's had involuntarily committed to an asylum. You're going to need a straightjacket and a padded room. DO NOT just duct-tape pillows to the walls — you're going to need actual asylum-grade padding.

9 ROLE PLAY: He plays himself, as the 22nd president of the United States. You play him also, but as the 24th president, wearing a big fake mustache . . . and nothing else. (Well, you can wear a top hat, but nothing other than that!)

10 ROLE PLAY: He plays anyone you want, because he's a skilled impersonator and does great impressions of his contemporaries in politics.

11 Having a THREE-WAY with Grover Cleveland and the current mayor of Buffalo.*

12 Listening politely while he TALKS ABOUT TARIFFS.

*716-851-4841

WILLIAM MCKINLEY

1897–1901 | Republican

When you find out that your spouse is very sick, it's tempting to lock him or her in the attic and then cover it up by telling people that the screaming coming from your attic is just a squirrel and don't worry about it. But that's just not William McKinley's style.

After McKinley's wife developed epilepsy, he cared for her with such tireless devotion that you can't help but fall in love with him and want to break up his marriage. That would be hard to do, though, because Ida McKinley is always at her husband's side. (She's really clingy like that. You would be so much better for him!) Ida would sometimes have seizures at parties or (ahem) inaugurations, but McKinley would just cover her face with a napkin and everyone would carry on as if it were totally normal for the president to smother the First Lady with a napkin.

William McKinley is a good guy, and he's proof that sometimes nice guys finish first. (If getting elected president and then being assassinated counts as "finishing first.")

Favorite Pickup Line

"I'd like to crucify you on my cross of gold, if you know what I mean."

(AUTHORS' NOTE: No one knows what he means.)

> McKinley defied convention by insisting that his wife be seated next to him at state dinners. This only made state dinners even *more* romantic.

Why You'll *Love* Him

He wears a red carnation in his lapel for luck, and often gives it away to little girls. This is so adorable and charming that you don't need more reasons to love William McKinley. But you are going to get them anyway!

He annexed Hawaii. If not for McKinley, we would all be honeymooning in Arizona.

He stopped a mob from killing his assassin. After McKinley was shot, an angry mob attacked the gunman. But McKinley called them off, because he's a better man than you. (This is especially true if you are not a man.)

He used to have a mountain named after him. In 1896, a gold prospector in Alaska spotted a towering peak, called "Denali" by the local Koyukon people, and decided to rename it Mt. McKinley, using the authorities vested in him as a gold prospector. But what a grizzled frontier prospector can giveth, the president of the United States can taketh away. In 2015 Barack Obama, cravenly pandering to the Koyukon vote, returned Mt. McKinley to its old name of Denali. During his presidential campaign Donald Trump promised to change it back to Mt. McKinley, because he is definitely not pandering to the Koyukon vote.

Timeline: The Assassination of *William McKinley*

SEPTEMBER 6, 1901
McKinley is shot by an anarchist in Buffalo, New York. Some legends claim that as he collapsed, he gasped, "The prophecy is complete."

SEPTEMBER 10, 1901
While McKinley is being treated, Vice President Teddy Roosevelt goes camping in the Adirondacks because, what the heck, why not?

SEPTEMBER 14, 1901
McKinley dies from his wounds. Roosevelt rushes to Buffalo to be sworn in. While there, he checks to see if buffalo wings have been invented yet. (They have not.)

REMEMBER THE MAINE?

No? Well, the **USS Maine** was a U.S. battleship sent to Cuba during turmoil between the Cubans and the Spanish Empire. It **blew up** and sank, and many Americans blamed Spain. Congress decided to **"declare war,"** which is something Congress used to do when the U.S. went to war with another country. Here are some fun facts to help you remember the *Maine*.

 It was named after a U.S. state called Maine.

 It was built as part of a naval arms race between the U.S. and Brazil. Presumably the U.S. eventually won this arms race, although we can't say we've actually checked.

The *Maine* is best known for blowing up. So in that respect, it's similar to the Death Star.

BEFORE

AFTER

McKinley pushed hard for the Tariff Act of 1890, raising import duties on tin plates and other items. Would this be good for you? Take this short quiz to find out.

	YES	NO
Are you the kind of person who buys a lot of tinware? (As opposed to the other kind of person, who buys a _huge_ amount of tinware.)	☐	☐
Are you a domestic tinware manufacturer?	☐	☐
Do you own or work in a tin mine?	☐	☐
Are you the tin man?	☐	☐

Answer: Your responses are irrelevant. The Tariff Act of 1890 would have been good for you because, candidly, you've been buying too much tinware.

WHEN HE WAS YOUNG

McKinley dropped out of college twice and never graduated, which means that dropping out of college is a proven route for reaching the White House. (He was also a wealthy attorney, which admittedly is a _more_ proven route.)

Vital Stats

Looks: 5

Just look at that cleft chin. You could fit a quarter in there! And you can stash the rest of your money in his eyebrows. Now you don't have to carry a purse!

Physique: 7

McKinley's family was in the ironworking business, so he's probably hiding a muscled, sooty body under all those layers of tuxedo.

Charisma: 8

Everybody loves William McKinley! Everybody except for that one assassin.

Looks like a villain in Titanic: 7

He's no Billy Zane, but he still looks like someone who'd order his manservant to hit you with an oar to make room on the life raft. If you're into that kind of thing!

SPECIAL INVESTIGATION:
WHICH PRESIDENTS ARE ALSO
SEXY VAMPIRES?

Due to anti-vampire and anti-sexiness prejudices, few presidents have included "My fellow Americans, it is time to reveal that I am a super-sexy vampire" in their inaugural addresses. But that doesn't mean that none of them were! Join us as we conduct a thorough, in-depth, well-researched investigation into which presidents might have been sexy vampires.

John Adams

☑ Vampire ☒ Sexy

Based on this portrait, Adams appears to be a prepubescent boy dressed up in a powdered wig and breeches. But the other Founding Fathers probably wouldn't have let a child sign the Declaration of Independence, so by process of elimination we conclude that Adams is actually hundreds of years old, but frozen in perpetual childhood by the dark gift of vampirism.

Thomas Jefferson
☑ Vampire ☑ Sexy

Have you ever wondered why there are a lot of paintings of Thomas Jefferson, but no photographs? It's probably because he is a vampire.

James Madison
☒ Vampire ☒ Sexy

Don't be fooled by his all-black wardrobe. People who wear all black are not necessarily mysterious and dangerous, no matter what nuns would have you believe.

James K. Polk
☑ Vampire ☑ Sexy

Doesn't it seem odd that Polk was so determined to secure control of the cloudy, rainy, sunless Pacific Northwest?

Andrew Jackson
☒ Vampire ☑ Sexy

Andrew Jackson is only bloodthirsty in the metaphorical sense. He would never actually drink anyone's blood, except maybe on a particularly hot and muggy day, or out of boredom.

Millard Fillmore
[√] **Vampire** [√] **Sexy**

These days, sexy vampire Millard Fillmore goes by the name "Alec Baldwin." Eventually "Alec Baldwin" will "die," and 50 or 100 years later he'll show up again in some new guise. Maybe next time he'll have a cool hat!

James A. Garfield
[√] **Vampire** [√] **Sexy**

Take a few minutes to stare into the eyes of James Garfield. Do you feel like you're drifting into a soft, beardy dream? That is just a distant echo of James Garfield's full vampiric powers. If you were staring into his eyes in person, you would have already taken your clothes off.

Theodore Roosevelt
[✗] **Vampire** [√] **Sexy**

Theodore Roosevelt is not a vampire. He is living forever, hidden deep in the Adirondack Mountains, for a different reason entirely.

Richard Nixon
[x] Vampire [x] Sexy

We don't think Richard Nixon is a vampire. But it's probably not for lack of trying.

Ronald Reagan
[√] Vampire [√] Sexy

"It's morning in America" is exactly the kind of campaign slogan a vampire would use, because he thinks it sounds positive and optimistic, because he doesn't remember what mornings are actually like.

Barack Obama
[x] Vampire [√] Sexy

We know Barack Obama isn't secretly an ageless, timeless vampire, because we know for a fact that he was born in Hawaii in 1961. We know this because as it turns out, if your name is Barack Obama and you're black, you have to produce a birth certificate to prove you were born in America. But we think Obama should at least *consider* becoming a vampire.

THEODORE ROOSEVELT

Wake up! You just fainted from all the manly pheromones that were released into the air when you turned to this page about Theodore Roosevelt. Also, while you were unconscious, someone came by and took your wallet.

Anyway . . . we're just going to keep writing about Theodore Roosevelt as if you were awake and able to read it. We're pretty sure that's what Roosevelt would have wanted.

It can be hard to wrap your mind around Theodore Roosevelt—partly because you hit your head when you fainted, but also because he is like six men rolled into one.

He's a bookish nerd who enjoys bird-watching, but he's also a brawny jock who was the first American to earn a brown belt in Judo. And also, maybe, the last. We haven't checked.

He's a conservationist who set aside millions of acres of land to preserve forests and wildlife, but he has also personally killed hundreds of exotic animals. (It's even more if you count birds. We don't count birds!)

Sometimes he seems like an overgrown child, like when you spot him walking around the White House lawn on a pair of stilts. On the other hand, not many children have won a Nobel Peace Prize for negotiating the end to the Russo-Japanese War. (But maybe that's just because the war is already over.)

Theodore Roosevelt is such a forceful and dynamic presence that it's difficult to capture in words. If you really want to get a sense of what Theodore Roosevelt is like, you should go stick your finger in an electrical socket. (But only after signing our release form!)

WHEN HE WAS YOUNG

In this rare photo, a young Theodore Roosevelt is coolly staring down an Imperial Spanish battleship, which eventually retreated, meekly.

Why You'll *Love* Him

He is manly. Roosevelt thinks that men are spending too much time working behind desks and not enough time tearing desks apart with their bare hands.

He is indestructible. Roosevelt once survived being shot in the chest—a part of the body that contains a lot of important organs. (We're talking to you, thymus gland!) He went on to give an hour-long campaign speech before seeking medical attention. His would-be assassin claimed to be taking orders from the ghost of William McKinley. And if the ghost of William McKinley cannot destroy you, then you can be destroyed by no man.

He loves animals. If you've ever said to yourself, "I wish I had a pet bear, snake, rabbit, owl, badger, parrot, lizard, pony, pig, flying squirrel, and a bunch of rats," then you might have found your soulmate in Theodore Roosevelt. Or you might be crazy. Probably both, if we're being honest.

He has a photographic memory. Say good-bye to the days of your boyfriend always forgetting what you look like!

He never swears. He also hates dirty jokes, which is why we haven't mentioned the Rough Riders.

Pop QUIZ

See if you can identify which things Theodore Roosevelt really did versus which stuff we just made up.

☐ Grew his own mustache

☐ Spent two years as a cattle rancher

☐ Scaled the Matterhorn

☐ Tracked down and captured the boat thieves who'd stolen his boat

☐ Led an uphill charge, on foot, in the Spanish-American War

☐ Spent a year on safari in Africa

☐ Explored uncharted parts of the Amazon

☐ Was parked with his girlfriend in the woods when an escaped serial killer with a hook attacked them; Roosevelt easily dispatched him, then resumed making out

ANSWER: These are all well-documented true facts about Theodore Roosevelt, except for the last one. But even with that one, we can't disprove it.

DIY PROJECT: FUN WITH TAXIDERMY

If you're looking for a hobby that is educational and wholesome, look no further than amateur taxidermy. Theodore Roosevelt practiced taxidermy as a boy, and just look where he ended up! (He ended up as president.) So grab whatever knife you usually use for skinning things, and let's get started!

1

First, find something that needs taxidermizing. This will probably be an animal, unless you want to start on something easier, like a banana, or a soccer ball.

2

Once you've chosen your subject, you will need to **murder it.** You might discover that this isn't as easy as you imagined it would be in your revenge fantasies. No matter how much you hate that woodpecker who put a hole in your siding, are you really capable of killing an innocent animal? If not, maybe it will help to put the animal on trial first so it can be found guilty.

3

Select a jury. You'll need to round up a dozen more woodpeckers from the neighborhood, plus two alternates. The best way to attract woodpeckers is to smear a bunch of suet everywhere, because woodpeckers love suet. Suet is the fat that's found around the kidneys of a cow. Which means you'll need to find a cow, accuse it of a crime, try it before a jury of cows, and hope that its crime was grave enough that it gets sentenced to death.

4

Manufacture evidence. After all the trouble you went to assembling a woodpecker jury, you can't afford for the accused to be found not guilty. That's why you should take the precaution of manufacturing evidence and planting it in the defendant's nest. (The details here will depend on the specific charges. For example, if the woodpecker is charged with murdering a cow, your job will be easy, because you just happen to have a dead cow in your driveway.)

5

Schedule a **sentencing hearing.** Don't worry; this is just a formality!

6

Carry out the **execution.** This animal is a convicted criminal, so now you can execute it with a clear conscience. Justice has been served!

7

Remove the animal's skin. Position the skin around a plaster mold of the animal, and then sew it back together again. Wait . . . you don't have a plaster mold? Whoops! You were supposed to make the plaster mold before you removed the skin. You'll have to start all over at the beginning.

It's never too early to start shopping for Theodore Roosevelt's birthday present. After all, his birthday is bound to come around eventually! To help inspire you, here are a few of the memorable gifts that Theodore Roosevelt has received over the years.

A CRATE FULL OF RACCOONS. It will have to be a pretty nice crate, though, to make up for the fact that it is full of raccoons.

BIG STICKS. Roosevelt's motto is "Speak softly and carry a big stick," so people are always sending him big sticks. He probably should have made his motto "Speak softly and carry a big ham."

HAM. Successfully anticipating all of Theodore Roosevelt's unspoken desires, one admirer sent him a ham carved into the shape of his profile.

A BADGER. A badger is the perfect gift for the man who has everything, because the badger will destroy a bunch of his stuff, and he will no longer have the burden of so many possessions.

Vital Stats

Looks: 7

If you're not attracted to Theodore Roosevelt, it's because you're not picturing him soaked in blood and perched over an elephant carcass. (This is assuming that you hate elephants.)

Physique: 10

Roosevelt's chest is so strong and muscled that it wants to explode out of his shirt. This is also what everyone else wants.

Charisma: 10

When he returned from a post-presidential year-long trip to Africa, hundreds of thousands of people gathered in the streets of New York City to welcome him back. There was a parade and people got a half day off work. If we're being honest, his charisma doesn't really fit on the 1-10 scale.

Depth perception: 0

Roosevelt would invite professional boxers to come to the White House and fight him, because of course he did. In one match, his opponent blinded him in one eye. And that's the true story of why Theodore Roosevelt gave up boxing and took up jujitsu!

1909–1913 | Republican

Guess who's calling your house right now?!

If there is one thing you probably already know about William Taft, it's that he's a really nice guy. But there's much more to him than that! So, so, so much more.

All Taft wanted in life was to serve on the Supreme Court, probably so he could wear a robe to work. He did not want to be president. But his wife, Nellie, had a different dream. Ever since visiting the White House as a teenager, she'd wanted to live there. And not as a mole-person hiding in the space between the walls, either! She wanted to be First Lady.

Forcing your husband to become the president of the United States against his will *sounds* like a great idea. But there is one major downside, at least in Taft's case. During his time in the White House, Taft was really, really depressed. Now, you're probably thinking, "What do I care if my husband is depressed?" But believe it or not, it's hard to enjoy reorganizing the White House china cabinet while your husband is sitting in the corner, crying quietly into his bucket of scrambled eggs.

Fortunately for Taft, no one gets to be president forever. (At least, not as of this printing.) Taft did not win a second term, because his ex–best friend Teddy Roosevelt ran as a third party candidate and split the Republican vote. Taft happily took a position teaching law at Yale, he lost a bunch of weight, and eight years later, he was appointed chief justice of the United States. And, just like all Supreme Court justices, he never wore pants again.

Why You'll *Love* Him

He is an adoring husband. Taft absolutely doted on his wife, even though she seems horrible. Just imagine how much he would dote on you, someone who is only a little bit horrible!

You can push him around. Not literally though, unless he's on a skateboard or something.

He has curves that won't quit. You can try asking them to quit, but they will say "no thanks!"

He has a great laugh. Taft has a deep, jolly laugh, just like Santa Claus. But his laughter hides a dark and crippling depression, also like Santa Claus.

He'll let you choose his political appointees. Now you can get revenge on all of your enemies by giving them boring government jobs.

How to Win His Heart

💜 **Be smart.** Taft is the kind of guy who will love you for your brain. But not in the sense that he's a zombie who wants to eat your brain, like so many other Supreme Court justices.

💜 **Criticize him.** Taft's parents were always criticizing him, so it's only natural for him to seek that same quality in a spouse. It probably feels comfortable and familiar, like a pair of well-worn slippers that shouts insults at you.

💜 **Go sledding.** Taft met his future wife at a sledding party. While this doesn't necessarily mean you will meet William Taft at a sledding party, it also doesn't mean you won't. (But you probably won't.)

💜 **Keep Him Awake.** Sometimes Taft falls asleep at public functions, so he'll be really grateful if you keep him awake by falling asleep first and snoring loudly.

💜 **Be ambitious.** Taft likes ambitious women. And if you stop to think about it, you probably have at least some ambitions. If nothing else, you've resolved to distract yourself from the alternating nihilism and vacuity of modern politics by reading this book.

JUST LOOK AT YOUNG TAFT WHEN HE WAS BUT A WISP OF A MAN, AND A CUSTOM-BUILT, 900-GALLON BATHTUB WAS ONLY A GLINT IN HIS EYE!

Sort-of Fun Fact

Before he was president, Taft served as governor of the Philippines *and* governor of Cuba! Doesn't that make you miss having an empire?

Favorite Pickup Line

"There's room for two in this 900-gallon bathtub! . . . Oh wait, no there isn't."

Vital Stats

Looks: 3

Taft's looks are all about that mustache. Just try *not* thinking about how it would feel brushing against your skin, like the rough-but-tender snout of a big, sexy walrus. (There, see! You're thinking about it!)

Physique: 1

Even Taft said that "too much flesh is bad for any man." Though maybe he just meant he was going to stop storing so much human flesh in his icebox.

Charisma: 2

Taft tends to be quiet and thoughtful, and quiet people aren't usually very charismatic, unless they are really good at wriggling their eyebrows.

Stuffed animals inspired by him: 3

After Roosevelt's presidency inspired a craze for teddy bears, toy makers tried to popularize a stuffed possum in Taft's honor. They chose a possum because possum is Taft's favorite food. No one can figure out why this didn't catch on.

135

PRESIDENTIAL

★ OILED HAIR! ★

TREND REPORT

Hair oil is one styling product that every president should have in his presidential medicine cabinet. Check out these 10 presidents who used hair oil to give themselves a cool, oily look.

JAMES K. POLK believes that women like it when a man shows a lot of forehead. (He is mistaken.)

RONALD REAGAN'S oiled hair is why hair oil was invented, and also why hair was invented. This is a head of hair you want to curl up in with a good Tom Clancy novel.

JAMES A. GARFIELD will tell you that it's not easy keeping your beard hair frizz-free during muggy Washington summers. (He's lying, though. You just slather it in oil!)

HERBERT HOOVER'S oiled hair is combed down his back and coiled around one leg—all held tightly in place with a half-pint of Brylcreem. This is the kind of eccentricity presidents could get away with in the days before television.

RICHARD NIXON doesn't use hair oil—these are all-natural secretions. He never shampoos, because he prefers to feel dirty.

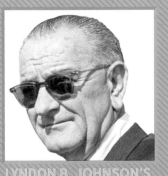

LYNDON B. JOHNSON'S hair is a tattoo made to look like oiled hair. But it shows a lot of dedication to the look, so we'll let him "sneak across the border and launch undeclared war" on our oiled-hair list.

HARRY TRUMAN is a salt-of-the-earth midwesterner who doesn't keep with East Coast dandyism like hair oil. When he wants to hold his hair in place, he uses good, honest spit.

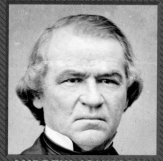

ANDREW JOHNSON was the only senator from a Confederate state who stayed loyal to the Union. It was because he greased his hair with whale oil and needed to keep the oak-and-copper whale oil pipeline between New Bedford and Richmond flowing.

GEORGE H. W. BUSH keeps his hair well lubricated so that should the need arise, he will be able to escape the Soviets by sliding through an air duct.

DWIGHT EISENHOWER is only here to warn you about the military-industrial hair oil complex and its tightening grip on American democracy. Too late, Dwight Eisenhower!

WOODROW WILSON

1913–1921 | Democrat

Everyone has "sexy professor" fantasies—why else would so many people waste their time on college? But it's not very often that you get the opportunity to combine your "sexy professor" fantasy with your "sexy president" fantasy, because no matter how many times you ask, your professor refuses to run for president.

Well, we have good news! In their boundless wisdom, the American voters have already created a sexy professor/president hybrid, and his name is Woodrow Wilson. Prior to becoming president of the country, Wilson was the president of Princeton University, which is considered by many to be among the top schools in New Jersey. Underneath his bookish exterior, you'll find a man who is, in fact, very bookish, but also passionate.

Plus, Wilson is hiding a naughty secret! Unfortunately, the secret is that he's a huge racist. (And it isn't actually that much of a secret.)

Here's a Tip

You don't want your child to be born a Yankee, do you? Ugh, no, of course not. Neither did Woodrow Wilson's first wife, Ellen, which is why she traveled all the way from upstate New York to Georgia during the final week of her pregnancy. Oh, and it was 1886, so she had to travel by stagecoach and it took several days.

All of her effort to avoid having a Yankee child was worth it in the end, though, when her Georgia-born daughter grew up, moved to India, and became a Hindu nun.

WOODROW WILSON'S HANDSOME FACE IS ON THE $100,000 BILL— THE LARGEST U.S. CURRENCY NOTE. IF YOU HAVE A BILL WITH WILSON'S FACE ON IT, CONGRATULATIONS! YOU EITHER SUCCESSFULLY ROBBED A FEDERAL RESERVE BANK, OR YOU SUCCESSFULLY ACCEPTED A COMICALLY LARGE COUNTERFEIT BILL AS PAYMENT.

Why You'll *Love* Him

He endorsed the nineteenth amendment, which gave women the right to vote. If you *don't* want women to be able to vote, then we have to be honest: You are not the target demographic for this book.

He's in the New Jersey Hall of Fame. He was inducted the same year as Judy Blume! Woodrow Wilson and Judy Blume, together at last.

He has his PhD. It's always better to date a guy who already has his PhD, so you don't have to support him while he *gets* his PhD.

He comes ready-made with a belittling nickname. Wilson's real first name was "Thomas," and he went by "Tommy" until he got to college. So if you ever need to take him down a peg, try calling him "Tommy," or "Tommy-boy," or "Hey, four-eyes!"

He won the Nobel Peace Prize. Woodrow Wilson won the Nobel Peace Prize after WWI for creating the League of Nations, a proto-UN intended to prevent another cataclysmic world war. And the great thing about winning a Nobel Peace Prize for preventing world war is they're not allowed to take it back.

He'll let you be president. Wilson had a stroke halfway through his second term that left him unable to move or speak, and he didn't mind his wife Edith being the secret acting president for the rest of his term. Or at least if he did mind, he didn't say anything about it.

DOES HE KEEP HIS *promises?*

☒ Keep the U.S. out of WWI.
Wilson tried pretty hard to keep the United States out of the pointless bloodbath that was WWI. But after Germany kept sinking American ships, Teddy Roosevelt said, *"If he does not go to war I shall skin him alive."* And when Teddy Roosevelt threatens to skin you alive, he's not speaking figuratively.

☒ Ban child labor.
Wilson did pass a law that would have eliminated child labor. But even with a team of ace child-lawyers defending it, the Supreme Court declared it unconstitutional.

SCANDAL!

At one point or another, most people are accused of murdering their spouse, and Woodrow Wilson is no different. Eight months after his wife Ellen died unexpectedly, he married local widow Edith Galt, and rumors swirled that the two had conspired to murder Ellen. And *still* they swirl, thanks to irresponsible rumor-mongering books like this one!

Immediately prior to becoming president of the United States, Wilson was president of the American Political Science Association. This set a pretty unreasonable bar for every subsequent president of the American Political Science Association.

Wilson is hot-tempered. According to one story, he almost punched someone who bumped into him at a train station and had to calm himself down by saying, "You can't behave this way, you're the president of Princeton University." It just goes to show how little he understood about being the president of Princeton University.

Wilson abolished eating clubs at Princeton to try to reduce the power of elites. It worked, and elites forevermore had no influence or special access at Princeton.

How to Win His Heart

Wilson is a huge bigot! But this unfortunate fact provides some useful strategies for seducing him and "graduating from the Woodrow Wilson school of public and international affairs," so to speak.

♥ **Don't be African-American.** Wilson wrote that in the antebellum South, "The domestic slaves, at any rate, and almost all who were much under the master's eye, were happy and well cared for." It's just *so sad* that Wilson never got to be a slave, since he thought it was such a happy and well-cared-for life.

♥ **Don't be African-American.** Wilson described the end of Reconstruction as "Negro rule under unscrupulous adventurers had been finally put an end to in the South, and the natural, inevitable ascendancy of the whites, the responsible class, established." You can see how, if you are African-American, comments like this would eventually drive a wedge between you and Woodrow Wilson.

♥ **Did we mention don't be African-American?** Wilson resegregated the federal workforce, firing black officials and introducing Jim Crow–style separate bathrooms and lunch tables in federal buildings. He told the black civil-rights leaders who confronted him to chill out, because "Segregation is not a humiliation but a benefit." Well, OK! Thanks for clearing that up, President Wilson.

♥ **Oh and also don't be Italian or Japanese or Hungarian or Polish or Chinese.** Wilson described Italian, Hungarian, and Polish immigrants to the U.S. as having "neither skill nor energy nor any initiative of quick intelligence," and he supported restricting immigration from China and Japan because "We cannot make a homogeneous population out of people who do not blend with the Caucasian race." He wasn't a big fan of Catholics, either, but please just take our word for it, because this section is starting to feel a little preachy.

All too many U.S. presidents have had the shattering experience of rejection by their cousins, and Woodrow Wilson is no exception. While in law school at the University of Virginia, he proposed to his ridiculously named cousin Hattie Woodrow. She turned him down, presumably on the grounds that she'd already had enough of the name Woodrow. Some historians think this spurning is why Wilson dropped out of law school. And, of course, this is all too common at UVA. They should probably start mentioning it in 1L orientation: "Fellas, don't fall in love with your cousins. They'll only break your heart."

WHEN HE WAS YOUNG

Believe it or not, Woodrow Wilson didn't learn to read until the age of 10. So if someone tells you that you'll never be president because you didn't learn to read until you were 10, they're probably right, because it's very unlikely that would happen twice.

Vital Stats

Looks: 7

While in law school, Wilson wrote a limerick about his own looks that began with "For beauty I am not a star / There are others more handsome by far." We know it's hard to believe that a law student taking the time to write limericks about himself ended up dropping out, but it's true.

Physique: 5

Wilson plays baseball, but that doesn't really tell us much about his physique. Come back and talk to us if he starts playing soccer.

Charisma: 7

Wilson is a good public speaker, but we are deducting points for the fact that his PhD dissertation was titled "Congressional Government: A Study in American Politics," and he probably liked to talk about it.

Having a PhD: 10

Wilson is the only U.S. president to have earned a doctorate. Most PhD graduates don't have time for politics, because they are too busy teaching high school English.

HOTTEST HEADS OF STATE EXPLAINS:

If I open an account at a Federal Reserve Bank, can I get checks with Hello Kitty on them? Because my bank won't give me Hello Kitty checks, and I'm like WTF, YOU'RE A BANK.

Unfortunately, you can't get any kind of personal checks from the 12 banks in the Federal Reserve System. That's because the "Fed" isn't a consumer bank—it's a central bank.

Ugh, OK, I'll bite. What is a central bank?

We're so glad you asked! A central bank is a government bank that, among other things, manages a country's money supply. Using a few different tools, a country's central bank can increase or decrease the amount of money in circulation.

I would like more money, please.

Well, sure, but it's not that simple. If everyone gets a bunch more money, without anything else changing, it just means that the money is worth less. If you gave everyone a trillion dollars, it wouldn't mean everyone was suddenly super rich, it would just mean that hamburgers would start costing a billion dollars each. That's called inflation. The Fed usually wants to keep inflation under control, so sometimes it takes steps to reduce the money supply.

I don't care if they want to reduce the money supply. Those jackbooted thugs at the Fed better not try to confiscate the Susan B. Anthony dollars I've been hoarding under my mattress.

Actually, central banks usually don't need to change the amount of currency in circulation in order to change the size of the money supply. That's because the money supply is different—and bigger—than the supply of actual, physical coins and bills.

Huh?

Well, it gets pretty complicated. But in the U.S., for every dollar in physical cash, there's almost four dollars in money that exists in bank accounts, investments, debt, and so forth.

Huh?

Think about the scene in *It's a Wonderful Life* where there's a run on the bank. All of those people thought they had a certain amount of money in their bank accounts—let's say a nickel, because it was the 1930s. If anyone had asked them, "How much money do you have in savings?" they would have said, "I'm proud to report that I have one shiny nickel saved at the bank." But the bank probably lent that same nickel to a borrower. Both the depositor and the borrower would have said they had a nickel, even though they were actually talking about the same nickel. And that's how five cents is turned into ten cents, through the magic of banking. It's a system that works great, as long as all the people involved don't ask for their money in cash at the same time.

The Federal Reserve System

I've never seen *It's a Wonderful Life*.

It's one of the best Christmas movies about the financial services sector. Now, remember when I said that for every U.S. dollar in cash, there are around four dollars in circulation? The Fed can help control that ratio by doing things like raising or lowering interest rates. A lower interest rate will create more money from the existing amount of cash, while a higher interest rate will shrink the money supply.

That sounds like witchcraft. Is the Fed a coven of witches?

Probably not. But it's definitely true that the complex and powerful ability to create money out of thin air has raised a lot of suspicion and conspiracy theorizing over the years. Whether or not to have a national bank was one of the most controversial policy debates during the 19th century. Alexander Hamilton helped create one—

Yes, yes, I know. Every fan of musical theater knows that.

And then it was allowed to expire 20 years later.

Wait, what? Well, that's a bummer.

Then another one was created in 1816, but Andrew Jackson killed it in 1836, partly because he didn't have a very good sense of what it is banks do, and partly because he just liked killing things. The current Fed wasn't created until 1916.

I'm starting to sense that this book has a pronounced anti-Jackson bias. Why did he dislike the idea of a central bank?

A lot of the opposition in the U.S. to a central bank, then and now, has less to do with monetary policy per se, and more to do with a general suspicion of "money" that doesn't exist in the physical world and thus feels ephemeral, as well as a general hostility toward concentrated economic power. But we think if people knew more about how central banks work, they wouldn't feel quite so hostile toward the idea.

I am actually feeling a lot *more* hostility now that I've been tricked into hearing about central banks when all I wanted to do was order some Hello Kitty checks.

Oh. Sorry.

WARREN G. HARDING

1921–1923 | Republican

You probably don't know much about **Warren G. Harding, except that he looks like sex on wheels.** Or maybe feet. It's hard to tell from this photo whether he has feet or wheels.

But if you'd like to get to know him better, there's an easy way to do it: Go to the Library of Congress and read the thousands of pages of steamy love letters that he wrote to his mistress. Go ahead—we'll just admire Harding's eyebrows while you're gone.

All done? Great. Now you know Warren G. Harding extremely well. Also, your cheeks are a little flushed.

Considering what an erotic and sensual man Harding is, it shouldn't surprise you to learn that he was a very popular president. In fact, he won the popular vote by the largest margin in American history! Which, unfortunately, does not reflect well on our ability to judge the competency of presidential candidates. Harding was not a very good president, and many consider him to be one of the worst presidents of all time. Which isn't really fair, since "all time" isn't over yet. Let's just say he's one of the worst presidents *so far.*

Favorite Pickup Line

"I'd like to return to normalcy all over you."

SCANDAL!

You'd think that after meeting some guy on vacation in Hawaii, you could trust him enough to make him director of the Veterans' Bureau, right? Well, no. Harding learned this lesson the hard way, when his director of the Veterans' Bureau was caught taking drugs and alcohol that were meant for veterans' hospitals and selling them to drug dealers and bootleggers. Some of whom, in his defense, might have been veterans.

Why You'll *Love* Him

He knows how to have a good time. The way to have a good time is to play poker, drink, and chew tobacco. There—now you know how to have a good time, too! And that's why we've included a cuspidor on this page, just for you.

He'll send you love letters. The letters are NSFW, so definitely don't bring them to work with you and read them aloud at your weekly staff meeting.

He'll write you poetry. Unfortunately, he's under the mistaken impression that "paradise" rhymes with "thighs."

He can't say "no." Harding once told a group of reporters, "It is a good thing I am not a woman. I would always be pregnant. I cannot say no." And that is how you flirt with a group of reporters.

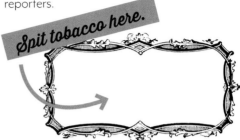

Spit tobacco here.

DIY PROJECT: LEARN CODE

Harding came up with a bunch of code words to use in his love letters to Carrie Phillips, so if the letters were intercepted, people would just think, "Wow, these are really weird love letters." To prepare for the possibility that Harding will send *you* love letters, you should go ahead and learn his secret code now. Once you've committed it to memory, tear out this page and eat it. (You'll also be eating a bunch of photos of Warren G. Harding, as an added bonus.)

REPAIR This is the word Harding uses to indicate what date he'll be arriving in New York, in case you want to meet him in New York for a tryst, or rob his house while he's out of town.

GRATEFUL = All my love to the last precious drop. For example, Harding might write, "I want to fill you up with grateful."

GATE = I want paradise in your embrace. Harding missed a great opportunity here to rhyme "paradise" with "thighs."

DELIVER = I am asking for your embrace. Which could be confusing if he ever actually wants you to deliver something.

DOLPHIN = Things have gone wrong here. And they have indeed, if Warren G. Harding is writing to you about dolphins.

DESIRE = I send you eight kisses. So if he sends you a telegram that says, "Desire! Desire! Desire! Desire!" that means he's sending you 32 kisses. No one at the telegraph office will suspect that the two of you are having an affair.

DEARER = I'd like to bring you the scepter tonight and make you my queen. He doesn't explain what "scepter" is code for, so you'll just have to guess!

MRS. POUTERSON This is his code name for Carrie Phillips. Or, depending on whom you ask, his code name for her vagina. I bet you didn't even realize that vaginas needed code names!

JERRY This is his penis.

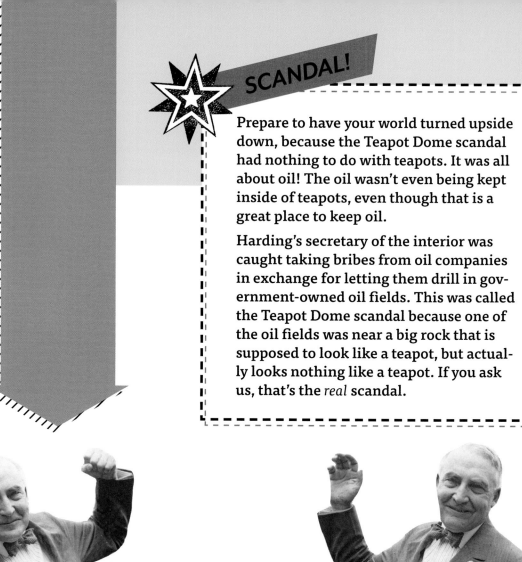

SCANDAL!

Prepare to have your world turned upside down, because the Teapot Dome scandal had nothing to do with teapots. It was all about oil! The oil wasn't even being kept inside of teapots, even though that is a great place to keep oil.

Harding's secretary of the interior was caught taking bribes from oil companies in exchange for letting them drill in government-owned oil fields. This was called the Teapot Dome scandal because one of the oil fields was near a big rock that is supposed to look like a teapot, but actually looks nothing like a teapot. If you ask us, that's the *real* scandal.

Here's a Tip

If you'd like to have an affair with Warren G. Harding, there are a few dos and dont's you should keep in mind to help you have the best affair possible.

DO: Pursue him. Harding was pursued fairly aggressively by his wife, Florence, his mistress Carrie Phillips, and his other mistress Nan Britton. And look at how it worked out for them! Or just take our word for it that it worked out fine.

DON'T: Talk about Germany all the time. If the FBI suspects you're a German spy, like they did Carrie Phillips, then it might not be such a good idea to go on and on about how much you love Germany. (Because it's boring.)

DO: Blackmail him. When Carrie Phillips threatened to reveal her affair with Harding, the Republican Party paid her off and sent her on all-expenses-paid trip to Japan! It's just like winning *The Price Is Right*, but without the hard part where you have to guess how much dining room furniture costs.

DON'T: Destroy evidence. The key to a good blackmail is to have evidence. Carrie Phillips saved over a thousand love letters from Harding, some written on Senate stationery. And Harding didn't want to get in trouble for stealing office supplies! In contrast, nobody believed Nan Britton about *her* affair with Harding, because she destroyed all of his letters, and the only evidence she had was a baby with really good eyebrows.

SCANDAL!

A few Harding appointees seized a German-owned company and transferred it to a new owner in exchange for bribe money. It was easier to get away with this kind of stuff in the aftermath of WWI, which you already know if you've ever tried seizing Volkswagen.

Vital Stats

Looks: 7

This is what happens when you let women vote!

Physique: 4

According to a 1946 article in *Life* magazine, Harding had a "'high stomach'—his paunch sat way up, crowding his breastbone." And before you say, "I'd rather a high, tight paunch than a low, sagging one," no you wouldn't.

Charisma: 2

If you read any of Harding's speeches, you might come away with the sense that he does not know what order words are supposed to go in. H. L. Mencken compared Harding's inaugural address to "a string of wet sponges," although in Harding's defense, how you feel about a string of wet sponges depends a lot on context.

Modesty: 8

Harding was always telling people that the job of president was totally beyond his abilities. At the time, people thought he was just really modest. Now we are not so sure.

CALVIN COOLIDGE

Maybe you're not interested in a president who annoys you by talking all the time, or even by talking some of the time. Enter Calvin Coolidge.

There is something undeniably attractive about a man who doesn't talk. If you don't believe us, just try talking to any man for any length of time without becoming overwhelmed with revulsion. It's hard, right? And that is just one of Coolidge's many attractive qualities; he is also brooding, controlling, and spends much of the day asleep. Like a cat! And people like cats, right? Or at least they tolerate them.

But there's more to Calvin Coolidge than silence and controlling behavior. He also enjoys practical jokes! As president, his favorite joke was to call for his staff and then hide somewhere, like under his desk or behind the curtains. His aides would search frantically for him, all while quietly reconsidering the choices they had made in life. Good one, Calvin Coolidge!

How to Win His Heart

💜 **Don't drive, talk politics, or wear pants.** Coolidge forbade his wife from doing all of these things. So make sure not to tell him what you think about politics while wearing a pantsuit and running him over with your car. He will definitely not be impressed!

💜 **Give him daily Vaseline scalp massages.** Coolidge liked to start the day by having breakfast in bed while someone massaged his scalp with Vaseline. If you play your cards right, that "someone" could be you!

Here's a Tip

Coolidge first met his wife, Grace, when she spotted him through a window, shaving while wearing only his underwear and a hat. So if you're single, take a page from Grace Coolidge's book and try spying on half-naked men through windows. When you get caught, just explain to the arresting officer that you're trying to find a husband. You'll both have a good laugh, and then you'll be able to resume your courtship.

Grace Coolidge was the subject of gossip after she and her handsome Secret Service agent took a "hike" in the "Black Hills of South Dakota" and got "lost" for "several hours."

The press insinuated that the First Lady was having an affair, as did we, with our excessive use of quotation marks. But the boring truth is that nothing was going on between Grace Coolidge and her Secret Service agent. And even though using an excessive amount of quotation marks is fun, it is wrong and we promise to never do it again. Or at least not until we get to Bill Clinton.

SEE HOW QUIET HE IS? IT'S NOT JUST BECAUSE THIS IS A BOOK. HE'S ALWAYS LIKE THAT!

Why You'll *Love* Him

He sleeps for 14 hours a day.
Nothing is sexier than a man who is extremely, extremely well rested.

He refers to every meal as "supper."
Ha! That will never get old.

He has a pygmy hippopotamus.
This could mean any number of things!

Vital Stats

Looks: 6
You just want to wipe that stern expression off his face with a kiss or, alternatively, a damp washcloth.

Physique: 6
Coolidge stays fit by riding a mechanical horse, often while wearing a cowboy hat, and possibly while shirtless.*

Charisma: 2
He gets one point for his weird practical jokes and one point for pity. (Our pity, for him. There is no evidence that he himself felt pity for anyone.)

Pets: 10
Coolidge had so many bizarre pets that you can't help but wonder if he misunderstood the nature of the president's duties.

*Although there is no evidence that Coolidge rode his mechanical horse while shirtless, this might be because presidential historians are selfishly keeping all of the shirtless Calvin Coolidge photos for themselves.

WHICH PRESIDENT HAS A *Secret Crush* ON YOU?

America has had a lot of presidents—more than we can even count! Or let's just say more than we care to count. With so many presidents, at least one of them is probably harboring a secret crush on you. But how to find out which one? Just complete the quiz below using a number 2 pencil and then insert this page into a Scantron machine. Probably nothing will happen, but you never know!

1. OMG. You opened your mailbox this morning and found a note . . . from a secret admirer! What does it say?

a. "I am watching you all the time. Even right now, while you read this note. (Hi!)"

b. "I'd like to have you over to my place for an 'Easter Egg Roll,' if you know what I mean. (I mean literally we would roll eggs around on the White House lawn.)"

c. "IT IS I, GEORGE WASHINGTON. I CANNOT TELL A LIE, EVEN A LIE BY OMISSION, AND THEREFORE I MUST IDENTIFY MYSELF AND CONFESS THAT I HAVE FEELINGS FOR YOU THAT ARE ROMANTIC IN NATURE."

d. "I luv you so much that I would comit bigamy for you. Go ahead—ask me to comit bigamy and see what hapens. Becuz I will tell you what is going to hapen: Bigamy!"

e. You did not receive a note that meets this description.

2. You're having drinks with a friend when the waiter stops by your table. "A former president asked me to deliver this drink to you," he says with a wink. "Before you ask, I don't know which former president because he was wearing a ski mask." How romantic! What drink did he send you?

a. A bottle of gin.

b. A glass of lemonade.

c. A glass of Mount Vernon whiskey, served on a cocktail napkin that says "THIS DRINK IS FROM ME (GEORGE WASHINGTON). I DISTILLED IT MYSELF! NO, I'M SORRY: THAT WAS A LIE. MY SLAVES DISTILLED IT FOR ME."

d. A glass of regular whiskey. But the stirrer is a hickory tree branch and there are leaves and clumps of dirt floating in it. So . . . that's probably a clue.

e. Nothing like this has ever happened to you.

3. You went to the movies with Alexander Hamilton last weekend, and a certain former president is totally jealous and acting crazy! What does he do?

a. He wiretaps Hamilton's phone.

b. He continues quietly being the better man.

c. He challenges Hamilton to a dance-off.

d. He shoots Hamilton in a duel. (It was bound to happen eventually!)

e. Again, nothing even remotely like this happened.

4. OMG again. Two Secret Service agents just dropped off a package at your house. You open it to find:

a. Your diary. You were wondering where that went!

b. A "Someone in Ohio Loves You" bumper sticker. So . . . that only narrows it down to eight presidents.

c. It appears to be his teeth.

d. Alexander Hamilton's blood-soaked waistcoat.

e. You did not receive a package from the Secret Service, unless they were really well-disguised as UPS guys.

5. You just got a text message from a number you don't recognize. It says:

a. "What's going on? What is this thing I am holding?"

b. "I also do not understand what is going on! Where do I insert the paper in this miniature typewriter? I am jamming a piece of paper against it but nothing is happening!"

c. "WHAT DEPRAVED WIZARD INVENTED THIS ENCHANTED PORCELAIN THAT ALLOWS ME TO MAKE WORDS APPEAR OUT OF NOTHING? I AM HURLING YOU INTO THE BRINY WATERS OF THE POTOMAC FROM WHENCE YOU CAME, ENCHANTED PORCELAIN! TELL YOUR MASTER I'LL SEE HIM IN HELL."

d. "Idzujxfo. Ijrfjjtztiok tgzmksr" (NOTE: *This is the letter sequence that is formed when a cell phone is being smashed with a cane.*)

e. "AT&T Free Msg: Your bill is past due. To make a payment now, reply 1 and press send. To schedule a payment for a later date, reply 2 and press send."

ANSWER KEY

Mostly A's: Richard Nixon
Richard Nixon is seriously crushing on you! This must have been what he was trying to get at in his Checkers speech.

Mostly B's: Rutherford B. Hayes
If you love beards and unpretentious sobriety, then you are going to love Rutherford B. Hayes! If you only love one of those things, then you will still love Rutherford B. Hayes, just not as much.

Mostly C's: George Washington
You've hit the Founding Fathers jackpot! George Washington has it all: He's tall, he's rich, and he's aloof. He's the Mr. Darcy of colonial America.

Mostly D's: Andrew Jackson
This is one "union" you're not going to want to "secede" from, or you'll be left with a "trail of tears"! (Seriously though, this guy is scary.)

Mostly E's: Calvin Coolidge
If you haven't been receiving gifts and love notes from a former president, don't feel bad. It's only because Calvin Coolidge is really shy!

151

HERBERT HOOVER

1929–1933 | Republican

When the stock market crashed in 1929, wouldn't it have been nice to have a president who was great at organizing large-scale relief efforts? Who had been elected precisely for that reason? Whose nickname was literally "Master of Emergencies"? Well, the funny thing is, we *did*. (Even though it did not seem very funny at the time.)

Herbert Hoover is a brilliant engineer and businessman who used his money, connections, and skill to organize massive aid efforts, first in war-torn Europe, then in flood-torn America. In the early 1920s, he probably saved millions of Russians from starving during the famine accompanying the Russian civil war. And to be clear, he did these kinds of things as a private citizen. In his free time, with his own money, as a hobby. (As opposed to your "hobby" of trying to stay caught up on flossing.)

So, how *did* having a disaster management expert as president work out when the Great Depression hit? Well, there's a clue in the fact that it's called "the Great Depression" instead of "that one time in the 1920s when the New York Stock Exchange had a big sell-off but then everything got back to normal."

DOES HE KEEP HIS *promises?*

✓ **"A chicken in every pot."**
What Hoover *didn't* tell people was that there were going to be a lot fewer pots.

✓ **Continued prosperity.**
Hoover absolutely delivered on this promise. But like some kind of trickster genie who loves verbal ambiguity, he never told the American people how *long* prosperity would continue. (It continued for nine months.)

✓ **Prohibition.**
Hoover promised that if elected, he would keep Prohibition in place. This helped him get elected because . . . actually, we don't know why that would help him get elected. Sometimes we don't understand this country at all.

Why You'll *Love* Him

He's rich. Hoover didn't accept a salary as president. Although it's possible he just wanted to be in a position to say, "Well, you get what you pay for," in case his presidency didn't work out. (It didn't.)

Hoover claimed to be the first student at Stanford, since he was the first student to spend the night in the dorms. If spending the night in a dorm room makes someone a student, then you might have been a student at a lot of different colleges without even realizing it!

He doesn't feel constrained by traditional ideas about romance, In fact, he proposed to his wife by telegram. For you kids reading this, "telegrams" are an ancient technology that involved sending messages where you ended each sentence with "stop." They're no longer used, and the modern equivalent of proposing by telegram would be proposing to someone via text. So now that's on the table.

WHEN HE WAS YOUNG

A rare photo of Herbert Hoover slowly vanishing because he went back in time and accidentally disrupted the first time his parents met.

FUN FACTS THAT COULD BE DOUBLE ENTENDRES

- HOOVER WAS AN ACCOMPLISHED "GOLD MINER," if you know what we mean. And as a mining engineer, he used "the froth flotation process" to solve "THE SULPHIDE PROBLEM." If you try this at home, you're going to want to change the sheets afterward.

- You're using a dental dam in the bedroom to keep things safe, right? No? Well, maybe it will feel a little more fun if you refer to it as your "HOOVER DAM." Which you use to "light up the Las Vegas strip." No? OK, well that's all we've got.

- If you're romantically involved with someone who is old enough to say "Hoovering" instead of "vacuuming," you can probably make some kind of dirty joke to them about Hoovering. "SHALL I HOOVER UNDER THE CUSHIONS?" "YOU LOOK A LITTLE DUSTY, I'D LIKE TO HOOVER YOU OFF." Or something like that. We'll let you figure out the details. (Note: Hoover vacuums had nothing to do with President Hoover except that the president of the Hoover Company was also named Herbert Hoover. Apparently Herbert Hoover used to be a pretty popular name! Can you guess why it no longer is?)

FISHING
FOR FUN—
And
To Wash Your Soul

HERBERT HOOVER
Edited by William Nichols

RANDOM HOUSE
New York

How to Win His Heart

We're just going to tell you right at the outset that you are not cool enough to win Herbert Hoover's heart. Hoover's wife, Lou, is a fearless, globe-trotting adventurer. It was basically like if Indiana Jones became the First Lady. (Which, incidentally, was the alternate ending on the 1984 BetaMax director's cut edition of *Raiders of the Lost Ark*.) Here are just a few of the things that make her so awesome and that make you look so boring by comparison.

Polyglotism. Lou Hoover spoke eight languages, including Mandarin. And that's not even counting the sign language she invented so she wouldn't have to address her servants directly.

Death-defiance. When Lou and Herbert were besieged in China during the Boxer Rebellion (yes), she insisted on delivering tea to the front lines (yes) on her bicycle (yes) and had one of the tires shot out (yes).

She went to Stanford. We're throwing this one in there to underscore that you're probably not even good enough to get into Stanford, let alone good enough to learn eight languages or bike-courier tea through a war zone. Sorry, no Herbert Hoover for you! You won't be "moving to Hooverville," so to speak.

"

It was when I said, 'We in America today are nearer to the final triumph over poverty than ever before in the history of any land,' and then the stock market crashed and the Great Depression began. But what people didn't realize is that I meant the final triumph will happen like a thousand years from now, and so every day, we're nearer to it. Even in the time it took you to read this, we got a little closer. It's too bad you won't be around to see it!

"

"

Oh wait! I just remembered that in 1938, I said 'I do not believe a widespread war is at all possible in the near future,' and then WWII began the next year. Ha, ha! I guess I'm not very good at predicting things!

"

Sort-of Fun Fact

When he was head of the U.S. Food Administration during World War I, Hoover invented "Meatless Mondays" as a way to make sure troops had enough meat. He also invented "Wheatless Wednesdays" to make sure they had enough bread. And he promoted the slogan "When in doubt, eat potatoes," because he apparently *didn't* want the troops to have enough potatoes. Those poor troops!

Vital Stats

Looks: 5

Hoover looks exactly like Orson Welles. And, as everyone knows, Orson Welles is a solid 5 out of 10.

Physique: 4

On the one hand, President Hoover played sports with his staff every morning. On the other hand, the sport was "Hooverball." (If you're wondering what Hooverball is, you'll find out when you get hit in the face by a six-pound medicine ball tossed over a volleyball net by a sweaty White House staffer.)

Charisma: 3

Hoover was quoted as saying, "If a man has not made a million dollars by the time he is forty, he is not worth much." This works not only as a condescending sneer from the president who presided over the 1929 stock market crash, but also as a birthday greeting for your friends, parents, children, etc.

Getting assassinated: 0

Argentine anarchists tried to assassinate Hoover while he was crossing the Andes from Chile. But they were foiled when his wife, Lou, rappelled through the train window and killed them all with throwing knives. Just kidding! They were foiled by the police. (Maybe with throwing knives—we don't know a lot about police procedure in early 20th-century Chile.)

1933–1945 | Democrat

Are you ready to learn all about FDR? If so, you should go read one of the many fascinating biographies of him. FDR's presidential terms were among the most action-packed in American history, and he had *four* of them. That's a lot of history! We're not going to have room here to cover things like his pre-presidential political career, or the New Deal. That's because we need room to address whether or not he used the navy to ferry his dog around, and whether or not he was good in bed.

It's going to be disappointing when FDR invites you to join him for a **FIRESIDE CHAT,** and it turns out to be about **ECONOMIC RECOVERY.** And also he's just talking to you over the radio. And also it's the **GREAT DEPRESSION,** so you weren't able to afford any wood for a fire. And also you live in a box.

Pop QUIZ

Some people claim that FDR knew about the Japanese surprise attack on Pearl Harbor in advance but let it happen anyway because he wanted an excuse to drag America into war. That sounds pretty crazy . . . but could it be true?

Answer: No.

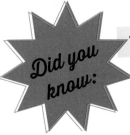

"FDR" ARE JUST HIS INITIALS?

People assume that FDR is like KFC —an acronym that doesn't actually stand for anything other than subrational emotional engagement with a brand. But FDR *does* stand for something! Let's dig deeper.

THE "F" STANDS FOR FRANKLIN.
This would be a good title for an FDR biography. If you're consulting this book while doing research for your own FDR biography, feel free to use *The "F" Stands for Franklin* as your title.

THE "D" STANDS FOR DELANO,
after his grandfather Warren Delano, Jr., a wealthy opium trader. Even if your grandfather wasn't an opium trader, this is a great explanation to give for your middle name. "Oh, the M? It stands for Marie. I'm named after my grandfather Marie, the opium trader."

THE "R" STANDS FOR ROOSEVELT.
Roosevelt means "field of roses" in Dutch (a language) and is pronounced "rose-e-velt." Unless you're FDR, and you decide to pronounce it like "*ruse*-e-velt." Arbitrarily changing the pronunciation of your own name is not a power the Founders intended for the president. But if we limited presidents to only what the Founders intended, they wouldn't have much to do.

WHEN HE WAS YOUNG

Go ahead. Admit it. You want this man to "electrify your Tennessee Valley."

SCANDAL!

FDR was deeply devoted to his Scottish Terrier, Fala. And while he was running for a fourth term in 1944, Republicans spread the false rumor that he had sent a navy battleship, at great cost, to pick up Fala in Alaska.

FDR *should* have said, "I pulled us out of the Great Depression, and I'm about to win WWII. I could use a battleship to raze Anchorage to the ground and still get reelected, so good luck with this dog angle, nerds."

But at the time, he was taking political advice from noted wimp and Herbert Hoover lookalike Orson Welles, who advised him to respond with humor. So FDR said, "I don't resent attacks, and my family doesn't resent attacks, but Fala does resent them!" This line had his audience rolling in the aisles, because amid the blood and chaos of the 1940s, it didn't take much.

Did you know:

Sort-of Fun Facts

FDR met Grover Cleveland as a five-year-old, and Cleveland told him, "I have one wish for you, little man: that you will never be President of the United States." Cleveland said that to *all* the kids he met, because he hoped to crack the secret of immortality and rule from the White House forever.

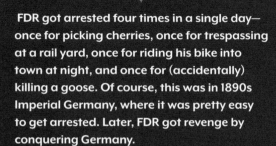

FDR got arrested four times in a single day—once for picking cherries, once for trespassing at a rail yard, once for riding his bike into town at night, and once for (accidentally) killing a goose. Of course, this was in 1890s Imperial Germany, where it was pretty easy to get arrested. Later, FDR got revenge by conquering Germany.

FDR got Prohibition repealed in his first year as president. The Great Depression had started four years earlier, and it seemed cruel to force Americans to endure any more of it sober.

After the U.S. entered WWII, the government rounded up tens of thousands of people of Japanese descent and put them in internment camps, but very few people of German or Italian descent, even though there were a lot more of them in America. Why this discrepancy? Who knows! (Well, actually, we think we know. This fact isn't all that fun after all!)

Here's a Tip

If you learn one thing from FDR, it should be "Never go to Canada." Although he claimed to love America, at age 39 FDR went on vacation to Canada. While there he developed polio and became paralyzed from the waist down. Now, we haven't checked to see what percentage of American visitors to Canada develop polio . . . but why risk it?

Roosevelt spent the rest of his life in a wheelchair, and he went to great pains to hide this fact from the public, probably because he didn't want them to find out he had vacationed in Canada. And when we say "great pains," we mean it literally. With both legs in heavy steel braces to keep them locked straight, he trained himself to walk for short distances by swiveling his hips and torso. This allowed him to appear onstage at the 1928 and 1932 Democratic conventions, "walking," to undermine the (accurate) rumor that he was paralyzed.

FDR  or TRUMP?

FDR and Donald Trump are a lot alike. They're both rich heirs, they're both from New York, and they both became president of the United States. How will you ever tell them apart? Here are a few simple questions you can ask to figure out if you're talking to FDR or Trump.

"What do you think about vaccines?"

Even though he's irrepressibly positive, FDR will express some regret that the polio vaccine didn't exist in 1921 to prevent him from becoming paralyzed.

Trump will tell you not to trust doctors who say that vaccination is safe.

"What is 'America First'?"

FDR will note that there was an influential isolationist movement in 1940 called the "America First Committee," fronted by famous aviator Charles Lindbergh. It wanted to keep the U.S. from providing military aid to England in its war with Hitler, and it explicitly argued that American Jews controlled the media and government and were trying to draw the U.S. into WWII for "their own interests," as opposed to "ours."

Trump will recognize "America First" as a slogan he chose for his presidential campaign.

"Do you think you should be allowed to serve more than two terms as president and radically expand executive powers?"

OK, they might agree on this one.

> During WWII, my good friend Winston Churchill warned me that after the war, Josef Stalin would seek to have the USSR dominate Eastern Europe. I told him, 'I just have a hunch that Stalin is not that kind of a man.' Hah! I can only hope future U.S. presidents learn from my mistake, and don't simply rely on their hunches when it comes to Kremlin strongmen.

Just another day at the Oval Office!

159

Marriage Advice
FROM FRANKLIN AND ELEANOR ROOSEVELT

FDR and Eleanor had more of a frosty political partnership than a loving marriage. But an essentially loveless marriage for *them* means better chances with FDR for you, because you can learn from Eleanor's mistakes.

DON'T SLEEP WITH FDR. Eleanor described sex with FDR as "an ordeal to be borne."* You already have enough ordeals in your life, so don't add this one. (If despite our advice you do have sex with FDR, then don't do what Eleanor did and tell your daughter that sex with her father is an ordeal to be borne.)

DON'T MOVE INTO A townhouse connected by sliding doors to your mother-in-law's townhouse. Having constant visits from your beautiful, wealthy, and controlling mother-in-law Sara—who tried to break up your engagement to her son by taking him on a long Caribbean cruise—sounds like a good living arrangement, because you'll get free babysitting. But keep in mind that one of Sara's babysitting techniques is to tell your children, "I am more your mother than your mother is."

DON'T INTRODUCE FDR to your social secretary. FDR had an affair with Eleanor's social secretary Lucy Mercer, and Eleanor's discovery of their love letters permanently fractured their marriage. If it's too late and you've already introduced FDR to your social secretary, try telling her that having sex with FDR is an ordeal to be borne.

> *In defense of FDR's skills in bed if not his perceptiveness, Eleanor might have been at least a *little* bit gay.

DOES HE KEEP HIS *promises?*

In short, no.

[X] Running for election in 1932, FDR promised **"an immediate and drastic reduction of governmental expenditures."** If you're thinking, "Wait a minute, I *don't* think FDR drastically reduced federal spending," then congratulations! You're ready to pass 11th-grade U.S. History.

[X] FDR also promised **"the removal of government from all fields of private enterprise except where necessary to develop public works and natural resources in the common interest."** Little did Americans know that when he said this, it happened to be Opposite Day.

[X] Running for reelection in 1940, FDR told U.S. soldiers, **"You boys are not going to be sent into any foreign war."** Though technically, maybe it wasn't a foreign war anymore after America got involved.

Here is a **rare photo** of FDR and Herbert Hoover taking a **romantic** carriage ride around Central Park at Christmastime. Just kidding! It's actually them at FDR's inauguration in Washington. But it was still pretty romantic.

WE ASKED . . .
ARE YOU RELATED TO HUMAN DYNAMO THEODORE ROOSEVELT?

We couldn't help but notice that you have stolen the name of our most vigorous and muscular president, Theodore Roosevelt.

Actually, it's my name, too. Theodore is my fifth cousin. We're both members of the extensive and storied Roosevelt family, whose history in New York dates to Dutch settlers in the mid-1600s.

Fifth cousins, huh? Have you ever met him?

Oh, yes. He gave my wife Eleanor away at our wedding.

Is that some kind of Dutch tradition? Women are given away by their groom's fifth cousin?

No. He was giving Eleanor away because he is her uncle. *She* is my fifth cousin, too. Actually, her maiden name was "Roosevelt."

We guess that saves her the trouble of telling you she's not going to change her name. So, you married your cousin. Was this wedding in a clapboard shack back in the hills somewhere?

Marrying your cousin is a lot like collecting jars of your own urine—you're much more likely to do it if you're either very poor or very rich. For instance, my parents were very rich and *they* were sixth cousins. So if you ever find yourself marrying your cousin, you'll know you've really made it big-time, or fallen very low. And if you can't tell which, just look around. If you're on a massive, sprawling estate, you're probably rich! Or, a rich person is about to hunt you for sport.

Vital Stats

Looks: 8

If you can look handsome in pince-nez glasses, you're pretty handsome. Also, you might be a member of the Roosevelt family, because Franklin and Teddy are pretty much the only two men who have ever pulled it off.

Physique: 8

Here is FDR's actual itinerary from the last day he had full use of his legs: 1) Go swimming and sailing in the ocean in Canada (which is presumably freezing); 2) help locals fight a forest fire; 3) jog a mile home. Not walk. Jog.

Charisma: 10

FDR is outgoing, warm, and personable. He loves talking to people and hearing about their problems, and he is magnetic both one-on-one and over the airwaves. His charisma was enough to win an unprecedented four terms as president, and many historians consider him to be the most charismatic president in history. But amazingly, he was not popular in high school, because he didn't play sports. That's high school for you.

Keeping secrets: 7

FDR didn't manage to keep his affair with Lucy Mercer a secret from Eleanor, but he did manage to run for president four times without most Americans finding out he was in a wheelchair. (He knew the voters would admire a man who had succeeded despite many obstacles, and he didn't want to have an unfair advantage in the election!)

FDR
Childhood Photo Album

We hate the way modern PC culture feminizes boys, watering down their natural aggression and competitiveness. In other news, here is a childhood photo of the man who crushed the Nazis and ushered in 50 years of American global dominance.

A young FDR sets out into the neighborhood on "Operation Make Friends."

47-96-14

FDR was a well-behaved boy, so no one suspected him of the Hyde Park Riding Crop Murders, even though he constantly carried around a silver riding crop, and whispered to it in French.

Can you believe this 18-year-old brute was bound for Harvard? You probably guessed he was a longshoreman, or a lumberjack, or the member of a post-apocalyptic biker gang.

HARRY S. TRUMAN

1945–1953 | Democrat

Farmer, haberdasher, railway timekeeper, mailroom clerk, auto club membership salesman . . . it wasn't until he became president at age 60 that Harry S. Truman finally found something he was half decent at.

And he was half decent at it! Winning WWII, helping establish the UN and NATO, desegregating the military—these are all things that Harry S. Truman did.

So if you've been eyeing the guy in the mailroom at work, but you're worried that his shoddy mailrooming might be a sign that he's not destined for great things, take heart! Any day now, he might get fired from the mailroom and start selling AAA memberships. And if nothing else, that means you can probably sweet-talk him into a discounted membership.

Well, maybe. It's worth a try!

Sort-of Fun Facts

Truman graduated from Independence High School, which was later renamed . . . William Chrisman High School. Yeah. They renamed it after the guy whose daughter donated land for it, instead of the graduate who went on to become president.

Truman is legally blind in one eye. So when he wanted to join the army as an artillery officer, he cheated on the vision test by memorizing the line of letters. Because it's not like someone operating a giant cannon needs to see *that* well.

Truman is known as "the Senator from Pendergast." What does that mean? Well, imagine Jimmy Stewart's character in *Mr. Smith Goes to Washington*, except instead of the freshman senator representing integrity and honor, he's representing Kansas City's corrupt and powerful Pendergast political machine.

Why You'll *Love* Him

He will defend you from music critics. The *Washington Post* never gets tired of making trouble for our hardworking presidents, and in 1950 they published a mediocre review of Truman's daughter's singing. Truman responded by sending a letter to the music critic threatening that if they ever met, "You'll need a new nose, a lot of beefsteak for black eyes, and perhaps a supporter below!" Some people accused Truman of unpresidential behavior, because they had forgotten what Andrew Jackson was like.

> Truman loved the army so much that he stayed in it for decades, until FDR finally forced him to resign his commission, on the grounds that, **"COME ON DUDE, YOU'RE A U.S. SENATOR NOW."**

Let's Talk About Clothes

Would you like to look as dapper as a young Harry S. Truman on his wedding day? It's easy!

Shave everything except for a long, dark forelock. (And we do mean everything!)

Stuff all that hair in the front pocket of your jacket, because you might need it later.

Boom, you're done. Wow, for a second there we thought you were Harry S. Truman!

Pop **QUIZ**

Can you guess what the "S" in Harry S. Truman stands for?

a. **"Sexy,"** because he is sooooo sexy.

b. **"Stevedore,"** from his days working as a rough-and-tumble longshoreman for Missouri River barges.

c. **Nothing,** because it was a bizarre ploy to trick both of his grandfathers into thinking he'd been named after them.

d. **"Danger."**

Answer: (c) His grandfathers were named "Andrew Shipp" and "Solomon," so Truman's parents made his middle name "S." But they could also have made it "Grandfather."

Harry S. Truman will always be true to you, even if Hollywood starlet Lauren Bacall is draped over his piano trying to seduce him while he plays scales, over and over again, deep into the night.

- Like Germany during WWII, you could "SURRENDER TO TRUMAN ON HIS BIRTHDAY."

- If you have access to the right kind of equipment, maybe Truman can satiate your hunger with a "BERLIN AIRLIFT."

- After you've gone on a couple of dates with Truman, you'll probably be ready to let him reprise his Korean War strategy of "CROSSING THE 38TH PARALLEL."

How to Win His Heart

💜 **When he asks you to marry him, turn him down.** This is what Bess Wallace did, and Truman kept asking and asking until she said yes.* Saying no to Truman will be the hardest thing you ever do, but it will be totally worth it. Unless it plays out differently this time, in which case, sorry—you just missed your one chance at true love, with Harry S. Truman.

*Interestingly, *a lot* of presidents had to propose more than once before convincing their girlfriends to marry them. What is it about future presidents that women find so repulsive? It's probably that they haven't been elected president yet.

WHEN HE WAS YOUNG

Truman's workout buddies in the army told him to stop focusing so much on his quads but he did not listen.

DOES HE KEEP HIS *promises?*

"

After FDR died and I became president, I compared my situation to having a load of hay fall on you. Specifically, I told a group of reporters, 'I don't know if you fellas ever had a load of hay fall on you, but . . .'

Afterward, it occurred to me that coming from the first president from Missouri, this analogy might have reflected poorly on my state. Specifically, those reporters might have concluded that a Missouri boy can't handle having a big load of hay fall on him. But please, let me assure you, the *exact opposite* is true.

"

☒ **Universal healthcare.** This campaign promise did not quite work out, as you might have already noticed if you don't have any health care. But in recognition of his efforts, Harry and Bess Truman got the first two Medicare cards ever issued. So unfortunately, that story your grandfather told you about getting the first Medicare card was a lie. Unless your grandfather is Harry S. Truman. In which case, thank you for reading this book, Clifton, Harrison, or Thomas!

Vital Stats

Looks: 7

Harry S. Truman looks like a turtle, but a relatively handsome one. Just relatively, though. There are a lot of very handsome turtles out there.

Physique: 8

While president, Truman got up at 5 a.m. almost every day and walked 1–2 miles, then swam laps in the White House pool. And he usually tried to squeeze in a "nap" with Bess in the afternoon.

Charisma: 4

It took Truman eight years to beat the Nazis, establish NATO, and convert the U.S. economy to a peacetime footing. And that's the same amount of time it took him to convince someone named "Bess" to marry him.

Doing shots at breakfast: 10

Truman did a shot of bourbon every morning, accompanied by a light breakfast. And if Truman could lead the free world fueled by nothing but a shot of hard liquor on an empty stomach at 6 a.m., then it is definitely OK for you to have a third mimosa at brunch. If the server looks at you funny, just tell him "I am President Harry S. Truman!"

1953–1961 | Republican

In troubled times, the safest pick for the White House is someone with the proven ability to invade Europe. That's why in 1948, voters went with Dwight D. Eisenhower, the commanding general of the Allied forces that landed at Normandy and defeated the Nazis in Western Europe. Eisenhower proceeded to heal the wounds of a nation recovering from cataclysmic war with the power of plainspoken speech and the best political slogan in human history: "I Like Ike."

While the 1950s are remembered and/or imagined by many Americans as a halcyon period of suburban tranquility and prosperity, Eisenhower largely focused on foreign affairs, leaving domestic policy to his "trusty" sidekick, Vice President Richard Nixon. Eisenhower positioned the United States to face off against the Soviet Union by strengthening NATO, expanding the country's nuclear arsenal, and helping countries like Guatemala and Iran get exciting new governments.

Eisenhower was known for having a sunny disposition, a friendly manner, and an optimistic outlook on America. Weirdly, back in the 1950s, that's what people wanted in a president.

Eisenhower is also known for being our baldest president. We guarantee that if you ask a hundred people on the street to state a fact about Eisenhower, the top answer will be "bald." After "no thank you" and "please stop following me."

"Did you LIKE watching America STRIKE the WARLIKE REICH? Would you not DISLIKE a new TURNPIKE, with no TAX HIKE? Vote for Dwight David Eisenhower!"

Alternate 1952 *Campaign Slogan*

Why You'll *Love* Him

He's not too into politics. Eisenhower had never voted until he ran for president. If this reminds you of Zachary Taylor, then you've been reading this book far too closely. But you've also learned a secret route to the White House: Join the army, and don't vote. If we've done the calculations right, this strategy will give you a 2/44 chance of becoming president.

He's a sound financial planner. Ike first proposed to Mamie with a miniature replica of his West Point class ring. For some crazy reason, this wasn't good enough, and he needed to then go buy a more traditional engagement ring. He didn't have enough money to buy a diamond ring, so he developed his own payment plan: "I'll just buy it on credit, then go win a bunch of money at poker." Later, we put this man in charge of saving Western civilization from fascism.

He might rename Camp David after you. Eisenhower renamed the presidential retreat previously known as "Shangri-La" after his grandson David. But you can probably get him to name it after you instead. The first step will be to drive a wedge between President Eisenhower and his grandson.

He doesn't let doctors tell him what to do. In high school, Ike developed a serious bacterial infection on his leg, and his doctor urged him to have it amputated. Ike refused, the leg healed, and he was fine. And we have to say—it feels like we've heard a million stories like this where the patient was fine, and none where the patient died. What if "You need to amputate or the infection might kill you" is a condition invented by the medical device industry to sell more bone saws?! (Ha ha but seriously, follow your doctor's advice.)

DOES HE KEEP HIS *promises?*

☑ **Be Clean.**
Running against Adlai Stevenson in 1952, Eisenhower promised that an Ike-ministration would be "clean as a hound's tooth." Eisenhower fulfilled this promise by picking Richard Nixon as his running mate, since Nixon was typically coated in saliva and bits of meat.

✗ **End the Korean War.**
Here's a fun fact: The Korean War never ended! There was a suspension of hostilities, but no treaty, and the two sides still occasionally shoot at and kill one another. As of June 25, 2018, the Korean War will be 78 years old. But age is just a number, and the Korean War feels young. HBD Korean War!

Pop QUIZ

While stationed in the Philippines, Eisenhower was known as "The Bridge Wizard of Manila." Can you guess why?

a. He was a very talented bridge player.
b. He built a lot of bridges.
c. He blew up a lot of bridges.
d. He was an actual wizard.
e. All of the above

Answer: The answer is (a), but we want so badly for it to be (e).

Highway TO HELL

By developing the Interstate Highway System, President Eisenhower connected the United States . . . in fear! Here are just a few of the terrors Eisenhower conjured into the world.

- Black ice
- Rest stop murders
- Large Marge
- Serial killers pretending to be cops
- Hitchhiker serial killers
- Hitchhikers who later turn out to be ghosts
- You're driving on the highway alone, late at night, and then in the rearview mirror you see a ghost in the backseat.
- You get tired late at night and stop to spend the night in a small town, and you meet a few people, but later you learn it was an abandoned town and they were all ghosts.
- You were killed in a highway crash, but you have blocked out the memory of it, and now you just endlessly drive the same stretch of highway, in a ghost car, not realizing that you are a ghost.

How to Win His Heart

♥ **Wear a lot of pink.** Mamie Eisenhower loved pink—specifically, a pale shade that came to be called "Mamie Pink." Because we were a more charmingly impressionable country in the 1950s, this started a nationwide craze for pink. So if you live in a building that was built in the 1950s and you have bubblegum pink tiles in your kitchen or bathroom, you can "thank" Mamie Eisenhower.

♥ **Be good at packing and unpacking boxes.** Mamie Eisenhower once said she moved 27 times in 37 years, and that would be a weird thing to make up.

♥ **Be patient.** Every anniversary, Eisenhower gave his wife one piece of silver to add to her tea set. It took about a decade to complete, at which point she was finally able to hurl a cup of tea in Eisenhower's face for making her wait so long for tea.

Can You Defeat Eisenhower at Bridge?

Here's a round of bridge that Dwight Eisenhower (South) won against the chief justice of the United States (West) and the secretary of the air force (East). He made his contract of 6 ♠, which (as we're sure you know) is a small slam. Now see if you can match wits with Eisenhower by making 6 ♠ yourself—or outplay him and go for the grand slam of 7 ♠ !

NORTH
♠ K 9 8
♥ A K J 5 3
♦ Q J 10
♣ 8 3

You're playing as SOUTH, and WEST leads with the three of diamonds. Good luck!

WEST
♠ 5 2
♥ 8 2
♦ 9 8 7 3
♣ K 7 5 4 2

EAST
♠ 6 4
♥ Q 10 9 4
♦ A 6 2
♣ J 10 9 6

SOUTH
♠ A Q J 10 7 3
♥ 7 6
♦ K 5 4
♣ A Q

●	●	●	●
1 ♥	PASS	2 ♠	PASS
3 ♠	PASS	4 NT	PASS
5 ♦	PASS	6 ♠	PASS
PASS	PASS		

SCORING

How many tricks did you take?

0-4: It appears that you just threw down a bunch of random cards and were lucky 0 to 4 times.

5-8: Are you drunk? It's fine if you're drunk, we're just curious.

8-11: Well, not terrible. But you probably won't be invited back to play again.

12: Great job! You are exactly as good at bridge as Dwight Eisenhower.

13: Amazingly, you are better than "The Bridge Wizard of Manila." That means that *you* are now The Bridge Wizard of Manila! Go to the DMV and request a driver's license with your new name; bring this book as proof.

I Like Ike
(As a Nickname)

Famously, Dwight Eisenhower's nickname was "Ike." Less famously, this was short for "Eisenhower," rather than "Dwight." And since Ike is such a perfect nickname for "Eisenhower," all of President Eisenhower's six brothers also went by "Ike"! Can you guess which of the following was Dwight Eisenhower's specific "Ike" nickname around the Eisenhower house in Kansas?

LITTLE IKE

BIG IKE

FLIRTY IKE

TOUGH IKE

MEAN IKE

FAT IKE

SLIPPERY FINGERS IKE

CANNIBAL IKE

IKE-WHO-WALKS-BETWEEN-THE-ROWS

Answer: President Eisenhower was "Little Ike," which probably contributed to his decision not to give his son the nickname Ike. Instead, Dwight and Mamie went with the time-tested boy's nickname "Icky."

Sort-of Fun Facts

"Eisenhower" means "iron hewer" in German. So if your name is Eisenhower, that's what it means.

President Truman, not knowing Eisenhower was a Republican, offered to run in the VEEP spot on an Eisenhower/Truman ticket. Eisenhower declined, thus denying America its chance at the first all-bald administration. Because apparently Eisenhower couldn't convince Richard Nixon to shave his head.

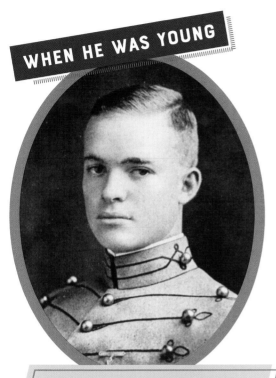

If you were the Germans, you'd surrender too.

SCANDAL!

You are probably still mad about the "U2 Incident," when iTunes forced you to download the U2 album "Songs of Innocence." But did you know there was *another* U2 incident, except with a hyphen? The U-2 Incident of 1960 occurred when the Soviets shot down a "U-2" high-altitude spy plane flying over their territory and captured its pilot, the CIA's Gary Powers.

Was this public humiliation by the Soviet military Ike's greatest disappointment? Probably not, because he later said that "not making the baseball team at West Point was one of the greatest disappointments of my life, maybe my greatest." Well, sure. That would be anyone's greatest disappointment. The West Point baseball team is a heartless machine consciously designed to inflict despair and regret.

Vital Stats

Looks: 4

Did you know that over time, people grow to look more and more like their favorite pastime? That is why the very handsome young Dwight D. Eisenhower gradually grew to resemble a golf ball.

Physique: 7

Eisenhower loved golf so much that he painted his balls black so he could play in the snow. And to prove that brevity is the soul of wit, here is a shorter version of that sentence: "Eisenhower painted his balls black so he could play in the snow."

Charisma: 8

In the 1956 election, Ike's plainspoken manner helped him trounce the more cerebral Adlai Stevenson, proving yet again that Americans want a president who seems smart, but not too smart.

Taking care of his health: 9

After suffering a massive heart attack during his first term, some argued that Ike wasn't healthy enough to serve a second term. But Ike's personal physician and—totally coincidentally—close political advisor told him that, in fact, a second term as president was *critical* to his recovery.

JOHN F. KENNEDY

1961–1963 | Democrat

You came here to see photos of WWII-era boats, right?

Let's not beat around the bush. We know why you're here, and it's not to hear about the Cuban Missile Crisis.

Why You'll *Love* Him

He's easy on the eyes. Unlike a lot of presidents, you don't mind looking at him.

You are drawn to men who compulsively cheat on you. As long as you're setting yourself up for heartbreak, it might as well be with JFK.

He's rich. Oh, but you don't even care about this! That's not the kind of person you are. You're only interested in him because of the cheating thing.

WHEN HE WAS YOUNG

There's just something about a man in uniform. (The "something" is that he has a job!)

How to Win His Heart

Be stunningly beautiful. Seducing JFK aside, this will help you in many aspects of life.

Convert to Catholicism. Finally, your decision to become a nun pays off!

Impress his dad. If you want to be with JFK, you're going to have to win over his dad. We hear his dad puts a lot of stock in the ability to have a bunch of affairs, so maybe start by telling him you plan to cheat on his son?

Be a good nurse. Did you know that it's possible for someone young and handsome and tan to also be extremely weak and sickly? It's (apparently) true! JFK was in and out of the hospital his entire life, and three times he was so sick that a priest administered last rites. So . . . do you enjoy taking care of sick people? If you're not sure, find some guy who is sick and try taking care of him. Then try taking his medicine and replacing it with slices of deli meat. Which did you enjoy more?

DIY PROJECT: SOLVE THE KENNEDY ASSASSINATION CONSPIRACY

You seem pretty smart. If you put your mind to it, we bet you can sort out this whole Kennedy-assassination-conspiracy thing once and for all.

Background: On November 22, 1963, John F. Kennedy was shot and killed while riding in an open convertible. The Warren Commission was tasked with investigating and concluded that a man named Lee Harvey Oswald, acting alone, fired three shots at the president from a sixth-floor window of the school book depository where he worked. Kennedy was struck by two of the bullets, one proving fatal.

Clues:

1 Two days after his arrest, Oswald was being transferred to county jail when he was shot and killed by nightclub owner Jack Ruby. A few years later, Ruby died of lung cancer. Ruby might have had ties to the mob, and some have suggested that the mob killed him as part of a cover-up. And if the mob knows how to give people lung cancer, then we're *all* in trouble.

2 Based on audio recordings and witness testimony, there is reason to believe that a fourth shot was fired at JFK from behind a nearby grassy knoll.* The police found three hobos hanging out in a train car back there, and observers noted that the hobos were clean-shaven and well-dressed. Which sounds a little suspicious, right? But maybe those observers were just jealous.

3 Lee Harvey Oswald spent some time living in the Soviet Union and even applied for Soviet citizenship. This might be evidence that he was working for the Soviets, or it might be evidence that he was crazy. (Or, we suppose, both.) It could also support the theory that Oswald was working for the CIA, because it's weird that he was able to move back to the U.S. without any difficulty. You can test this theory yourself by trying to defect to Russia, then returning to the U.S. and seeing how things play out at customs.

4 Two months before the assassination, Oswald traveled to Mexico City and visited the Cuban and Soviet embassies. The CIA was monitoring him there, and whatever they found out, they concealed it from the Warren Commission. Which means that it was probably something boring and they didn't want the Warren Commission to be bored.

Your conclusion (Don't forget to show your work!):

WHO KILLED JFK? (CHECK ALL THAT APPLY)

☐ Lee Harvey Oswald ☐ The Cuban government ☐ Some fancy hobos

☐ The CIA ☐ The Soviet government ☐ He died of natural causes

☐ The FBI ☐ J. Edgar Hoover

☐ The mob ☐ Lyndon B. Johnson

A knoll is a small hill, not to be confused with a gnoll, which is a sort of half-human, half-hyena. No gnolls are suspected in the assassination of JFK.

Do you want to give your children an edge in life? Or do you want to set them up for failure? Both sound like fun, but in case you decide on the former, here are some parenting tips from JFK's father, Joe Kennedy.

Assign each child a career path at birth. Children need structure and direction, and that's why part of being a good parent is requiring each of your children to pursue a pre-determined career path. For example, your oldest child can be assigned to "president," and the rest of your children can be professional basketball players. If one of your children dies fighting in World War II (unlikely, but you never know), then everybody moves up a spot.

Help your child win the Pulitzer Prize. After your child has gone to the trouble of writing (part of) a book, the least you can do is make sure he or she wins the Pulitzer Prize. Call around and find out if any of your friends are on the Pulitzer Prize board. You'd be surprised! A lot of people are on the Pulitzer Prize board but never mention it, because they are being modest.

Bankroll your child's campaign for president. Running for president is expensive! All of those yard signs aren't going to pay for themselves. (And if they do, you should be concerned.)

Challenge your children to see if they can have more extramarital sexual conquests than you. Joe Kennedy told his oldest sons all about his many affairs and challenged them to see if they could sleep with more women than he had. And nothing drives children to succeed like setting high expectations.

Vital Stats

Looks: 10

Finally, there's a reason to watch the State of the Union address. You might even want to watch it alone, with the lights dimmed.

Physique: 6

JFK had digestive problems, glandular problems, and back problems so severe that he sometimes had to use crutches. Just to get through the day, he had to take a battery of medications. He hid all of this from the public, but there were still rumors. During the 1960 election, burglars broke into his doctor's office looking for evidence that would expose his health problems. Who could possibly be behind something like that? The answer, of course, is American hero Richard Nixon.

Charisma: 10

How *else* could he get so many women to sleep with him?

Preventing nuclear war: 5

When Russia started installing nuclear missiles in Cuba, JFK stopped them without starting a nuclear war. He also kind of started the whole thing, though, by putting his own nuclear missiles in Turkey. (Which, FYI, is really close to Russia. You might even say that Turkey is the "Cuba" of Russia! It wouldn't be very accurate, though.)

match the Mistress to her Potus

John F. Kennedy liked to tell people, "If I don't have sex every day, I get a headache." So for him, Jackie's frequent travel made affairs a medical necessity. After all, aspirin wasn't invented until . . . oh, ha ha, it was invented in 1897. Well, still, it's hard to blame JFK, because having sex is more fun than taking an aspirin.

DRAW A LINE MATCHING THE PHOTO OF EACH PRESIDENT TO HIS ALLEGED MISTRESS(ES)

Ellen Rometsch

Pamela Turnure

Mimi Alford

Judith Exner

Angie Dickinson

Marlene Dietrich

Blaze Starr

Jill Cowen

Priscilla Wear

Gunilla von Post

Marilyn Monroe

John F. Kennedy

Note: We've included a line between Marilyn Monroe and JFK, because everyone already knows they had an affair. In fact, the cosmic connection between them is so strong that sometimes, a line will just mysteriously appear linking pictures of them. You can test this at home: Draw pictures of JFK and Marilyn Monroe on the walls of your house, and see if a line materializes, uniting them in eternal love.

MIMI ALFORD + JFK

Mimi Alford started having an affair with JFK on her fourth day as an intern at the White House, after being invited to a party at the president's private pool. So if your boss invites you to a pool party at his house on the fourth day of your internship, don't worry: He probably just wants to sleep with you.

JUDITH EXNER + JFK

JFK was introduced to Judith Exner by Frank Sinatra during a visit to Las Vegas. People knew Frank Sinatra for his music, but his true love was matchmaking. It's terrifying to think how many headaches JFK would have suffered through if not for Frank Sinatra's tireless matchmaking.

ANGIE DICKINSON + JFK

Another magical Frank Sinatra match, although their affair is only rumored.

MARLENE DIETRICH + JFK

When he was 20 and she was 60! Dietrich told JFK ahead of time "Don't muss my hair, I have to perform." To which JFK probably replied, "Ditto."

ELLEN ROMETSCH + JFK

Ellen was a sex worker and probable East German spy who lived in a hotel on Capitol Hill. She visited the Kennedy White House for naked pool parties because hey, why not have naked pool parties at the White House and invite some communist spies?

BLAZE STARR + JFK

You're not going to believe this, but Blaze Starr was a stripper.

PAMELA TURNURE + JFK

Pamela Turnure was Jackie Kennedy's press secretary and bore a close resemblance to the First Lady. So, is it better or worse to be cheated on with someone who looks like you? This is a great question to pose if the conversation starts to slow down on a first date.

GUNILLA VON POST + JFK

JFK met Swedish aristocrat Gunilla while vacationing on the French Riviera. And that right there is why you're not having an affair with a president. You're not a Swedish aristocrat who vacations on the French Riviera. Get on that.

THIS IS "FIDDLE." THIS ONE IS "FADDLE."

PRISCILLA WEAR (LEFT) + JFK
JILL COWEN (RIGHT) + JFK

JFK had two cute, young secretaries nicknamed "Fiddle" and "Faddle."

LYNDON B. JOHNSON

1963–1969 | Democrat

Do you like being pressured into doing things? Sure, we all do. That's why Lyndon B. Johnson was so popular and beloved, except for the whole Vietnam thing.

LBJ is known for "The Treatment," a process by which the large man would literally get inches from your face and talk until you agreed to do what he wanted. As Johnson's press secretary described it, "When that man started to work on you, all of a sudden, you just felt that you were standing under a waterfall and the stuff was pouring on you." If you feel a little flushed after reading that sentence, then LBJ might be the guy for you!

Johnson used his legendary powers of close-talking to ram through all kinds of good policies, including the Civil Rights Act, the Clean Air Act, the Social Security Act . . . and honestly too many other things for us to list. This isn't a history book, folks.

> If Vietnam taught us anything about what it would be like to date Lyndon B. Johnson, it's that even when facing a complete disaster that will ruin lives, he still refuses to pull out.

TRUE FACTS THAT ARE ALSO

DOUBLE ENTENDRES

- After the Pearl Harbor attack, the navy assigned sailor LBJ to "INSPECT THE SHIPYARDS."

- He was the first serving U.S. president to "GO DOWN UNDER" and "VISIT AUSTRALIA."

- He amazed Texans along the campaign trail with what he called "THE JOHNSON CITY WINDMILL." (It was a helicopter. This would have to be a double entendre for something pretty un-sexy, high-fiving in bed.)

Why You'll *Love* Him

He spent two years in the Senate as "majority whip." *Two years in the Senate as Majority Whip* would also make a great title for an erotic history of LBJ's time in the Senate. See you on the bookshelves, Robert Caro!

He's not clingy! In fact, he's *so* not clingy that he constantly sleeps around. He once bragged he'd "had more women by accident than Kennedy ever had on purpose." (We don't know exactly how that can happen by accident, but we assume it's a constant risk for close-talkers like LBJ.)

It's rumored that LBJ deliberately peed on the shoe of one of his Secret Service agents. So you could probably get him to pee on you, too, if you join the Secret Service.

You'll never have to see him cheating on you. LBJ had a buzzer installed in the Oval Office so that the Secret Service could alert him when his wife was coming, so she wouldn't walk in on him having sex with his secretary. Because it was pretty embarrassing the *first* time that happened.

He wears a cowboy hat.

WHEN HE WAS YOUNG

"Hi, I'm Lyndon. Welcome to the navy! Now, confidentially—do you want to form an alliance with me against the guys on the other bunk?"

Vital Stats

Looks: 2

His wife, Lady Bird Johnson, said that when they first met, it felt like a moth being drawn to a flame. We're going to go ahead and assume that in this scenario, he is the moth.

Physique: 7

Do you like your men tall and lanky? LBJ is 6' 3½". And it tells you a lot about him that he isn't content with just telling people he is 6'3".

Charisma: 3½

Once, in the Oval Office, he reportedly grabbed the Canadian prime minister by the lapels and said, "Don't you come into my living room and piss on my rug!" And the prime minister *hadn't even pissed on his rug yet!*

Low center of gravity: 9

LBJ installed showerheads in the White House that were so powerful, Richard Nixon said they almost knocked him down. And Nixon's heart was made from the superdense core of a dead star, so that's saying a lot.

1969–1974 | Republican

Richard Nixon is thought of as a Machiavellian figure who relentlessly crushed his enemies and pursued power. But few today remember how relentlessly he crushed (on) and pursued young schoolteacher Pat Nixon. Did he propose on their first date? He did. After she turned him down, did he persuade her to let him drive her to dates with *other* guys? He did. Did he keep on proposing to her, over and over again, until she said yes? He did.

But please: Don't fall for Richard Nixon simply because he proposes on the first date and then obsessively stalks you until you finally relent and marry him. Because there's some bad stuff about Richard Nixon, too.

How to Win His Heart

💜 **Skip the dirty talk.** While working as an attorney, Nixon avoided taking divorce cases because he didn't like to hear women talking about sex. But we're guessing you won't have a hard time not talking about sex with Richard Nixon.

💜 **Try to be in a play with him.** Nixon *twice* proposed to women who were cast in plays with him. So he either has a thing for actors, or for women who are in his immediate vicinity.

💜 **Have the best-looking legs of any woman in public life today.** *Women's Wear Daily* said Pat Nixon had the "best-looking legs of any woman in public life today." But that was in 1969, and we're talking about *today*, so you've got a shot to edge Pat out for this coveted recognition and catch Nixon's eye. Start by mailing a photo of your legs to *Women's Wear Daily* at 475 Fifth Ave, 3rd Floor, New York, NY 10017. No need to include an explanation—they'll know why you're sending it.

Why You'll *Love* Him

He writes a lot of love letters. To Pat, he wrote, "Every day and every night I want to see you and be with you. Yet I have no feeling of selfish ownership or jealousy. Let's go for a long ride Sunday." He might have been referring to driving her to a date with another guy, but still: If there's one sure way to wow your date, it's having Richard Nixon drop you off.

If he falls for you, he'll call you "thee" instead of "you," which is a Quaker thing. Unfortunately, this is going to make you wonder, "Hey, *wait just a gosh-darned minute,* how come Quaker president Herbert Hoover never called me 'thee'?"

He won't make you wear fancy clothes. When Nixon gave his famous "Checkers" speech in which he refused to return an inappropriate campaign contribution (specifically, his dog Checkers), he assured a worried nation that his wife Pat didn't own a mink coat, but rather a "respectable Republican cloth coat," whatever that is. Every girl dreams of growing up to marry someone who brags to strangers about how she doesn't have a nice coat.

Sort-of Fun Fact

Pat Nixon's real name was Thelma, but she went by "Pat" because she was born the day before St. Patrick's Day, and also because her real name was Thelma.

YOU'D BETTER START THINKING NOW ABOUT WHAT TO SAY IF NIXON ASKS YOU TO GO BOWLING WITH HIM.

Alternate History Timeline:

In 1969, Nixon vetoed a NASA plan that would have put a manned base on the moon by 1980. What would have happened if he *hadn't* vetoed the moon base?

1979 — Moon base completed.

1980 — Soviet Union concedes defeat, asks to be annexed by California. Ronald Reagan elected Governor of Moscow Oblast.

1984 — President Nixon completes fourth term. He points out that he is in violation of the Twenty-second Amendment, but everyone shushes him and says, "But you're doing so great!"

1994 — Space elevator connecting Houston and the moon completed. Neighborhood around the space elevator station on the moon starts gentrifying.

2003 — To celebrate his 90th birthday, Chancellor Nixon tries out his new biomechanical legs by climbing Olympus Mons. Experts at the Department of Martian Terraforming tell him the atmosphere isn't ready for a climb without supplemental oxygen; he adds them to the enemies list.

2018 — Space Emperor Nixon grants an imperial pardon to Carl Bernstein and Bob Woodward for sedition; they are released from Moon Reeducation Camp #45.

DOMESTIC BLISS

In Nixon's famous "KITCHEN DEBATE," he argued in a kitchen with Soviet Premier NIKITA KHRUSHCHEV over whether capitalism or communism had better kitchens. And you could have spirited conversations with Richard Nixon in your kitchen, too! For example: "RICHARD NIXON? WTF ARE YOU DOING HERE, GET OUT OF MY KITCHEN!"

Favorite Pickup Line

"Nixon's the One!"

Nixon might try to use his 1968 campaign slogan when he sidles up to you at the bar. But before you agree to let him drive you to your dates with other guys, you need to ask yourself, "the one *what*?"

Who Said It?

Did you know that Richard Nixon was named after 12th-century English **King Richard the Lionheart?** See if you can identify who said the following quotes—Richard Nixon or Richard the Lionheart. (Oh, and we also threw in a quote by **Patrick Swayze** from when he wore a Nixon mask in *Point Break*. So that's an option, too.)

1. "You can do what you want, and make up your own rules. Why be a servant to the law, when you can be its master?"

2. "When the President does it, that means that it is not illegal."

3. "I am born of a rank which recognizes no superior but God."

4. "This is a great day for France!"

Answer key: 1. Patrick Swayze; 2. Richard Nixon; 3. Richard the Lionheart; 4. You probably thought this was Richard the Lionheart, since he spent most of his life in France. But this was actually Nixon speaking at the funeral of French national hero Charles de Gaulle, because he thought it was a can't-miss opportunity to stick it to de Gaulle.

WE ASKED . . . WHAT WAS YOUR MOST EMBARRASSING MOMENT?

"

I lack the capacity for shame. But other people might say it's the time I helped sabotage President Johnson's peace talks with the North Vietnamese because I thought a successful ceasefire would make it harder for me to win the 1968 presidential election. This probably extended the war by a few years. But I don't know . . . even as I'm saying it now, it doesn't sound all that bad to me!

"

Pop QUIZ

What is "The Nixon Doctrine"?

a) Giving allies aid rather than entering combat directly on their behalf.

b) Recording all of your own conversations, just in case.

c) Proposing on the first date.

d) Resigning the presidency.

e) Being tricky.

f) All of the above.

Answer: It's (e). If the teacher grading your AP History exam tells you it's (a), have them come talk to us.

WHEN HE WAS YOUNG

A young Richard Nixon gazes into the future, **and it's dark.**

SCANDAL!

It's hard to pick just one Nixon scandal, but let's talk about these drapes.

DOES HE KEEP HIS *promises?*

☑️ **Allow dancing.** In college, Nixon became class president by promising to end the school's ban on dancing, and the yearbook gave him credit for "living up to his promises." So if you're a college student looking to vote for a fun-loving class president, consider writing in "Richard Nixon." Or "I want to dance." Or "No one knows how lonely I am." Whatever. It's student government.

❌ **Unavailability for kicking around.** After losing the 1962 California gubernatorial election, Nixon promised the press "You don't have Nixon to kick around anymore." But he has done a terrible job of keeping this promise. The press will still be kicking Richard Nixon around when the sun goes supernova and swallows the Earth.

❌ **Not being a crook.** Nixon told the country, "I am not a crook. I've earned everything I've got." But if you end up accepting a presidential pardon, you're at least *kind of* a crook. And why the gratuitous dig at crooks, anyway? Who's to say crooks *haven't* earned everything they've got? Do you think a high-tech art museum heist is easy?

Vital Stats

Looks: 5

Notoriously bitchy fashion critic George Orwell once wrote, "At age 50, everyone has the face he deserves." Nixon was a handsome young man, but over the decades his craftiness began to visibly weigh on him. And when we say, "visibly weigh on him," we mean "on his cheeks."

Physique: 4

Also on his pectoral muscles.

Charisma: 3

Nixon sought respect rather than love, and he didn't connect with people personally. He once said, "Even with close friends, I don't believe in letting your hair down." So if you're ever alone with Richard Nixon and he suddenly lets his hair down, you can at least console yourself with the knowledge that he doesn't consider you a close friend.

Nickname: 3

Nixon was nicknamed "Tricky Dick" because of his underhanded campaign tactics. If you ever meet a guy nicknamed Tricky Dick and you're worried about how he got that name, "underhanded campaign tactics" is really the best-case scenario.

Can you cover up
WATERGATE?

Do you think you would have fared better in Nixon's shoes? Now is your chance to find out!

On June 17, 1972, five burglars were caught trying to bug the Democratic Party's headquarters, which was located in the Watergate Hotel in Washington, DC. This set off an investigation that ultimately led to President Nixon's resignation. But what a lot of people don't realize is that Nixon didn't get in trouble for the break-in itself. It's actually perfectly legal to spy on the Democratic Party! No, Nixon got in trouble because he tried to cover it up (and, more important, failed).

IT'S TIME TO COVER UP THIS WHOLE WATERGATE THING. HOW DO YOU WANT TO START?

Do nothing. →

YOU LOSE!
The good news is that there's no evidence you ordered the Watergate break-in. So you might not have to resign, or be impeached, or live forever in infamy. The bad news is that the whole point of this flowchart was to pull off a successful cover-up and you failed. Better luck next time!

Pay the burglars hush money.

Uh oh, investigators have traced some of the hush money back to your re-election campaign. This looks bad!

Have the CIA tell the FBI to stop investigating the break-in.

Sweep it under the rug by taking everyone involved and sweeping them under a giant rug.

OK, you managed to fit all of the Watergate conspirators underneath the Oval Office rug. But now they're complaining about being hungry, and some plucky *Washington Post* reporters are sniffing around, wanting to know why your rug is so lumpy. What are you going to do?

Slip some sandwiches under the rug to keep everyone quiet.

Great. But now those reporters who were sniffing around and want to know why the Oval Office smells like corned beef all the time. What now?

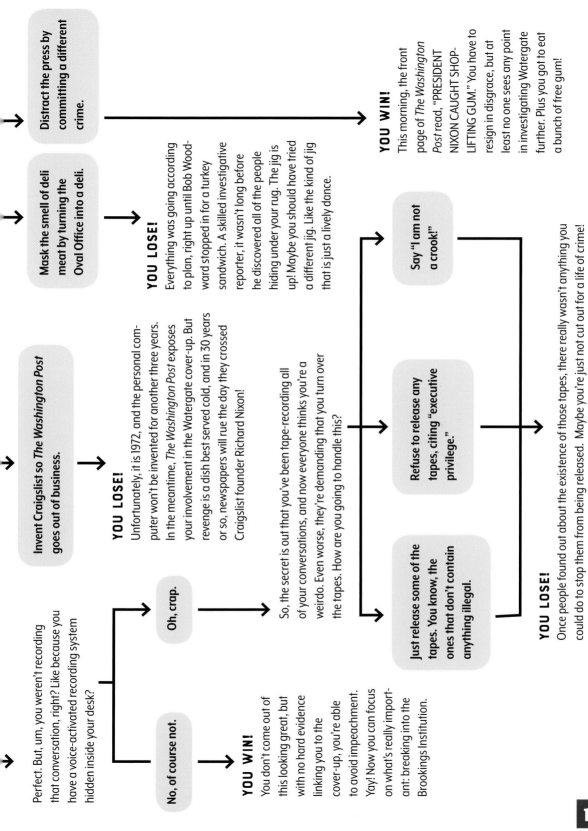

Distract the press by committing a different crime.

Mask the smell of deli meat by turning the Oval Office into a deli.

Invent Craigslist so *The Washington Post* goes out of business.

Perfect. But, um, you weren't recording that conversation, right? Like because you have a voice-activated recording system hidden inside your desk?

Oh, crap.

No, of course not.

YOU WIN!

This morning, the front page of *The Washington Post* read, "PRESIDENT NIXON CAUGHT SHOP-LIFTING GUM." You have to resign in disgrace, but at least no one sees any point in investigating Watergate further. Plus you got to eat a bunch of free gum!

YOU LOSE!

Everything was going according to plan, right up until Bob Woodward stopped in for a turkey sandwich. A skilled investigative reporter, it wasn't long before he discovered all of the people hiding under your rug. The jig is up! Maybe you should have tried a different jig. Like the kind of jig that is just a lively dance.

YOU LOSE!

Unfortunately, it is 1972, and the personal computer won't be invented for another three years. In the meantime, *The Washington Post* exposes your involvement in the Watergate cover-up. But revenge is a dish best served cold, and in 30 years or so, newspapers will rue the day they crossed Craigslist founder Richard Nixon!

So, the secret is out that you've been tape-recording all of your conversations, and now everyone thinks you're a weirdo. Even worse, they're demanding that you turn over the tapes. How are you going to handle this?

YOU WIN!

You don't come out of this looking great, but with no hard evidence linking you to the cover-up, you're able to avoid impeachment. Yay! Now you can focus on what's really important: breaking into the Brookings Institution.

Say "I am not a crook!"

Refuse to release any tapes, citing "executive privilege."

Just release some of the tapes. You know, the ones that don't contain anything illegal.

YOU LOSE!

Once people found out about the existence of those tapes, there really wasn't anything you could do to stop them from being released. Maybe you're just not cut out for a life of crime!

GERALD FORD

1974–1977 | Republican

Gerald Ford is the classic handsome, popular jock who peaks in high school, and then gradually declines over the years, until he finally becomes president.

George Washington is a great dancer, and Teddy Roosevelt is great at surviving gunshots to the chest, but no president can match Ford for sheer athleticism. He was a standout football star in high school, he played both center and linebacker for the University of Michigan, and he turned down the chance to play in the NFL. If we had decided to settle the Cold War through trial-by-combat, he probably could have picked up Brezhnev and thrown him across the room, Abraham Lincoln–style.

Unfortunately for Ford (and all of us), this opportunity never came up, and the biggest tackle he needed to make as president was tackling the legacy of a criminal predecessor and dishonored party. Other missed Ford administration tackles included "inflation" and "walking onstage without tripping," and these failures prevented nice-guy Ford from winning the 1976 presidential election against the ruthless Jimmy Carter.

In the end, Ford has never really escaped his reputation as a dumb jock. But people forget that he graduated from the Yale Law School, so he probably wasn't any dumber than the *average* Yale graduate.

How to Win His Heart

♥ **Be hot.** Ford worked as a model in college, and both of his serious relationships were with women who'd been successful fashion models. So if you've been looking for an excuse to finally launch your career as a fashion model, here it is!

♥ **Be a hot mannequin.** When Ford met his future wife Betty, she was working as a "department store fashion consultant." Is "department store fashion consultant" code for "mannequin," and was Betty Ford a beautiful mannequin brought to life by love, as in the movie *Mannequin?* Yes.

♥ **Don't be a dancer, or a divorcée, or both.** Ford and Betty put off their marriage until after his first congressional campaign, because he was worried what voters would think about him marrying a divorced ex-dancer. It was a simpler time.

Why You'll *Love* Him

He was good enough to beat Reagan.

If you want to know how different the 1970s were, consider this: In the 1976 GOP primary, Ronald Reagan was defeated by Gerald Ford. The only way Reagan could lose a GOP primary today is if somehow his opponent was *also* Ronald Reagan. And, with continued advances in cloning technology, we might live to see this primary.

He made Eagle Scout.

Can you guess how many of the U.S. presidents have been Eagle Scouts? 100%? 110%? 2000%? Wrong. Only Gerald Ford, and he basically only became president by accident. If you think this is a scathing indictment of the Eagle Scout program, you're right. Statistically speaking you have a better shot at the U.S. presidency if you become a Freemason, or a Quaker. *(This message brought to you by the Freemason Coalition to Recruit Quakers.)*

He will stand up for his friends. Or sit down for them, depending on the situation.

In 1934, Georgia Tech's football team refused to play Michigan unless African-American player Willis Ward was benched. Michigan acquiesced, and an outraged Gerald Ford quit the team in protest. But then Ward urged him to play and beat Georgia Tech, so he rejoined the team. Ford knocked an epithet-spewing Georgia Tech lineman out of the game with a vicious hit. Michigan won the game. Ward went on to become a judge, Ford went on to become president. And did we mention that both of them were really handsome? Get on it, Hollywood.

SCANDAL!

If you're hoping that Ford will keep a photo of you in his wallet, sorry: there's no room. That's because it's already holding a copy of the Supreme Court decision *Burdick v. United States*.

Now you're probably wondering, "What is *Burdick v. United States*"? (Or, depending on your age, "What is a photo?" or "What is a wallet?") Well, one of Ford's first actions as president was pardoning Richard Nixon for—

to use a legal term of art—"being a crook." This was controversial. But because *Burdick v. United States* said that accepting a pardon was the same as admitting guilt, Ford felt he had at least gotten Nixon to admit guilt, and he carries around the decision to prove it.

Nixon, on the other hand, probably doesn't carry anything in his wallet but a few stolen credit cards and a lock pick set.

Gerald Ford is the origin of the expression "walk and chew gum at the same time." Specifically, LBJ accused Ford of being too dumb to do this. Except he said "fart and chew gum" and the press sanitized it, because American society was not ready to learn about the brutal expletive "fart."

He never won a national election. Ford was appointed vice president after Nixon's first vice president, Spiro Agnew, resigned in disgrace over bribery allegations and also maybe because his name was an anagram for "grow a penis." Nixon needed a vice president with a good, clean reputation whose name was an anagram for a good, clean phrase like "frog ladder," so he picked Ford. Then *Nixon* resigned in disgrace, and blam! Gerald Ford became president without ever having won a national election. The lesson is that before you choose a name for your child, check to see what the anagrams are. We cannot stress this enough.

Timeline: *Jock President*

1935 Ford turns down offers to play for the Detroit Lions and the Green Bay Packers, instead taking a position as boxing coach at Yale. Even a lucrative NFL career couldn't tempt this jock away from a full-time job punching nerds.

1942 After the attack on Pearl Harbor, Ford joins the navy, helping to win the war in the Pacific by serving as his aircraft carrier's Athletics Officer and coaching sailors in nine separate sports. Historians still ponder "what if" scenarios where the Japanese win because Ford only coached seven or eight sports.

1974-77 As president, Ford often has the United States Navy Band play the Michigan fight song instead of "Hail to the Chief" before state events. Unless you're a Michigan fan, you should be rolling your eyes right now.

1975 Ford trips and falls while walking onstage and thus launches a thousand jokes making fun of him for being clumsy. Live by the sword, die by the sword (of jockishness).

A blond, shirtless Gerald Ford jumps for the ball as part of preparations for the bombardment of Japanese fortifications on Iwo Jima.

Just look at how *dreamy* Gerald Ford was, before his *looks* were *ravaged* by age and the stresses of *boat ownership.*

PRESIDENT LESLIE KING?

Did you know that Gerald Ford was born Leslie King Jr.?

You might be wondering why any man would change his name from "Leslie." Well, as Tolstoy wrote in *Anna Karenina* (but in Russian), "Each unhappy family is unhappy in its own way." And the way that Leslie King Jr.'s family was unhappy is that his father Leslie Sr. was (allegedly) a violent alcoholic who threatened the newborn future president and his mother Dorothy with a butcher knife. No guy is perfect, but Dorothy decided she could probably do better. She fled with her baby and later married paint salesman Gerald Ford Sr., who raised Leslie as his son and whose name the future president eventually took as his own.

Leslie Sr. never paid child support, but he made amends by showing up unannounced at the restaurant where Ford worked in high school and giving him $25. Which you have to admit is a pretty good tip, especially in 1930.

Vital Stats

Looks: 6

This is tricky, because in his youth, Ford was literally a cover model. But as he became a middle-aged dad, his looks slid inexorably toward "middle-aged dad." This is in contrast to presidents like George W. Bush who stayed handsome into old age. Which just goes to show that if you want to preserve your looks, don't become a politician. Become a multi-millionaire baseball team owner. There—now you can't say this book didn't give you any useful beauty tips.

Physique: 10

Did you take a good look at that photo of Ford playing basketball shirtless?

Charisma: 7

Ford is well liked by most people who know him. He's not flashy, but he is fair, reasonable, honest, trustworthy, zzzzzzzzz . . . oh, sorry, we fell asleep listing Ford's boring personal qualities.

Getting assassinated: 0

There were two assassination attempts against Gerald Ford, both by women, both in California. Which just goes to show you that the Beach Boys' song "California Girls" is 100 percent correct about women in California.

1977–1981 | Democrat

If you like peanut jokes, you've come to the **right page!** Because now we're going to talk about Jimmy Carter: nuclear engineer, U.S president, Nobel Peace Prize winner, and peanut farmer.

"Big Peanut" had been trying to get its salty claws into the White House for decades, and in Jimmy Carter they finally had their guy. Carter presented himself as a man of the people, but some historians suspect that he was actually a puppet being manipulated by the purse strings of powerful Georgia peanut tycoons. (To be clear, when we say "some historians," we are referring to ourselves, and "historian" is, frankly, a stretch.)

But there's still a lot to love about Jimmy Carter, if you're in the market for a man who is thoughtful, optimistic, and alarmingly frank about the lust hidden deep within his heart (more on that later!).

And Jimmy Carter managed to accomplish some great things. Just not, you know, as president.

Here's a Tip

During the energy crisis of the late 1970s, Carter urged Americans to wear sweaters at home to reduce energy consumption. (Apparently he could not care less about the energy used to *make* sweaters.) If you're ready to take your advice about winter clothing from a Georgian, then go right ahead and put on a dorky sweater. Or you can listen to *our* winter weather advice: **CRANK YOUR THERMOSTAT UP TO 85 AND WALK AROUND IN A SWIMSUIT.** It will encourage you to keep it tight all year long, and it will help create jobs at struggling oil, gas, and coal companies.

Why You'll *Love* Him

Carter has been to North Korea on several post-presidency diplomatic missions. If you're ever in North Korea and see someone who looks like a farmer, it might be Jimmy Carter!

He cares about the things that really matter. Not money, or prestige, or international travel. But rather, peanuts. In 1964, Carter was a New York–based naval officer specializing in nuclear engineering. But when his father fell ill, he brought his wife back home to tiny Plains, Georgia, to pursue the alternate life path of "impoverished peanut farmer living in public housing." Rosalynn Carter is a very lucky woman!

He'll let you sit in on cabinet meetings. Maybe bring a book.

He's a homeowner. When he was 13, Jimmy Carter saved up and bought *five* houses in his hometown, then rented them out to local families. So if you ever think your life couldn't get any worse, just think "At least I'm not suffering the indignity of renting from a 13-year-old."

Pop QUIZ

Some people say Carter's presidency was doomed by "stagflation." But **what is stagflation?**

a) Simultaneous weak economic growth and high inflation rates.

b) A minor deity worshipped by the ancient Celts with the head of a stag, and the body of high inflation rates.

c) The sinister clique of ruthless peanut-industry bagmen who stalked Carter at every turn, demanding payback for putting him in office.

d) a and b

Answer: No one knows what stagflation is. Ask ten different ancient Celts and you'll get ten different answers.

WHEN HE WAS YOUNG

Cut out this photo and carry it with you. The next time your parents ask you why you're still single, show it to them. Tell them it's your new boyfriend, and his name is *Midshipman Jimmy,* and he lives in the past.

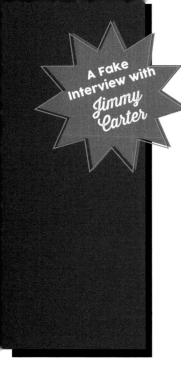

A Fake Interview with *Jimmy Carter*

Q: President Carter, What do you consider your greatest accomplishment?

A: Definitely when I deregulated the sale of hops, malt, and yeast, and thus launched the home and craft brewing movement.

Q: Oh. Really? Not the time you won the Nobel Peace Prize for your post-presidential diplomacy, human rights and global health work?

A: Nope. Microbreweries.

Q: What about when you successfully negotiated the Camp David Accords that secured peace between Egypt and Israel?

A: Huh? Oh, that. I'd forgotten all about that. Yeah I guess that was good. But not as good as a nice, bitter IPA.

Q: What about when you negotiated the SALT II nuclear arms reduction treaty with the Soviets?

A: I *guess* I'm proud of SALT II. But I'm not as *excited* about it as I am about washing down a big handful of salty peanuts with a nice brown ale.

Q: President Carter, we'll be honest—we didn't realize you were much of a drinker. We'd heard that at most, you'd have a glass of white wine every now and then.

A: What was that? Sorry, I didn't hear you, these guys are making me do a keg stand. If you want to interview anyone at the Carter Center, don't call after 2pm.

DOES HE KEEP HIS *promises?*

✗ Clean up the mess in Washington.
Someday some politician really *is* going to clean up the mess in Washington, and we'll discover that without the mess it's just a crumbling husk.

✓ Restore sweaters to the White House.
This wasn't technically a promise, but he did it anyhow. Carter goes above and beyond the call of duty if it involves wearing sweaters.

✗ "Real leadership, for a change."
Carter's presidency isn't thought of as hugely successful, so we're going to have to give him an "✗" for delivering on this campaign slogan. On the other hand, we give him three or four checks for "weirdly passive-aggressive campaign slogan."

A rare photo of the moment when Jimmy Carter used the power of positive thinking to fly into the air and stay aloft for a full 10 minutes.

Carter is one of only two American presidents to have been interviewed by *Playboy*. Can you guess the other one? What if we told you he's been interviewed by them more than once? What if we told you he's appeared (clothed) in a *Playboy* soft-core porn video, pouring champagne on a Playboy bus? We bet you can guess!

Anyhoo, back to Carter. Jimmy Carter has not, as far as we know, appeared in any porn videos. But he *did* tell the magazine, "I've looked on a lot of women with lust." Which was weird, because all they'd asked him was "Did you have any trouble finding our office?"

FUN FACTS THAT ARE ALSO DOUBLE ENTENDRES

- When things start getting dirty, Carter might ¨DECLARE A FEDERAL EMERGENCY IN LOVE CANAL.¨

- If Jimmy Carter puts on some smooth music and offers you a massage, get ready for an ¨OIL SHOCK.¨ (The shock is that he's having a hard time acquiring enough massage oil.)

Vital Stats

Looks: 6

On a long submarine voyage, Jimmy Carter will start to catch your eye. But no fraternization onboard the boat, sailor! Unless the boat is the submarine ride at Disneyland. In which case, it's your vacation—if you want to spend it making out with Jimmy Carter on a submarine, we're not going to stop you.

Physique: 8

Carter has a fit, compact physique, earned through decades of wresting peanuts from the earth's clammy grip.

Charisma: 6

Carter's quiet integrity is the perfect antidote if you've just broken up with a slimy Richard Nixon–style boyfriend. But once the rebound period is over, you'll get bored with quiet integrity and be back to wanting a smooth-talking, oiled-haired Californian.

Bloodlust: 9

Through the so-called Carter Center, Jimmy Carter is the mastermind behind extensive, global efforts to murder the parasites that cause malaria, river blindness, schistosomiasis, and Guinea worm disease. Those poor guinea worms never did anything to Jimmy Carter—they simply want to be left in peace, and allowed to live in and occasionally burst forth from people's bodies. And yet he is hell-bent on wiping them from the face of the earth. Jimmy Carter: Enemy of Nature.

match the Mistress to her Potus

♥ **1963-2018** ♥

Some people think that infidelity ended in 1963, when zi
codes were invented. But in fact, to this day people have a
and that includes presidents.

DRAW A LINE MATCHING THE PHOTO OF EACH PRESIDENT TO HIS ALLEGED MISTRESS(ES)

Lyndon B. Johnson

Bill Clinton

George H.W. Bush

Gerald Ford

Donald Trump

Ellen Rometsch

Jennifer Fitzgerald

Helen Gahagan Douglas

Marla Maples

Gennifer Flowers

Madeleine Brown

Alice Glass

Monica Lewinsky

 +

MADELEINE BROWN AND LBJ

Madeleine Brown wrote a book about her claimed 20-year affair with LBJ titled *Texas in the Morning*. So, you're welcome—now you're thinking about having sex with LBJ in the morning, in a brightly lit room, dead sober. But here's a consolation: She also claimed LBJ had known about the Kennedy assassination in advance. That is probably a lie, so it might also be a lie that anyone has ever had morning sex with LBJ.

 +

ALICE GLASS AND LBJ

In 1973, Lady Bird Johnson received a letter from this former mistress, requesting the return of a gift she'd given LBJ—a brass-and-crystal eagle once owned by Thomas Jefferson. And Lady Bird did return it. If you ever get a chance to time travel, consider going back to 1973 and convincing Lady Bird to instead run it over with her car.

 +

HELEN GAHAGAN DOUGLAS AND LBJ

Douglas was a Hollywood actress-turned-congress-woman, and she coined the nickname "Tricky Dick" when she and Richard Nixon were running for the same Senate seat. Another tricky dick in her life was LBJ's.

 +

ELLEN ROMETSCH AND GERALD FORD

Remember East German spy Ellen Rometsch, who slept with JFK? According to one source, she also slept with then-congressman Gerald Ford, and FBI director J. Edgar Hoover blackmailed Ford with an audiotape of the rendezvous. Hoover might not have totally understood the FBI's counterintelligence role.

 +

JENNIFER FITZGERALD AND GEORGE H. W. BUSH

Rumors swirled after then-Vice President Bush shared a cottage with his personal secretary during a visit to Geneva in 1984. Both deny the affair, and frankly, it seems likely that the vice-presidential travel budget simply wouldn't cover two Swiss cottages.

 +

GENNIFER FLOWERS AND BILL CLINTON

During Bill Clinton's affair with Gennifer Flowers, did he ever get used to seeing the name Jennifer spelled with a "G"? Or did it continue to feel forbidden and naughty?

 +

MONICA LEWINSKY AND BILL CLINTON

But is it really an affair if you don't have "sexual relations," but just oral sex? I mean, we're not a bunch of Puritans, are we?

 +

MARLA MAPLES AND DONALD TRUMP

You're probably putting a finger to your temple and saying, "Wait, wasn't he married to Marla Maples?" The answer is yes, he was, technically. But he started sleeping with her while still married to his first wife, Ivana. Before you judge him too harshly, keep in mind it was widely reported in the New York tabloids that he thought Ivana's breast implants felt unnatural.

1981–1989 | Republican

America was coming off a series of bad relationships with presidents. It had tried a peanut farmer, a jock, and a crook, but none of them really seemed to act like a president. And when you're looking for someone who will act like a president, there's one obvious choice: an actor.

Ronald Reagan had parlayed a sports radio broadcasting job into a successful Hollywood movie career, and he parlayed *that* into a job giving pep talks to GE employees and hosting the "GE Theater" weekly variety show. The GE gig was lucrative, but Reagan knew that money isn't everything. So after a few years he stepped off the notoriously grueling career track at GE and took a major pay cut by accepting a position as the governor of California.

But Reagan had his eyes on bigger prizes than Sacramento, if that's even possible. And the nation was ready for him. In 1979, Jimmy Carter gave his nationally televised "malaise" speech, in which he said that a crisis of confidence was undermining America. He was right, and the speech resonated. But a few months later, Americans got to choose whom they wanted to inspire a renewal of national pride and confidence. A farmer who wanted you to keep your house cold in the winter? Or . . . glamorous movie star Ronald Reagan?

Once elected, President Reagan cut through the national malaise like a hot, cheerful knife through gloomy butter. Drawing on all the skills he learned from serving on the men's basketball cheerleading squad at Eureka College, he put a few extra drops of Grecian Formula in his hair, popped a few jelly beans, and got to work. And almost before he knew it—in fact, sometimes without his knowledge entirely—bold measures were underway to defeat communism and restore American confidence.

Favorite Pickup Line

"You and I are going to spend our sunset years telling our children, and our children's children, what it once was like in America when men were free."

(NOTE: *Reagan originally used this line in 1961 to warn Americans that creating Medicare would end freedom in America. But it also works great as a pickup line, if you want to quickly establish that you're ready for a long-term relationship, and that you're looking forward to a future dystopia.*)

Why You'll *Love* Him

He is literally a movie star! You've seen *Brother Rat*, right? And its popular but highly controversial sequel, *Brother Rat and a Baby?*

He dated a woman (Nancy Reagan) who dated Clark Cable. That means that if you sleep with Ronald Reagan, it's like you're sleeping with Clark Gable! At least in the STD-transmission sense.

He made 77 rescues as a high school lifeguard. Of course, those figures are probably self-reported. So it's possible he inflated his own numbers by blowing his whistle, swimming up to some cute girl, and saying "Hey, are you OK? By the way, my name is Ronald, but you can call me 'Dutch' because I look like a fat little Dutchman."

He told the greatest joke in American history. When conducting the sound test for his weekly radio address, President Reagan said, "My fellow Americans, I'm pleased to tell you today that I've signed legislation that will outlaw Russia forever. We begin bombing in five minutes." The audio was leaked and the Soviet military went on alert, but (spoiler alert) they figured out it was a joke and it did not start WWIII.

Reagan was nicknamed *"Dutch"* because his father, correctly, said he looked like a *"fat little Dutchman."* Other fat little Dutchman presidents include: Martin Van Buren.

How to Win His Heart

Be matronly. Even as a hot young starlet, Reagan's future wife Nancy Davis was typecast as a housewife, and her studio's promotional materials said that her "greatest ambition was 'a successful happy marriage.'" Reagan liked to call her "Mommy." You were probably going to become pretty matronly anyway, so you might as well put it to a good use: bedding Ronald Reagan.

Fight communists together. Reagan and his first wife informed on communist-sympathizing actors to the FBI. Can't you picture spending a romantic evening with Reagan, curled up on a bearskin rug in front of a roaring fire, calling the FBI and telling them your coworkers are communists?

Charlton Heston called Ronald and Nancy's relationship "the greatest love affair in the history of the American presidency." But that was only because he didn't yet know about Donald and Melania.

Reagan was almost 70 when he entered the White House, and this was controversial. By 1980, a president alerted to an apparent Soviet missile launch would have less than 15 minutes to decide whether to launch U.S. missiles in response. And if deciding whether or not to launch nuclear missiles is as hard as deciding what to watch on Netflix, then that's really not a lot of time.

The "Ronald Reagan Legacy Project" aims to name one thing in every state—bridges, airports, roads—after Ronald Reagan. You can help out by naming something in your house after Reagan . . . or even part of your own body! "The date was going great, until she turned around and saw that I'd taken out my Reagan." "I gasped with pleasure as he pressed himself against my Reagan." "I have a weird rash on my Reagan." And so forth.

Get the Look!

Reagan's look is ˮCOWBOY.ˮ But a cowboy who cares about looking good. And whose idea of looking good is lots and lots of HAIR PRODUCT, so that not a single hair is out of place, even for a second. And whose SMILING, friendly demeanor belies incredible power to INFLICT VIOLENCE. (Actually, this would be a good Cormac McCarthy character.)

Timeline: Wartime President/Governor/Actor

Ronald Reagan believed in "peace through strength," and he demonstrated his commitment to the peacemaking power of strength by constantly using strength to go to war against one thing or another.

1937 **WAR ON (FICTIONAL) CORRUPTION.** Reagan stars in his first feature film, *Love Is on the Air*, about a radio announcer who proves that you *can* fight city hall, as long as you're in a rom-com.

1937 **WAR ON SOLDIERS NOT HAVING ENOUGH INFORMATIONAL MOVIES TO WATCH.** Reagan enlists in the army, but his poor eyesight relegates him to the "First Motion Picture Unit." However, his bad eyesight doesn't prevent him from helping to discover a young Marilyn Monroe. And she, in turn, helps the young army officer discover *himself*. Sexually.

(Maybe.)

(OK, probably not. But just imagine!)

1940 **WAR ON (FICTIONAL) WEST POINT.** Reagan portrays Notre Dame football player George Gipp in *Knute Rockne, All American.* In that movie he is nicknamed "the Gipper," and his teammates are urged to "win just one for the Gipper" in the big game against Army. Years later, Reagan begins using "the Gipper" as a nickname in real life, and encouraging White House staff to "go out there and win one for the Gipper," because he understands that reality is an illusion.

1970 **WAR ON HIPPIES.** During student unrest at California universities, Governor Reagan says, "If it takes a bloodbath, let's get it over with. No more appeasement." This, perhaps, is a man who over-embraced the cautionary lessons of the 1938 capitulation at Munich.

1982 **WAR ON DRUGS.** President Reagan re-declares Nixon's "War on Drugs." And that's why there's no longer any illegal drug use in America. Sorry, teens.

1983 **WAR ON STARS.** President Reagan announces plans to build a space-based missile defense system. Democrats mock this as "Star Wars," because comparing a policy proposal to a wildly popular movie is a surefire way to undermine it.

1983 **WAR ON GRENADA.** The Pentagon holds a contest to see who can come up with the most over-the-top code name for invading a nation whose population is smaller than Columbia, Missouri. The winner is "Operation Urgent Fury."

1985 **WAR ON SANDINISTAS.** Until he got caught supporting the Contras, Reagan's approval had been going *up* and *up*, but it started going *down* and *down*, as the *left* attacked him and the *right* defended him. The *left's* attacks began to prevail against the *right's* defenses, and it was looking like Reagan would *b a* failed president, but finally he was able to *start* moving past it.

1987 **WAR ON WALLS.** At a joint appearance with Gorbachev in Berlin, Reagan urges the Soviet premier to "tear down this wall." Gorbachev, obligingly, goes home to get his sledgehammer.

HOROSCOPE

After an assassination attempt against Reagan, Nancy increasingly turned to her astrologer for advice about how to keep him safe. She was roundly mocked for this. And if you believe in physics, it's easy to mock the idea that celestial movements determine our individual destinies here on Earth. But be honest: if you opened up the newspaper and your horoscope said, "Someone will try to assassinate you in front of the Washington Hilton," you would probably stay home.

SPEAKING OF WHICH: LET'S TAKE A LOOK AT TODAY'S HOROSCOPE. NO MATTER WHAT YOUR ASTROLOGICAL SIGN, SOMETHING TELLS US THAT YOUR FORECAST WILL CONTAIN AN INTERESTING TIDBIT FROM REAGAN'S PRESIDENCY!

ARIES

You will sign the Intermediate-Range Nuclear Forces Treaty with the Soviets at 1:33 p.m., because 33 is your lucky number, and this treaty is going to need all the luck it can get.

TAURUS

The stock market will rise 180 percent over the course of your presidency. But—and telling you this is a violation of the astrologer's code of ethics—it's vital that you sell all your stocks on October 18, 1987. Don't ask us why!

GEMINI

You will dream about having an evil identical twin. *Or was it a dream?* If it was just a dream, then why is there drool all over your desk, just like in your dream??!!

CANCER

You will transfer your presidential powers to Vice President George H. W. Bush for eight hours while you're under sedation to have a cancerous bowel polyp removed. Bush will manage to go the whole time without vomiting on any foreign leaders, but you shouldn't assume this means a President Bush will never vomit on a foreign leader. (He will.)

LEO

On safari in Africa, you will shoot and skin a lion, then donate its pelt to the Smithsonian. (Oh wait . . . sorry, that was Teddy Roosevelt's horoscope! Your horoscope for today is that you will try out a new kind of shampoo.)

VIRGO

You will finally give your first substantive remarks on AIDS after more than 20,000 Americans have already died from the disease, and your comments will consist, in part, of supporting abstinence education. AIDS isn't going to know what hit it!

LIBRA

Today you will nominate Sandra Day O'Connor to the Supreme Court, making her the first woman to sit on the nation's highest court. Later, she and the authors of this book will move across the country at the same time, and the moving company will carry their stuff in the same truck. What? Yes, it's true! For all J.D. knows, they accidentally swapped his Xbox with hers.

SCORPIO

You and Mikhail Gorbachev will agree to set aside all of this Cold War stuff if aliens invade the U.S. or the U.S.S.R. You will not agree on what to do if aliens invade China.

SAGITTARIUS

Someone is going to try to assassinate you in front of the Washington Hilton. So maybe don't go to the Washington Hilton today. Or whatever, you can go if you want to. We're not going to tell you how to live your life.

CAPRICORN

You will proclaim this National Dairy Goat Awareness Week. You don't give people a lot of notice, though, so everybody has to scramble to come up with goat-related festivities.

AQUARIUS

You will quip that hippies "look like Tarzan, walk like Jane, and smell like Cheetah," without realizing that Tarzan almost certainly smelled a *lot* worse than Cheetah, even though Cheetah was, confusingly, a chimpanzee.

PISCES

While staying at the house of Prince Karim Aga Khan IV during nuclear talks with the Soviets, you will accidentally kill his son's pet goldfish and send a White House aide on a frantic search through Geneva for a replacement goldfish. On the plus side, no one will ever ask you to pet-sit ever again.

A Time for Choosing:

Reagan entered the national stage in 1964 when he gave his famous "A Time for Choosing" speech. He wrote it himself, and it was compelling and effective. But we don't want you to take time away from more important things (reading this book) to go read his speech. So as a special favor, we've diluted "A Time for Choosing" down to its best lines.

"SOMEWHERE A PERVERSION HAS TAKEN PLACE."

"WE BOUGHT A TWO MILLION DOLLAR YACHT FOR HAILE SELASSIE."

"I'M NOT SUGGESTING HARVARD IS THE ANSWER TO JUVENILE DELINQUENCY."

"AND STILL THEY CAN'T TELL US HOW 66 SHIPLOADS OF GRAIN HEADED FOR AUSTRIA DISAPPEARED WITHOUT A TRACE AND BILLIE SOL ESTES NEVER LEFT SHORE."

"SHOULD CHRIST HAVE REFUSED THE CROSS?"

"THIS IS THE LAST STAND ON EARTH."

"YOU AND I HAVE A RENDEZVOUS WITH DESTINY."

Vital Stats

Looks: 8

You have to admit, Ronald Reagan is a man who ages well. If you do not admit it, Ronald Reagan will keep invading Grenada until you admit it.

Physique: 3

Do you like the long, hydrodynamic, hairless swimmer's body? But on a 70-year-old? Well, like it or not, that's what you're getting.

Charisma: 10

Reagan was known as "The Great Communicator," and he was especially convincing over the radio and onscreen. After he left office, all across the country people awoke as if from a dream, and said, "Wait a minute . . . I think I've spent the last few years believing the U.S. could start and win a limited nuclear war against the Soviets, but that can't be right."

Mentor: 8

When Bill Clinton asked Reagan for advice on being president, Reagan taught him how to give a good, crisp salute.

HOTTEST HEADS OF STATE EXPLAINS:

Can you explain it in the form of a dumbed-down analogy?

Sure! Let's say you give your son a dollar and tell him not to use it to buy any candy. He gives the dollar to a friend, and the friend uses the dollar to buy candy and gives it to your son. By using a go-between, your son technically followed the rules, right?

No, definitely not.

Well nevertheless, this is basically what the White House did. Rather than sell arms to Iran directly, they sold arms to the Israelis, who immediately turned around and sold them to the Iranians. And because the Iranians had influence over the Lebanese hostage-takers, the Americans said, "Hey, since we're getting you these anti-tank missiles, could you do us a solid and lean on your boys to free their hostages?"

I know you think using colloquial language makes this topic feel less bewildering, but it does not. Did their plan work?

Sort of, eventually. But first, it occurred to the Reagan administration that there was a third problem they could also solve by selling weapons to Iran.

At this rate, I can't believe America had any problems left by the time Reagan left office. What was the third problem?

The CIA had been funding and training an armed group seeking to overthrow the leftist government in Nicaragua. These rebels were called the "Contras," short for *contrarrevolucionarios.* They were pretty ruthless, even by counterrevolutionary standards, and Congress passed a law telling the administration to stop. But Reagan didn't want to stop! So his people came up with another interesting legal theory.

The Iran-Contra Affair better have involved an actual affair. Can you please tell me about it? And don't spare the saucy details!

Well . . . OK. The whole thing started in the mid-1980s, when the Reagan Administration tried to solve two problems at once.

That sounds efficient! It's nice to see a politician who actually follows through on promises to reduce waste and inefficiency. What were the two problems?

First, armed groups in Lebanon had seized a number of American hostages.

I just got a wave of '80s nostalgia for the days when terrorists simply took hostages. What was the second problem?

Congress had banned arms sales to Iran after the Islamic Revolution in 1979. But then Iran was invaded by Iraq, and the Reagan administration was worried that if the U.S. didn't sell the Iranians arms to defend themselves, they would drift into the Soviet sphere of influence.

Did it occur to anyone to just topple the Iraqi government and thus bring peace and democracy to the region?

No, although National Security Council (NSC) staffer Col. Oliver North later claimed that Reagan had him convey the message "Saddam Hussein is an asshole" to the Iranians. They came up with a much more elaborate plan, based on some convoluted legal reasoning.

The Iran-Contra Affair

Please don't use another candy metaphor.

OK, fine. Let's say you tell your teenager, "You get a weekly allowance. But you are not allowed to buy beer." And your teenager takes this to mean that she *is* allowed to buy beer, as long as she doesn't use her allowance money. Reagan's staff decided that if the White House could make its own money, it could spend it however it wanted. And, as luck would have it, they already had a moneymaking operation in place.

The White House Gift Shop! Now I feel guilty for buying all those commemorative plates!

No. They had their operation selling weapons to Iran. Oliver North realized they could raise the prices on weapons sold to the Iranians and use the profits to fund the Contras.

I don't see how this could possibly go wrong. But I guess it must have, or else I would never have heard of it.

As anyone with a favorite child knows, keeping a big secret is hard. And word of the Iran-Contra operation began coming out pretty quickly, in a variety of ways. An Iranian general leaked it to a Lebanese magazine. A planeload of U.S. arms bound for the Contras crashed in the jungle. And—most hilariously—Oliver North's secretary mixed up a bank routing number, and as a result $10 million for the Contras was accidentally wired into the bank account of a very confused Swiss man.

Oh man! Well honestly, anyone could make that mistake. I hope everything turned out OK for her!

A couple years later, she was dating Rob Lowe.

Well, she can go straight to hell, then. So what happened to Reagan?

When the story first broke in November of 1986, Reagan said, "We did not, repeat, did not, trade weapons or anything else for hostages." A few months later he gave another speech saying (essentially) "Well actually, it turns out we did trade weapons for hostages." And although there were extensive investigations, to this day it's hard to know how much he knew. He was not a details guy, his health was deteriorating, and Oliver North was a pretty slippery character.

Oh yeah, Oliver North. What ever happened to him?

He was convicted on three felony counts, but they were overturned because he'd been granted immunity for cooperating with prosecutors. He went on to have a cameo on the '90s TV show *Wings*. And he was a contestant on *Jeopardy* in 1997, where he was beaten like a gong by journalist Andrea Mitchell.

I'm going to go see if I can stream *Wings*.

We are watching *Wings* right now, as we write this. In fact, it's possible we might have accidentally included some plot elements from *Wings*.

GEORGE H.W. BUSH

1989–1993 | Republican

If we told you that a U.S. president had 1) enlisted in the wartime navy on his 18th birthday, 2) promptly become its youngest aircraft-carrier aviator, 3) been shot down by the Imperial Japanese and rescued by a submarine, 4) joined the submarine's crew for a few months, 5) run the CIA, 6) presided over the defeat of the Soviet Union, and 7) skydived on his 90th birthday, what word would you use to describe him?

Perhaps . . . "wimp"?

No? Well, that's because unlike most people in politics, you're not horrible. In spite of all evidence to the contrary, George H. W. Bush struggled against the perception of wimpiness for much of his political career. Sure, he's a big preppie, he went to Yale, and his nickname is "Poppy." But there are a lot of tough preppies who went to Yale named "Poppy." If you don't believe us, just put down this book, enroll at Yale, and start asking around. No matter what you find, you'll come away with a world-class education and memories to last a lifetime.

NOTE: *As you'll learn in a few pages, George H. W. Bush had a son who was also named George Bush, who also became president. It's easy to get them mixed up! So, since George H. W. Bush was one of only three U.S. presidents to be knighted, we'll refer to him as "Sir George of Kennebunkport" from now on.*

Here's a Tip

For all of you kids out there deciding how to celebrate your 18th birthday, do what George H.W. Bush did: **JOIN THE NAVY!** Either that, or go buy some cigarettes. Then celebrate having legally bought cigarettes by enlisting in the navy!

Why You'll *Love* Him

Sir George was flying a bombing mission against a Japanese radio station when his plane was struck by antiaircraft fire and engulfed in flames. **But he waited to bail out until he had completed his mission and bombed the radio station.** Even then, the future politician hated the media!

Oh, sorry, did we say "plane"? We meant "Barbara II." **Sir George named his WWII fighter planes "Barbara I," "Barbara II," and "Barbara III."** Was there sexy Barbara Bush pin-up art on the sides of these planes? Tragically, there was not. Unless you think the word "Barbara" is inherently sexy all by itself.

(NOTE: *Pause here and recall that Barbara was, at this point, a college freshman, and reflect on your college boyfriends and the many ways they disappointed you.*)

Not only a great boyfriend and husband, Sir George gives wise fatherly advice. For instance, when asked why he didn't depose Saddam Hussein during the first Gulf War, he said it would have "incurred incalculable human and political costs. . . . We would have been forced to occupy Baghdad and, in effect, rule Iraq." Listen to your dad, kids.

If you think you're in love with George H.W. Bush now, wait until we tell you about the time he shaved his head in solidarity with the son of one of his Secret Service agents, who was undergoing chemotherapy.
OK, now we've told you about it!

Favorite Pickup Line

Bush: "Read my lips . . ."
You: "Oooh, well I don't mind if I—"
Bush: ". . . no new taxes."
You: "Oh."

WHEN HE WAS YOUNG

IT'S WEIRD THAT WE SEND TEENAGERS TO FIGHT IN WARS. BUT WHAT CAN WE SAY... TEENS LOVE WAR!

We sat down with Sir George of Kennebunkport to find out once and for all if his whole New England blue-blood schtick is for real, or if it is a cover for the fact that he is, in fact, a deep-cover communist spy.

Q: Mr. President, are you a communist spy? If you are, it's OK! After all, the Cold War is over.

A: I was there, I know it's over.

Q: But how do you feel about that? When the Berlin Wall fell, a reporter asked you why you didn't seem more excited. You claimed, "I am not an emotional kind of guy." Which is exactly what a communist spy would say, if he were secretly super sad that things weren't going so well with communism!

A: I just didn't think the moment called for a chest-beating display of triumphalism. Honestly, I am not a communist spy.

Q: Well then how do you explain . . . this photo?!

A: I was appointed by President Ford to be the chief U.S. envoy to China.

Q: Oh sure, that's what they all say. Well, what about the date you chose to announce your first candidacy for the presidency in 1979? May 1? *International Worker's Day?* You and your Moscow handlers must think we're pretty stupid!

A: Look, I hate to sound immodest, but I used to be director of the CIA. And I can tell you from experience that if you're trying to plant a deep-cover spy in a hostile government, you don't have them openly celebrate one of your own holidays. It would be a little obvious.

Q: EXCEPT THAT'S EXACTLY WHY YOU WOULD DO IT! BECAUSE NO SPY WOULD EVER DO IT, SO IT'S THE PERFECT THING FOR A SPY TO DO!

A: Well, OK. But aggressively trying to root out spies is *also* a pretty great cover for a spy, wouldn't you say? So how do I know *you're* not a spy?

Q: . . . this interview is over.

Timeline: George H.W. Bush, *Perfect Boyfriend*

💜 **1941**
Meets Barbara Pierce at age 17, at a Christmas dance.

💜 **1942-45**
Helps defeat the Axis powers, with torpedoes.

💜 **1948**
Graduates from Yale in two and a half years.

💜 **1948-58**
Was born rich but goes ahead and makes a fortune in the oil business in his 30s.

💜 **1959**
Ugh we can't even go on, Barbara is so lucky.

Vital Stats

Looks: 6
Wait until you see him in madras shorts!

Physique: 8
He was both the captain of the Yale baseball team *and* a Yale cheerleader. So no matter what your taste, the answer is "George H.W. Bush."

Charisma: 7
Bush is a personable and likable guy who makes friends easily. Which is why it must have sucked to constantly have his charisma compared to that of a Hollywood movie star like Ronald Reagan.

Picking vice presidents: 7
Yeah, you read that right — 7 out of 10 for picking Dan Quayle! If you think that's too high, why don't you go read a history of the vice presidents and then get back to us.

BILL CLINTON

1993–2001 | Democrat

Bill Clinton was dubbed by some supporters as "The Man from Hope." And not just because he was born in Hope, Arkansas! Clinton was able to connect with voters on an emotional, empathetic level, encouraging and inspiring them while also showing that he felt their pain. His administration oversaw one of the longest peacetime economic expansions in U.S. history, leaving the U.S. federal budget in the black for the first time in many years, and he had several international affairs victories.

But while Clinton was *born* in Hope, he was *raised* in Hot Springs, Arkansas, a resort town named for its hot mineral baths. He carried the spirit of hope throughout his life. But for better or worse, he also carried the spirit of hot tubs.

Favorite Pickup Line

"We have the largest watermelons in the world."

(This is the actual thing Bill Clinton was boasting about to a group of fellow Yale law students the first time his future wife Hillary ever laid eyes on him. And it worked! Although it's possible that bragging about agriculture production in a vaguely raunchy way only works on Ivy League women.)

WE ASKED BILL CLINTON: WHAT IS YOUR GREATEST REGRET?

I guess it was when a former employee named Paula Jones sued me for sexual harassment. I fought the lawsuit, and gave a deposition in which I lied under oath about my relationship with White House intern Monica Lewinsky. Republicans in Congress used this to impeach me. Then, I settled with Jones for nearly $1 million. So if I was going to end up settling anyway, I wish I had done it in the first place and skipped the deposition.

Well, or not lied under oath. Or not had the affair in the first place. But once you start tugging on that thread, where does it end? On second thought, I don't have any regrets.

On *"Switcharoo Saturdays,"* Clinton and Vice President Al Gore would trade suits.

How to Win His Heart

♥ **Go to the library.** Hillary met Bill by approaching him at the library. You can do this too, if you happen to see Bill Clinton at your local library taking advantage of the free wi-fi. In fact, it might work on other men, too. Just walk up to a man at the library and say, "Hi, my name is Hillary Rodham Clinton." And don't worry that he'll think you're mentally ill just because you claim your name is Hillary Rodham Clinton. If he didn't want to meet mentally ill people, he wouldn't be at the library.

♥ **Be a change-maker.** At the 2016 Democratic National Convention, Clinton described his wife as "the best darn change-maker I've ever met." If you want to borrow this phrase, because you're trying to draft the most awful wedding vows in history, go right ahead!

♥ **Be ambitious.** Hillary Rodham Clinton isn't just a long-suffering wife—she is also a highly accomplished politician in her own right, having served as a U.S. senator, secretary of state, and the Democratic presidential nominee in 2016. Bill Clinton doesn't really have just one "type," but clearly one of his many types is women who share his thirst for political power. So you're going to need to run for office. But don't begin by running for city council or state rep, because this doesn't show a lot of ambition. We recommend starting with president, and then working your way down.

♥ **Get close to him.** The Clinton Foundation is accepting applications for internships in its New York, Boston, and Little Rock offices.

CROSSWORD PUZZLE

Bill Clinton loves doing crossword puzzles, and he also loves reminiscing about his impeachment. (OK, that second thing might not be true.) Whether you're sitting in the doctor's office, stuck in gridlock, or doing hard time in the hole, why not while away the hours by doing a Bill Clinton impeachment-themed crossword puzzle?

ACROSS

2. A massive, glowing sphere of gas, such as the Earth's sun, but spelled with an extra "r"
4. Very large in size, such as a _____ right-wing conspiracy
5. To admonish sanctimoniously. Usually, but not always, a metaphor rather than a literal physical gesture
11. Would be more fun if it actually involved peaches
12. In French, *affaire*
14. A room where no one should have sex, and yet they do
16. Like a jury, but fancier. Or maybe bigger. Honestly we've never been 100% clear on this
18. We are not even going to try to define this impossibly ambiguous term. Who even knows what the meaning of this word is?
19. Like a nightstand box of tissues, but more "dressy"

DOWN

1. The only president other than Clinton to be impeached. Also, slang term for the ultimate source of most of Clinton's troubles
3. Statistically speaking, the most likely outcome when impeaching a president
6. An explosive surge of white, frothy . . . river water
7. Both the process of giving sworn testimony and, coincidentally, the process of toppling a leader from power
8. Definitely not the first White House intern to have sex with the president
9. Pertaining to a place where, apparently, sexual relations cannot happen
10. Affectionate term for the employee with whom you've been fooling around at work
13. The last person in the world who should be moralizing about infidelity
15. As in, "During deliberations, the bailiff will provide no more than one pizza party _____"
17. A young temporary employee sometimes paid not in money, but experience. Horrible, horrible experience

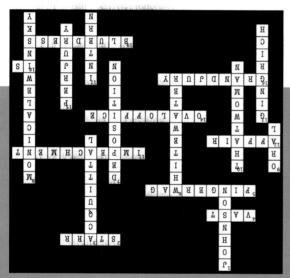

ANSWERS

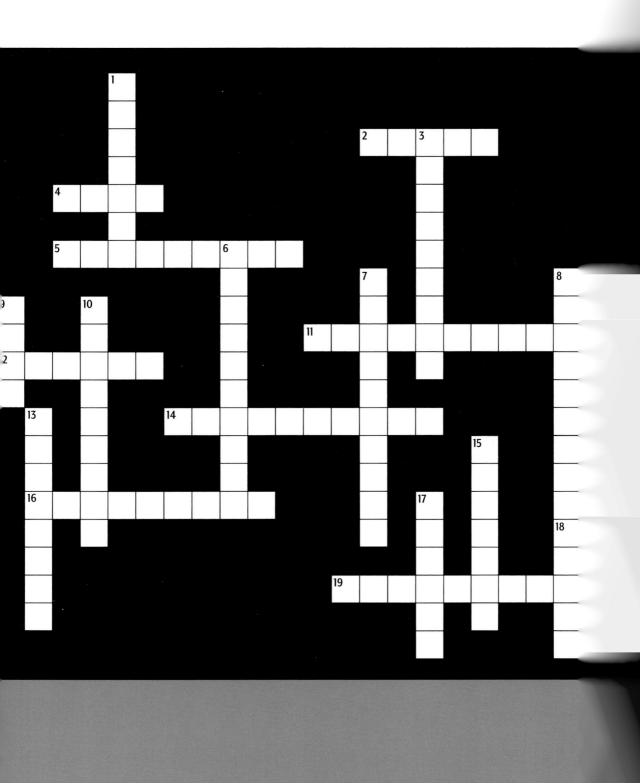

Sort-of Fun Facts

★ Bill Clinton plays the saxophone, which was invented in 1846 by a guy named Sax who also invented the "saxhorn" (!) and "saxtuba" (!!). Was the success of the saxophone over the saxtuba the point at which other timelines diverged from ours, the darkest? Yes.

★ Bill Clinton first became interested in the law when he was in high school and participated in a mock trial as the lawyer for the ancient Roman senator Catiline. Catiline was actually put on trial a few times . . . but we really hope that this was his trial for sleeping with a temple virgin.

★ Speaking of high school, Bill Clinton went to Hot Springs High School. If you ever stop procrastinating and finally write that screenplay for a mid-1980s teen sex romp, this is what you should name the high school.

★ After his presidency, Bill Clinton became very rich, in part by giving paid speeches for an average fee of $200K. It's hard to imagine any speech being worth $200K, unless it is titled "I Have Traveled Here from the Future, and I Have Stock Tips."*

★ Bill Clinton supported and signed the Defense of Marriage Act. Unfortunately for *his* marriage, this was not a bill to assign the president a 24/7 chaperone.

★ Bill Clinton served an unprecedented five terms as governor of Arkansas. Political analysts on both sides of the aisle agree that this is a *lot* of time to spend in Little Rock.

*Here are *our* stock tips, for free: Sell all your stocks. Buy canned food, iodine tablets, and edged weapons.

TRUE FACTS THAT COULD ALSO BE DOUBLE ENTENDRES

● Clinton earned well-deserved acclaim for "TAPPING A LOT OF WOMEN FOR HIS CABINET."

● Early in his career, Clinton argued against rigid, binary party identification, instead self-identifying with a more fluid "THIRD WAY."

● Clinton's policy on discussing marital status when he's out at the clubs is the same as his policy on gays in the military: "DON'T ASK, DON'T TELL."

After they graduated from law school, Bill took his girlfriend Hillary Rodham on vacation to Europe and proposed to her at sunset on the shores of Ennerdale Water in northern England.

That was possibly the most romantic sentence in this book. And yet Hillary said no! He proposed a few more times (hopefully not on that same vacation), but she continued to rebuff him.

She eventually relented a few months later, when he picked her up from the airport in Little Rock and said something along the lines of, "Hey, remember that house you said looked nice a few weeks ago? Well I bought it, so now you have to marry me." The moral of the story is that if you're going to eventually marry Bill Clinton anyway, you might as well say yes when he proposes to you lakeside rather than in the car driving back from the airport in Arkansas. (Unless you're holding out for a house in Arkansas.)

Vital Stats

Looks: 8

What you need to do is imagine seeing Bill Clinton for the very first time, before you've heard anything about cigars and blue dresses and so forth. See, he looks pretty handsome! Try to remember this lesson the next time you're swooning over a handsome stranger.

Physique: 5

Bill Clinton loves golf and jogging. But he also loves hamburgers and fries. One thing about Bill Clinton is that he has a lot of love to go around.

Charisma: 9

Bill Clinton is extremely sociable. As president he would often call people in the middle of the night, just to chat. So if your phone rings in the middle of the night, answer it, because it might be Bill Clinton! Also, the call might be coming from your basement, because he also likes to break into people's basements (maybe).

Knows how to use drugs: 2

By his own admission, Bill Clinton didn't inhale when he tried smoking marijuana. It's surprising that this kind of incompetence didn't sink his election bid, but you have to remember that independent candidate Ross Perot siphoned off a lot of Republican votes.

Are you BILL CLINTON?

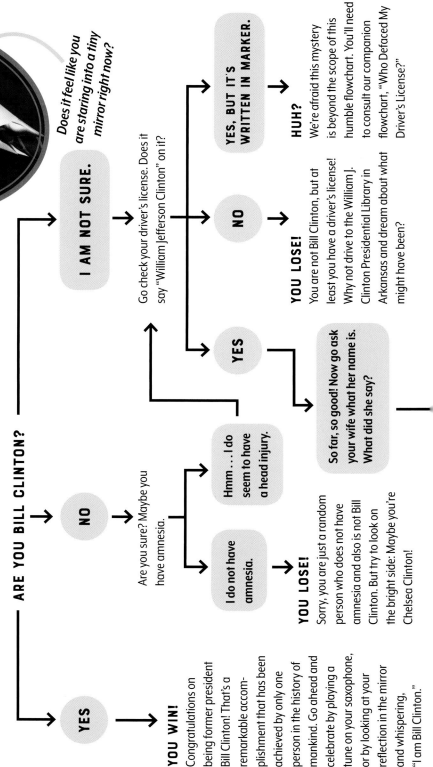

Like many presidents, Bill Clinton sometimes reads books. That means it's technically possible that Bill Clinton is reading THIS book, right now. And hey—YOU are ALSO reading this book right now. Does that mean that you are a former president Bill Clinton? Maybe! There's only one way to find out for sure.

ARE YOU BILL CLINTON?

YES

YOU WIN!
Congratulations on being former president Bill Clinton! That's a remarkable accomplishment that has been achieved by only one person in the history of mankind. Go ahead and celebrate by playing a tune on your saxophone, or by looking at your reflection in the mirror and whispering, "I am Bill Clinton."

NO

Are you sure? Maybe you have amnesia.

I do not have amnesia.

YOU LOSE!
Sorry, you are just a random person who does not have amnesia and also is not Bill Clinton. But try to look on the bright side: Maybe you're Chelsea Clinton!

Hmm . . . I do seem to have a head injury.

So far, so good! Now go ask your wife what her name is. What did she say?

I AM NOT SURE.

Does it feel like you are staring into a tiny mirror right now?

Go check your driver's license. Does it say "William Jefferson Clinton" on it?

YES

NO

YOU LOSE!
You are not Bill Clinton, but at least you have a driver's license! Why not drive to the William J. Clinton Presidential Library in Arkansas and dream about what might have been?

YES, BUT IT'S WRITTEN IN MARKER.

HUH?
We're afraid this mystery is beyond the scope of this humble flowchart. You'll need to consult our companion flowchart, "Who Defaced My Driver's License?"

"Why are you asking me that? What's wrong with you?"

"Brenda"

"Hillary"

Ugh, she's being difficult. OK, new plan: Go through your wife's wallet and locate her driver's license. What name is on it?

Hillary Rodham Clinton

Brenda Clinton

J.K. Rowling

I didn't find her driver's license, but I did find $40!

Hot dog, let's go shopping! What are you going to buy?

23 cans of tuna

Sauna pants

YOU LOSE!
You are not Bill Clinton, and even worse, you are married to someone named Brenda.

YOU WIN!
You aren't former president Bill Clinton, but you are married to billionaire author J. K. Rowling, which is just as good! Go make her explain to you why the wizards don't just use cell phones.

YOU WIN!
Even though you'll never know whether you are former president Bill Clinton, you've still won the greatest prize of all (sauna pants).

YOU LOSE!
Surely you saw this coming when you made the choice to buy 23 cans of tuna.

That's promising! But we better check one more thing, just to be sure. Bill Clinton is never without this carpet with his face woven on it that was given to him by the president of Azerbaijan. Take a look around your house. Do you see this carpet?

NO

Yes, I am wrapped up in it right now, like a burrito.

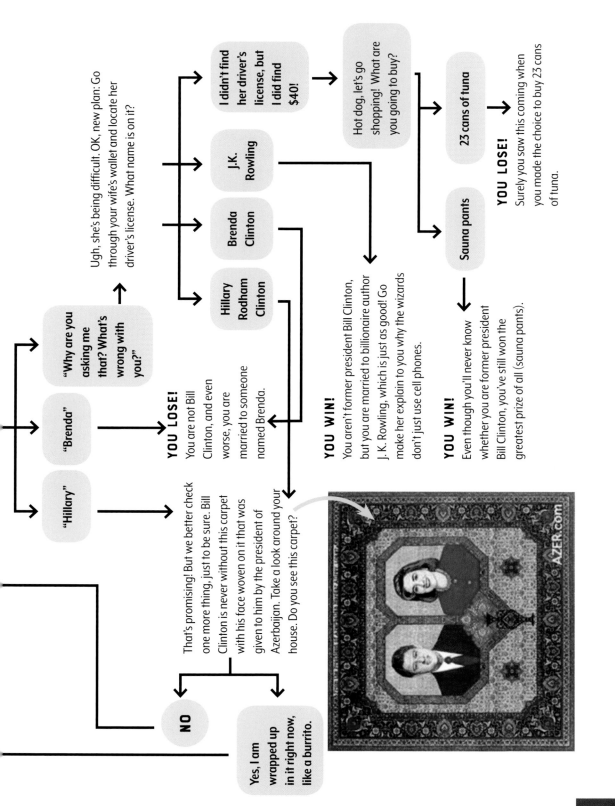
AZER.com

2001–2009 | Republican

If your goal was to finish this book, we have good news:

MISSION ACCOMPLISHED

Ha ha! Just kidding. But you're getting close! Just a few more "surges" of reading effort, and you can finally put this horrible experience behind you.

Speaking of which, let's talk about the 43rd president, George W. Bush. George W. Bush is seen by many as a plainspoken, no-nonsense, shoot-from-the-hip Texas cowboy. And indeed, he had a pretty stereotypical Texas cowboy background: Born in Connecticut, summered in Maine, head cheerleader at Phillips Andover, graduate of Yale University and Harvard Business School.

But while in the hearts of most Texas cowboys is a lonesome wolf's howl, or the endless wind scouring the prairie, or a nice, meaty cow, in Bush's heart lies ambition. Ambition to rise above his station as "son of a U.S. president," and become "U.S. president," so that for the rest of his life he could lord it over his brother Jeb at Thanksgiving.

But his elevation to the White House brought a dilemma the likes of which America hadn't faced since the earliest days of the Republic. Not "Is torturing people bad, or does it depend on the circumstances?" but rather "How are we going to distinguish between two presidents with the same name?"

People came up with a lot of dumb solutions, and in this book we'll use one of those dumb solutions, which is to call George W. Bush, the 43rd president, "43." But in the spirit of having powerful families exercise dynastic control of government, we'll use Roman numerals and call him George XLIII.

When George W. Bush was facing rising anger around the world, he should have just airdropped millions of copies of this photo of himself as a baby. What a cute baby!

Why You'll *Love* Him

He wrote a biography of his father.
If our son wrote a biography of us, it would mainly address how we don't let him watch enough TV and make him wear pants in public. This is also the general thrust of George XLIII's *A Portrait of My Father.*

He's a compassionate conservative.
You care about other human beings, right? Even if they live in other countries? George XLIII created a program aimed at helping prevent and treat AIDS, malaria, and neglected tropical diseases that has saved millions of lives in the developing world. (If you *don't* care about other human beings, try hitting yourself in the head with this book and see if that jars anything loose.)

He is an amazing marksman. During his successful run for governor of Texas, George XLIII went hunting and accidentally shot an endangered species of bird. Not to be outdone, years later his vice president Dick Cheney later went hunting and accidentally shot a 78-year-old lawyer. (The lawyer was *not* endangered, except in the sense that anyone who goes hunting with Dick Cheney is in at least a *little* bit of danger.)

He will be your permanent designated driver. George XLIII became a teetotaler the day after celebrating his 40th birthday. His advice to people thinking about getting on the wagon? "If Bush can quit, I can quit." That's very motivating! "If the president of the United States can do it, I can do it!" One day at a time!

He will coin a new nickname for you.
George XLIII is famous for coming up with new and colorful nicknames for the people around him. Will he nickname you "Pootie-Poot," like Vladimir Putin? Perhaps "Big Time," like Dick Cheney? Or maybe even "Turd Blossom," like Karl Rove? But only if he likes you as much as he likes Karl Rove.

He was the most popular president ever.* Bush registered the highest approval ratings in presidential history: 90% approval, right after the 9/11 terror attacks. The political lesson for future presidents is that we have always been at war with Eastasia.

* Unfortunately, he was also arguably the least popular president ever, registering the lowest approval ratings in presidential history: 25%, following years of quagmire in Iraq and the botched federal disaster response to Hurricane Katrina. The political lesson for future presidents is that if a catastrophic hurricane is coming, resign immediately.

SCANDAL!

The Iraq War may seem like a catastrophic mistake *now*. But it's important to remember that history will have the final verdict. For instance, perhaps 50 years from now, historians will say, "The Iraq War was good, because it initiated the chain of events that shattered the liberal democratic international order and paved the way for conquest by Zod the Tormentor, may he reign from his orbital throne forever."

TRUE FACTS THAT ARE ALSO DOUBLE ENTENDRES

As someone with the last name "Bush," George XLIII's life is basically one long string of double entendres.

- George XLIII is an expert in ¨LOOKING FOR DRILLING SITES,¨ and he used these skills to start his own company: ¨BUSH EXPLORATION.¨ We would bet any amount of money that George XLIII would snicker when telling people, "I'm the head guy in charge of Bush Exploration."

- His election, controversially, involved a lot of people examining ¨HANGING CHADS,¨ ¨DANGLING CHADS,¨ ¨FAT CHADS,¨ and even ¨PREGNANT CHADS.¨ Never let anyone tell you politics isn't a dirty, dirty business.

- After 9/11, George XLIII smooth-talked a nervous America into the ¨PATRIOT ACT,¨ which left a lot of people feeling exposed and violated.

- During his presidency, George XLIII and Laura often retreated to their ranch in Crawford, Texas so he could unwind by spending some time ¨CLEARING BRUSH.¨

"So remember, Bonesman: If anyone ever says 'Skull and Bones,' then no matter where you are you have to get up and leave the room."

How to Win His Heart

💜 **Hang out at backyard BBQs.** Laura Welch met George XLIII at a backyard BBQ in Midland, Texas, and within three months they were engaged. (Please note: If you find yourself flirting with a handsome young oil executive at a backyard BBQ in Midland, Texas, and his dad just wrapped up a stint as director of the CIA, it's possible you are a character on the popular '80s show *Dallas*.)

💜 **Go miniature golfing with him.** When they met, George asked Laura to go miniature golfing with him. If this happens to you, just smile and nod, and bite your cheek if that's what it takes to keep from laughing.

💜 **Be a sexy librarian.** Laura was a librarian when she met George, and you're probably closer than you realize to pulling off the sexy librarian look. You're already reading a book, and chances are pretty good you're wearing glasses. All that's left is to start sexily chewing on a pencil, and take off your top.

DIY PROJECT:
DECIDE HOW TO RUN THE GOVERNMENT

George XLIII's background in business helped him get elected to the White House. That's because throughout American history, the idea that we should run the government like a business recurs periodically, like a herpes outbreak.

Just so you know for next time, running the government like a business usually doesn't work out that well! But obviously we don't want a president who will run the government like a *government*, either. So what are our other options? Here are a few ideas that you can try suggesting during the next election cycle.

★ We need to run the government like a **BASEBALL TEAM.**

★ We need to run the government like an **APPLE ORCHARD.**

★ We need to run the government like a **SPACESHIP.**

★ We need to run the government like a **STREET GANG.**

★ We need to run the government like a **PYRAMID SCHEME.**

★ We need to run the government like a **MAXIMUM SECURITY PRISON.**

★ We need to run the government like a **BANK HEIST CREW.**

★ We need to run the government like a **RUNAWAY TRAIN.**

★ We need to run the government like a **DOOMSDAY CULT.**

Vital Stats

Looks: 9

George XLIII is very handsome! Say what you will about eugenics, but the Kennebunkport breeding program that has been working to produce the perfect politician for more than 100 years has, if nothing else, produced a very handsome politician.

Physique: 9

George XLIII jogs regularly, and during his presidency he could clock 7.5 minute miles, mile after mile. So whatever else you do, do not challenge him to a foot race, unless you're prepared to cheat. You probably don't need us to tell you how to cheat at foot races, but just in case: The trick is to put bees in his shoes.

Charisma: 8

Even for those who would describe his accent as "nails on a chalkboard," or perhaps "affected," George XLIII is a friendly and likeable guy. At any social gathering, he is the life of the party. And it is one of the wonders of democracy that voters occasionally decide to put the life of the party in the White House.

Lifelong learner: 7

During his presidency, George XLIII read 14 biographies of Abraham Lincoln. So if you need to get a message to George XLIII, try writing a biography of Lincoln and putting your message in the foreword.

BARACK OBAMA

2009–2017 | Democrat

If you're not already familiar with Barack Obama, it's probably because you just woke up from a long cryogenic slumber. The world must seem like a frightening and unfamiliar place! There's so much that you've missed—where do you even get started? If you want our advice, stop wasting your time on books and start learning how to use Twitter.

Let's Talk About Clothes

IF YOU WANT TO LONGINGLY STROKE HIS CHEEK WITH YOUR FINGERTIP, GO AHEAD! NO ONE IS LOOKING. (WELL, OK, A FEW PEOPLE ARE LOOKING.)

Obama wears only blue or gray suits in order to cut down on the "decision fatigue" that would result from having to start each day with trying to decide whether or not to wear a seersucker suit.

You can cut down on decision fatigue in your own life by throwing away all of your clothes and buying seven identical white bathrobes.

Why You'll *Love* Him

He's cool. You might have noticed that this is the first time that we've use the word "cool" to describe anyone in this book.

He's cool-headed. Just try to make Barack Obama lose his temper. Go ahead—give it a shot! You won't be able to do it, but at least you'll have fun trying.

He's good with babies. Babies love Barack Obama because they admire his many accomplishments.

PRESS HERE to Hear Barack Obama Singing Al Green's "Let's Stay Together"!

If you can't hear Barack Obama singing right now, your book must be broken! Don't return it for a refund though. Just buy a second copy and maybe that one will work.

LOVE STORY

Obama had just started a summer internship at a law firm in Chicago when he first met his wife, Michelle. (Except she wasn't his wife yet. That would have been weird!) Michelle was an associate at the firm, and she was assigned to be Obama's mentor. He had to ask her out a few times before she agreed to go on a date with him, because she thought it would be weird if the only two black people at the firm immediately started dating. (For the record, the firm is very quick to point out that there were like four other black people working there.)

Obama wisely planned a first date that would show he has all the qualities that women look for in a man. First he took Michelle to an art museum, so she would see that he is not an art thief. Then he took her to the movies, to show that he is capable of looking up movie listings. Finally he took her out for ice cream, because as long as he was on a date anyway, he figured he might as well try to set a world record for "longest first date."

Two years later, Obama proposed by taking Michelle to a fancy dinner and arranging for the waiter to put an engagement ring on her dessert plate. (The strong implication being that if she turned him down, she would not receive dessert.) ♥

DIY PROJECT:
LEARN HOW TO TWEET AT BARACK OBAMA

Things have changed a lot since you first stepped inside that icy cold cryogenic chamber. In the world you remember, if you wanted to tweet at Barack Obama you would just stand outside the Illinois Statehouse and yell "Tweet! Tweet! Tweet!" at him on his way into work. Now, thanks to social media, you can do essentially the same thing without having to leave the comfort of your cryogenics lab.

1 Let's start with the basics. "Twitter" is a "social networking service" where you can publicly post any message (or "tweet"), as long as it is extremely short. For example, you could tweet "Hello world, I just awoke from a long, cryogenic slumber." But you can't tweet all of the lyrics to "The Sign" by Ace of Base, even though that's the last song you can remember hearing as you drifted into unconsciousness. Someone in the lab must have left the radio on, and you could hear it playing faintly through the frosted door of your chamber, like a lullaby singing you to sleep.

2 After you've set up a Twitter account, you'll need to think of what you want to say to Barack Obama. How about "Who are you and what have you done with Bill Clinton?"

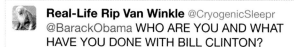

Real-Life Rip Van Winkle @CryogenicSleepr
@BarackObama WHO ARE YOU AND WHAT HAVE YOU DONE WITH BILL CLINTON?

3 Now all that's left is to wait for Barack Obama to respond. Maybe use this time to get caught up on *Lost*.

4 Hey look, he tweeted you back!

Barack Obama @BarackObama
@CryogenicSleepr Forget about Bill Clinton. You don't need him anymore. I am the only one you need.

5 Wait, is Barack Obama flirting with you?? You should flirt back! Send him another tweet.

Real-Life Rip Van Winkle @CryogenicSleepr
@BarackObama I HAVE A LONG WHITE BEARD.

6 OK...so your flirting skills have gotten a little rusty. We'll worry about that later. In the meantime, Barack Obama just tweeted back:

Barack Obama @BarackObama
@CryogenicSleepr I'd like to see that. We should meet IRL.

7 Woah, Barack Obama wants to meet you! See, "IRL" stands for "in real life." Though it could also stand for *"Isamaa ja Res Publica Liit,"* the Estonian political party. Maybe you should ask him to clarify.

Real-Life Rip Van Winkle @CryogenicSleepr
@BarackObama I SAW THE SIGN AND IT OPENED UP MY EYES I SAW THE SIGN. LIFE IS DEMANDING, WITHOUT UNDERSTANDING. I SAW THE SIGN, AND IT OPENED

8 Uh oh—looks like you panicked and started tweeting all of the lyrics to "The Sign," the one thing we specifically told you not to do. Maybe Barack Obama won't notice.

Barack Obama @BarackObama
@CryogenicSleepr Never mind. I don't want to meet someone who doesn't understand how to use Twitter.

9 Oh well! It's been a wild ride, but now it's over. At least you've learned some important lessons about Twitter, and also about life. (But mostly about Twitter.)

Barack Obama loves to play *Scrabble*. And if you want to beat him at *Scrabble*, it will take more than finally learning the rules of *Scrabble*. You're going to have to cheat. In case you're new to cheating at *Scrabble*, here are some ideas to help you get started.

1. Hide a dictionary in your bathroom. If Obama wants to know why you're going to the bathroom every five minutes, just explain that you have diarrhea.

2. Keep some extra *Scrabble* tiles up your sleeve. You can slip them onto your tile rack whenever Obama leaves the room. If he's not leaving the room often enough, keep telling him you think you hear a prowler.

DOES HE KEEP HIS *promises?*

√ Pass healthcare reform.
Have you heard of Obamacare? It's how the government ended up paying part of your maintenance costs during your suspended animation.

✗ Close Guantanamo Bay.
Obama tried to close the infamous military prison at Guantanamo Bay, but he was not successful. Is there more he could have done? Of course. For example, he could have arranged for all of the prisoners to move into Mitch McConnell's house.

√ End the use of torture.
Obama ended the use of waterboarding and other interrogation methods we always called torture until we started doing them. Unfortunately, the president does not have the power to end politically convenient redefinitions of the word "torture."

✗ Bring Republicans and Democrats together to usher in a new age of unity and compromise.
Wait, did this happen? We can't remember if this happened or not.

√ Withdraw troops from Iraq.
Obama did withdraw our troops from Iraq. Then he sent some back in because, you know, ISIS. But to be fair, he never promised to withdraw troops from Iraq *twice*.

Vital Stats

Looks: 9

This is a 10 if you like big ears—which we do, but we know that it's a controversial position to take.

Physique: 10

Would you like to learn the secret of how Obama stays in shape? It's a combination of weightlifting and cardio workouts. So now you have no excuse for not being in as good of shape as Obama! If only there were some way to unlearn this secret.

Charisma: 10

The best part of being married to Obama would be making him say "Yes we can" over and over again, whenever you wanted.

Averting financial crisis: 9

Remember back in 2009 when the financial crisis did not turn into a catastrophic global economic depression? Obama wishes that you would remember.

A GLORIOUS BOARD GAME

Race your friends to see who is the fastest president!

How to Play:

1. First, you'll need to obtain a six-sided die and some U.S. coins. (To maintain plausible deniability, please don't tell us *how* you obtained them. We don't want to know!) Each player chooses a coin to use as his or her game piece and places it on the "Inauguration" square.

2. The player with the best political views goes first, followed by the other players in order of "lifetime sexual partners," most to fewest. (In the case of a tie, knife fight.)

3. A turn consists of rolling the die, moving that many spaces, and following any instructions on the square you land on. This includes instructions other players might have surreptitiously written into empty squares, like "Give Derek your wallet."

4. Whoever reaches the "End of Term" square first wins the game, because as in life, the best president is always the fastest president. The winner gets to decide who the other players vote for in the next election.

5. Each coin comes with its own special abilities, as outlined on the next page.

PENNY

If you play as Abraham Lincoln, you can re-roll the die twice per game to reflect Lincoln's ability to bounce back from political setbacks. It's also your job to make sure no one "secedes" from the game. That includes bathroom breaks, so you'll need to take a firm hand.

QUARTER

If you play as George Washington, you always get the first turn. (Just ignore all of that stuff we said earlier about how to decide which player goes first.) You may also choose to make yourself king and not let any other player have a turn until you die .

1782 BIRCH CENT

Oh man . . . this is embarrassing, but that penny is super old. Gross! Go ahead and mail it to JD and Kate Dobson, c/o Henry Holt & Co., New York, NY, and we'll send you back a bright, shiny, new penny. That's just the kind of people we are!

NICKEL

If you play as Thomas Jefferson, you are allowed one act of brazen hypocrisy per turn. For example, you can write the Declaration of Independence while keeping human beings enslaved, if that's how things roll at your house.

DIME

If you play as FDR, once per game you can force another player to join the Tennessee Valley Authority. That player loses a turn while they build a hydroelectric dam or something. Also, you're allowed to "drop a dime" on the other players by literally dropping dimes on them.

HALF-DOLLAR

If you play as JFK, you start the game on the "JFK" space, to reflect how lucky you are to have been born rich and good-looking. You are also allowed to seduce other players, passers-by, or anyone who texts another player during the game.

DOLLAR

If you play as Dwight D. Eisenhower, add +1 to your die rolls, to reflect how fast you can move thanks to the interstate highway system. You also have to explain to the other players why you carry around a silver dollar.

YOU'RE READY TO
PLAY

INAUGURATION

Congratulations on your election! Or, congratulations on being vice president when your predecessor's term ended unexpectedly.

TIME FLIES

After your first month in office, you glance in the mirror. You've already aged five years, and even as you gaze on in horror, a new wrinkle creases your brow like a crack in a dam. Go back 1 space

PROHIBITION

For some reason you think it will be popular to reinstate prohibition. Your punishment will be your own sobriety for the rest of this game.

KENNEDY COMPOUND

If you're playing as JFK, start here. If you're not JFK and you land on this space, you are promptly frogmarched off of the Kennedy estate. But go forward 1 space, because at least you got to experience that fabled magic for a few seconds.

VETO OVERRIDDEN

The Senate has overridden your veto of a controversial bill. Flip your coin over to hide your face in shame for the rest of the game.

HOW ABOUT SOME SHIRTLESS LBJ WHILE YOU WAIT?

WAR!

Your approval rating goes up 30 points as the nation rallies around the flag. Enjoy it while it lasts, and roll again.

WHISKEY REBELLION

Go get yourself a drink, and "accidentally" knock the board over while you're getting up. Screw these guys and their rules, right?

MID-TERM ELECTIONS

The president's party usually loses mid-term elections, because after two years voters have started wondering "What the hell were we thinking?" Roll the die. On a 1–5, your party loses—go back 3 spaces.

A REPUBLIC, IF YOU CAN KEEP IT

Continuing a proud White House tradition, you successfully shift more power away from Congress toward the executive branch. Email your Member of Congress, and say "Hah! In your face, legislative branch!"

HOW IS THE MAYOR OF BUFFALO DOING?

It's been awhile since you called the Mayor of Buffalo! Lose a turn while you check in on him. 716-851-4841.

END OF TERM

Congratulations, you made it! Make sure to steal all the White House towels before the next president arrives.

AIR FORCE ONE

Russian nationalists hijack Air Force One, as in the movie Air Force One. Roll the die. On a 1–5, you defeat them and recapture the plane. On a 6, you yourself are a Russian nationalist, so everything is fine. Move forward 1 space.

ASSASSINATION ATTEMPT?

Lose a turn while you recover from what, in retrospect, was just food poisoning. (Unless you are playing as Andrew Jackson, possibly because you've hand-etched Andrew Jackson's face onto a coin. In which case you hit the White House chef with your cane and move ahead 2 spaces.)

CIVIL WAR

If you are Lincoln, move forward 4 spaces. If you're some other president . . . how do you think that president would have done in the Civil War? If you think they'd have done well, move forward 4 spaces, and if poorly, move backward 1 space.

FORD'S THEATER

Players playing as Lincoln must swap their penny for a sewing needle to represent Andrew Johnson, and begin moving backward. All other players enjoy a pleasant evening watching Our American Cousin.

DONALD TRUMP

2017– ____ | Republican

Donald Trump's story is the classic American "rags-to-riches story," except without the "rags" part.

Trump was born on the wrong side of the tracks, in Queens. But like so many heirs of super-wealthy Queens real estate developers, he had big dreams of becoming a *Manhattan* real estate developer. And with a little luck, and a little loan of a million dollars from his dad, and a little inheritance of a few tens of millions more, he made that dream come true.

Later, Trump met the love of his life, "attention," whom he courted assiduously and followed all the way into a successful career playing a skilled business executive on a popular TV show. He also married a series of models, divorcing them in turn as they aged out.

Trump would have been content to while away his remaining days in the gilt penthouse atop Trump Tower, eating taco bowls and reading his own dwindling news clippings. But he knew he had to enter politics when Barack Obama was elected president. There was just *something* about Obama that made it hard to believe he was a real American. Trump made it his mission to prove to the world that America's first black president was secretly born in Africa and thus ineligible for the presidency, and the rest is history.

As of this writing, the full story of Donald Trump's presidency cannot be told. Citizenship is a heavy burden, and part of that burden is that we need you to help us complete this profile. We recommend you use pencil because it feels like things are going to be pretty dynamic.

Get the Look!

Getting Donald Trump's look is easy. Go to an isolated rural crossroads at midnight, and wait for a stranger with red eyes and a sulfurous odor to emerge from the darkness. He's going to offer you a deal.

Books are heavy! If you've brought this book with you on your ascent of Mount Everest, feel free to lighten your load by cutting this page out.

WORD SEARCH

Sometimes, it can be hard to spot the undercurrents of a political campaign–even when they're right in front of your nose! Can you find all 16 of the terms related to Donald Trump's 2016 campaign for the presidency?

drain the swamp	NAFTA	ISIS	puppet
birth certificate	TPP	Iran	tax returns
Comey	lock her up	Twitter	MAGA
China	Kenya	sad	wall

U	N	Z	O	Z	Ш	B	M	U	K	P	H	W	Y	P	J
A	W	X	D	L	П	Q	Z	I	O	D	F	O	L	G	T
N	A	F	T	A	И	K	N	G	M	A	G	A	C	J	A
Y	L	P	V	B	O	P	S	D	П	E	T	P	P	F	X
I	L	O	C	K	H	E	R	U	P	H	P	U	V	W	R
S	B	L	S	E	D	M	A	X	O	S	Г	P	У	T	E
A	Z	C	W	N	O	Л	Q	A	M	S	S	P	P	J	T
D	X	L	X	Y	M	Ь	U	K	A	L	R	E	O	M	U
A	M	O	Ч	A	Z	C	Q	E	T	W	I	T	T	E	R
M	H	Z	M	W	P	O	L	P	R	X	A	I	L	Z	N
X	T	V	M	C	Ф	M	N	C	D	I	W	I	S	I	S
B	I	R	T	H	C	E	R	T	I	F	I	C	A	T	E
H	R	Z	I	I	Б	Y	R	B	U	M	D	G	R	J	T
H	A	F	Y	N	B	T	X	O	B	A	F	A	I	U	R
T	N	D	R	A	I	N	T	H	E	S	W	A	M	P	S
K	J	F	Д	E	З	И	Н	Ф	О	Р	М	А	Ц	И	Я

How to Win His Heart

♥ What Donald Trump wants more than anything else is **a woman who can join with him as an equal partner in life.**

♥ He wants **someone who is intelligent, who has her own opinions, and who isn't afraid to fight for them.** He wants **someone with a sense of humor, and who won't hesitate to use it to take him down a notch when he starts taking himself too seriously.** And most important, he wants **someone close to his own age,** so that he can benefit from the hard-earned wisdom and lived experiences that only come with time.

♥ Obviously, it doesn't hurt if he finds her **physically attractive.** But what he's *most* attracted to is who a woman is on the *inside.*

DOES HE KEEP HIS *promises?*

Donald Trump made one or two promises during his presidential campaign. But until the end of his administration, it will be impossible to know whether he ended up keeping them. Help us out by marking the box to indicate whether or not he made good on his word. We use ✓ and ✗ to indicate "yes" and "no," but if you want to use ✓ to mean "no" and ✗ to mean "yes," that's up to you—it's your book! (Unless you borrowed it from the library, in which case it's *even more* important that you fill in this section, to help keep your fellow citizens informed.)

☐ **"[I will] be the greatest jobs president that God ever created."**

Be careful, because this one is a little ambiguous. Did he mean he will create a *lot* of jobs? Or just one really *amazing* job, like "emperor."

☐ **Eliminate the national debt at the end of eight years.**

This one is easy, and President Trump has done it several times in the private sector. You just dissolve the entity that owes the money, and reorganize under a new structure.

☐ **"I'm going to be so presidential, you're going to be bored."**

But would the people accept a boring president? As the person commanding the most fearsome arsenal the world has ever seen, isn't it the president's responsibility to be entertaining and unpredictable?

☐ **"I promise I will never be in a bicycle race. That I can tell you."**

We hope he *doesn't* keep this promise.

☐ **"No one is going to touch us because I'm so unpredictable."**

It does seem possible that by the end of President Trump's administration, no one will want to touch us.

☐ **"The whole psyche [of the U.S.] will change."**

"Change" can mean a lot of things. "When I woke up this morning I'd *changed* into a giant cockroach." "Weather conditions are *changing* rapidly, brace for impact." And so forth.

☐ **"I will never let you down."**

Keep in mind that whether or not someone lets you down is really a function of *expectations*.

☐ **"All your dreams are going to come true."**

Note that Trump didn't limit this to your *good* dreams. It's very possible the Trump administration will include a lot of teeth falling out, plummeting from great heights, and people made to give speeches in the nude.

☒ **"I will give you everything."**

At the risk of being labeled pessimists, we're just going to go ahead and mark this one with an "X" now.

SCANDAL!

We don't know yet whether the Trump administration will have any memorable scandals. So in the meantime, we've written this Donald Trump Presidential Scandal Mad Lib. It's perfect for parties, or just passing time with your bunkmates at reeducation camp.

Even Donald Trump's fiercest critics were surprised when they learned that he had used the presidency to
_____ more than $_____ billion from a series of _____ while disguised, poorly, as a _____.
   verb   *number*   *plural noun*   *noun*
The first journalists to discover his actions were promptly _____ by allies of the president. But this did
                                                              past-tense verb
not solve his problem, as video of Trump being _____ upon by several _____ quickly began
                                                past-tense verb   *plural noun*
circulating on the Internet.

Seeking to distract the nation's attention from the blossoming crisis, Trump held a press conference at which he
brazenly _____ and, shocking the audience of staff and reporters, tore off his clothes to reveal a _____
          past-tense verb   *noun*
where his _____ used to be. As the nation reeled from this information, Trump issued an executive order
           body part
declaring a national emergency and extending his presidential term to _____ dozen years and barricaded
                                                                        number
himself at Mar-a-_____, refusing to talk to anyone except for paying club members.
                 Spanish term

It appeared that the stalemate would continue indefinitely. But only days later, construction workers in _____
                                                                                                          place
unearthed a buried _____ during the demolition of one of Trump's several failed _____. This
                    noun   *plural noun*
shattering discovery made it impossible for the compromised Trump presidency to continue.

When Trump finally bowed to public pressure and resigned, he revealed that his entire political career had been
an elaborate performance-art piece, designed to demonstrate that rather than being well informed and committed to democracy, the American electorate was _____ and _____.
                                                adjective   *adjective*

Vital Stats

Looks: 3

Donald Trump was pretty good-looking in his twenties, but we only rank presidents based on their looks when they became president. And in his twenties, Trump was so busy getting sued by the Justice Department for housing discrimination that he had no time to run for office.

Physique: 2

Unfortunately, the "heel spurs" that got Donald Trump his fifth draft deferment during the Vietnam War have apparently also kept him from any sort of regular workout routine. (Well, they've kept him from working out recently. He managed to grit his teeth through the pain and play football, tennis, and squash when he was getting his first four deferments for being in college.)

Charisma: 7

If you're the kind of person who watched *Back to the Future* and thought, "Michael J. Fox is *okay*, but tell me more about this *Biff* guy," then you might be susceptible to Donald Trump's . . . let's call it "charm."

Gropiness: 10

If you're attracted to men who brag about grabbing the genitals of strangers, then boy oh boy have we got the guy for you. Also, maybe you should talk to someone about that!

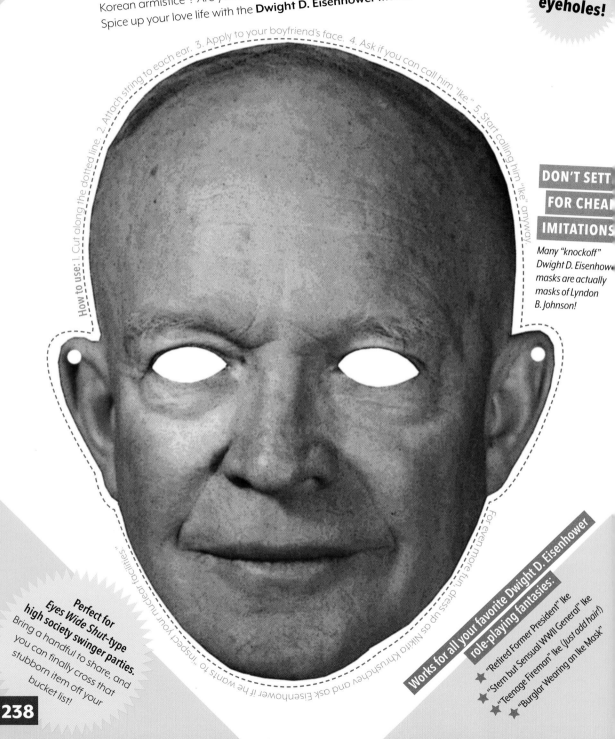

About the Authors

KATE DOBSON is a former assistant comics editor for the *Washington Post* and was head writer for *The Brown Jug*. When she's not writing, she enjoys serving food to her small children and, later, vacuuming that same food up off the floor.

J.D. DOBSON is a former U.S. Senate staffer, federal lobbyist, and crisis communications consultant. Now he makes candles that smell like politicians and hopes for the best.

KATE AND J.D. are married (to each other) and live in St. Louis, Missouri. In addition to this book, they have created:

TWO YOUNG HUMAN BEINGS

THOUSANDS OF HAND-CUT CANDLE WIGS

A TRULY IMPRESSIVE AMOUNT OF STUDENT DEBT

AND THE WEBSITE WWW.HOTTESTHEADSOFSTATE.COM.

123RF.com: Rampersad Ramautar © 113; Yuliia Sonsedska© 131; Patrick Guenette© 135

Alamy Stock Photo: MARKA: 178-178; ZUMA Press, Inc.: 195; Everett Collection Inc: 213

Andrew Jackson's Hermitage: 34, 38

Azer.com: 221

Bob McNeely, The White House: 200 (second and third from top, right)

Brooklyn Museum: 46 (top right)

Cardinal & White, Volume XX; yearbook of Whittier Union High School: 186

Clark Art Institute: 150

ClipartOf.com: 77

emojione.com: 50, 51, 53

FDR Presidential Library and Museum: 105 (bottom left)

Gage Skidmore: 49 (bottom right)

George Bush Presidential Library and Museum: 211, 212

Gerald R. Ford Library: 190, 193, **Gerald R. Ford Library,** photo by Ricardo Thomas: 199 (fourth from top, left), 200 (bottom right)

Google Cultural Institute: 44

Harry S. Truman Library & Museum: 165, 166 (top left)

Howell Conant, White House Photo Office; Richard Nixon Library: 182, 184

IIP Photo Archive: 12, 16, 20, 30 (bottom left), 30 (bottom right), 50, 124, 125 (top right), 125 (bottom left), 125 (bottom right), 126 (top left)

iStock.com: iStock.com /7romawka7: 9 (top, right); iStock.com/joecicak: 9 (bottom); iStock.com/RiverNorthPhotography: 11; iStock.com/traveler1116: 23; iStock.com/GeorgiosArt: 33; iStock.com/sx70: 100; iStock.com/Ferdiperdozniy: 104-107, 178-179, 199-201; iStock.com/zoljo: 109; iStock.com/eli_asenova: 133; iStock.com/parameter: 184; iStock.com/Sashkinw: 184; iStock.com/korsaralex: 213; iStock.com/DaddyBit: 232; iStock.com/mvp64: 233; iStock.com/Nastco: 233

James K. Polk Memorial Association: 58, 136 (top left)

JFK Presidential Library and Museum: 174, **JFK Presidential Library and Museum,** photo by Frank Turgeon Jr.: 175; **Cecil Stoughton, White House Photographs:** 178-179, 178-179; **Robert Knudsen, White House Photographs:** 178-179, 178-179

Kremlin.ru: 224

LBJ Library: 181, 199 (top left), **LBJ Library,** photo by Arnold Newman: 180, **LBJ Library,** photo by Yoichi Okamoto: 137 (top center), 199 (top left), 200 (top right), 232

Library of Congress: front cover, title page, 13, 37 (top right), 42, 45, 47 (left), 47 (right), 48 (top right), 48 (bottom right), 54, 59, 63 (left), 64, 67 (left), 67 (right), 68 (right), 70, 71, 74 (left), 74 (bottom right), 80 (left), 80 (right), 81 (bottom left), 81 (bottom right), 81 (top right), 82 (left), 85, 86, 88, 90, 94, 102, 105 (top left), 105 (second from top, left), 105 (third from top, left), 105 (fourth from top, left), 105 (bottom right), 106 (top), 106 (bottom), 107 (top right), 107 (second from top, left), 107 (bottom right), 108 (top left), 111, 112, 118 (top), 118 (bottom left), 118 (bottom middle), 118 (bottom right), 119 (bottom left), 119 (bottom right), 120, 122, 126 (middle right), 126 (bottom left), 128 (top), 128 (bottom), 131, 132, 133, 136 (bottom left), 136 (bottom right), 137 (top right), 137 (middle), 137 (bottom right), 138, 141, 144, 146, 146, 146, 148, 149, 151, 152, 153, 156, 157, 160, 161, 178-179, 188, 199 (third from top, left), 200 (top right); **Toni Frissell, Library of**

Congress: 69 (left), **Library of Congress, Veterans History Project:** 49 (top left)

lukeford.net: 199, 200 (bottom left)

Metropolitan Museum of Art: 32

Museo Nacional de San Carlos: 17 (bottom right)

National Archives: 183, **National Archives, Department of Defense:** 69 (right), 164, 199 (second from top, left), 220, **National Archives, Franklin D. Roosevelt Library:** 159, 162 (left), 162 (right), 163 (left), 163 (right), **National Archives, George Bush Library:** 137 (bottom left), 222, 222 **National Archives, Gerald R. Ford Library:** 63 (right), 210 **National Archives, Harry S. Truman Library and Museum:** 166 (top left), 166 (bottom right), **National Archives, Herbert Hoover Library:** 154 (bottom), **National Archives, Jimmy Carter Library:** 194, **National Archives, Richard Nixon Library:** front cover, 62, 68 (left), 137 (top left), **National Archives, Ronald Reagan Library:** 127 (middle right), 202, 204, **National Archives, Victor Jorgensen, US Navy:** 192, **National Archives White House Photo Office:** 127 (top left), 187, 215

National Institutes of Health: 214

National Portrait Gallery, Smithsonian Institution; transfer from the National Gallery of Art; gift of the A.W. Mellon Educational and Charitable Trust, 1942; Frame conserved with funds from the Smithsonian Women's Committee: front cover, 66, **National Portrait Gallery, Smithsonian Institution;** acquired as a gift to the nation through the generosity of the Donald E. Reynolds Foundation: 25, **National Portrait Gallery, Smithsonian Institution;** gift of Mrs. Harry Newton Blue; Frame conserved with funds from the Smithsonian Women's Commit: 100, **National Portrait Gallery, Smithsonian Institution:** 28, 30 (bottom middle), 101

New York Historical Society: 125 (top left)

Office of Public Affairs, Yale University, photographs of individuals, 1870-2005 (inclusive). Manuscripts & Archives, Yale University: 134

Official White House Photo by Pete Souza: 127 (bottom left), 227

Popular Science Monthly Volume 53, 1898: 130

Public Domain Images-PIXNIO: 232

Ronald Reagan Library: 136 (top right), 203

Rutherford B. Hayes Presidential Library & Museums: 93

Shutterstock: R2D2/shutterstock.com: 103; FelixLipov/shutterstock.com: 108 (bottom right); Alhovik/shutterstock.com: 131; digitalreflections/shutterstock.com: 138 (bottom); JosephSohm/shutterstock.com: 219

Thomas Nast: 82 (right)

Transylvania University: 46 (left)

US Army: 105 (top right), 107 (bottom left),

US Department of Defense: 199, 200 (middle left), **US Department of Defense,** photo by Navy Petty Officer 2nd Class Dominique A. Pineiro/Released: 160, 199 (bottom left), 200 (bottom right), 234

US Naval Historical Center: 122

US Navy, Dwight D. Eisenhower Museum: 168, 238

US Senate: 226

Wikimedia Commons: 46 (bottom right), 48 (left), 49 (bottom left), 60, 87, 98, 105 (second from top, right), 107 (third from top, left), 115, 178-179, 199, 200 (bottom left), 230